Copyright © 2020 Gideon Hirtenstein

ISBN:
978-1-952874-20-8 (paperback)
978-1-952874-21-5 (hardback)
978-1-952874-22-2 (ebook)

All rights reserved. No part of this publication may be reproduced, stored in a retrieval system, or transmitted in any form or by any means - electronic, mechanical, photocopy, recording, scanning, or other – except for brief quotations in critical reviews or articles, without the prior written permission of the publisher.

Photographs by: Jonathan Hirtenstein

OMNIBOOK CO.
99 Wall Street, Suite 118
New York, NY 10005
USA
+1-866-216-9965
www.omnibookcompany.com

First Edition

For e-book purchase: Kindle on Amazon, Barnes and Noble
Book purchase: Amazon.com, Barnes & Noble, and
www.omnibookcompany.com

Omnibook titles may be purchased in bulk for educational, business, fund-raising, or sales promotional use. For more information please e-mail info@omnibookcompany.com

4 SEASONS
400 SALADS

GIDEON HIRTENSTEIN
GIDI GOURMET, LLC.

GIDEON HIRTENSTEIN
Executive Chef

- Graduated Culinary School 1969; European Trained
- 3 years Military
- Worked in 4-5 Star Hotels
- Traveled around the world—47 countries
- Designed and made a Replica Cake of the first ship to sail from the Suez Channel from Israel for the Welcoming Party
- Certified by American Culinary Institute, 1985
- Executive Chef for the College of William & Mary
- Corporate Chef for Shamrock Service/Merged with GSI
- Traveling Executive Chef: Overseen multiple food service facilities, retirement homes, hotels, corporate parties, etc.
- Trained over 2,000 staff personnel: cook positions, kitchen management, etc.
- Published 1st book 1986—Israel
- Participated in entering personal recipes for "Great Chefs of Virginia Cookbook", by American Culinary Institute, 1987
- Participated adding recipes to Hampton Roads Chefs Association, 1990
- Gidi Gourmet International Cooking, published, 1992
- The Only Source, published 2016, Gideon Hirtenstein-Gidi Gourmet, Factual/Educational Book
- 30 Complete Menus—7 Course Meals, Gideon Hirtenstein-Gidi Gourmet, published 2017
- Hundreds of Thank You letters on file
- Owner of Gidi Gourmet, LLC. 1985-present. Executive Chef offering high class catering and others

NICOLE HIRTENSTEIN

- Participated in the test kitchen of Gidi Gourmet, LLC.
- On her 4th year of college
- Plans to continue on to PhD Program
- Participated in working on 2016-2017 Gidi Gourmet Books
- Highly creative on home cooking and is excellent at what she does
- Trained from an early age

Summary of Newest Book

4 SEASONS 400 SALADS

By Gideon Hirtenstein

This salad book is based on a variety of fruits, veggies, pasta, rice, eggs, poultry, seafood and much more.

The combination/principal of this book is to create healthy recipes with some that are quick and easy, and utilizing what you may have in leftovers. With the help of this book, you can create and utilize without waste, conserve by not overspending, and make entire meals by following these recipes. They are made up of what most average households have in stock. Your blender will be your right hand. All recipes are 6-8 servings, with the average salad cost being between $10-$20. More expensive salads, such as seafood and meat, will cost between $20-$25.

The preparation time for many of these salads will be approximately 30 minutes, based on the average salad.

Flavoring for any salad can be adjusted for personal taste preference. Garnishes can be adjusted by whatever is available—be creative!

In 1986 when writing my first book, I experimented with many combinations. This book became very successful– with 4 editions, and had good reviews in Women's magazines.

These recipes are for anyone, with many type of different eating preferences such as vegetarian, kosher, low salt, low cholesterol, etc.

VEGETABLES

Alfalfa Sprouts with Veggie Cream Dressing

Ingredients

12 oz. alfalfa sprouts
¾ cup white sharp cheddar cheese
2 persimmon, cubed
1 red pepper, chopped
2 Tbsp. dill

Dressing

¾ cup sour cream
¼ cup mayonnaise
¼ cup lemon juice
1 tsp. garlic
½ cup sundried tomatoes
¼ cup half and half
1 Tbsp. rosemary
Salt and pepper to taste

Garnish

6 lettuce leaves
1 tomato, sliced
½ cup orange, cubed 1 cup croutons

Instructions

Wash alfalfa sprouts in cold water and strain. Prepare a serving tray with lettuce leaves. Place alfalfa sprouts over the tray. Add sharp cheddar cheese, persimmon, red pepper, and dill. Prepare the dressing in a blender and mix on high speed for 1 minute. Before serving, pour dressing over the salad. Garnish with tomato rings around the tray. Add orange cubes and sprinkle with croutons.

Artichoke Bottom with Feta, Cream Cheese and Avocado Dressing

Ingredients

16 oz. artichoke bottoms, cooked or canned
8 oz. feta cheese
1 cucumber, cubed
2 scallion onions, chopped

Dressing

3 oz. cream cheese
1 avocado
¼ cup lemon juice
1 lime for juice
¼ cup olive oil
1 Tbsp. garlic
1 Tbsp. oregano
Salt and pepper to taste

Garnish

5 lettuce leaves
2 Tbsp. parsley, chopped
6–8 cherry tomatoes

Instructions

Boil the fresh artichokes and put something heavy on top of them so they do not float. Boil for approximately 25 minutes with a touch of salt and lemon juice. When they are done, strain them and let cool. Remove all the leaves from the artichoke. Scoop the artichoke out. If you are using canned artichokes, wash them with cold water. Prepare a tray with the iceberg lettuce. Place artichokes on the lettuce. Add crumbled feta, cucumber cubes and scallion onions. Put all dressing ingredients in a blender for 50 seconds on high speed. Before serving pour dressing on salad. Garnish with the parsley and place cherry tomatoes on top.

Artichoke Heart with Roquefort Kalamata

Ingredients

24 oz. artichoke hearts
8 oz. Roquefort cheese, crumbled
¾ cup seedless Kalamata olives, chopped
1 small red pepper, cut into thin strips
1 small carrot, coarsely grated
2 Tbsp. oregano, chopped
1 small lemon with skin, cut into rings
Salt and pepper to taste

Dressing

⅓ cup fresh lemon juice
⅓ cup olive oil
⅓ cup water
½ cup sundried tomatoes
1 Tbsp. garlic, chopped
Salt, pepper, and sugar to taste

Garnish

3 cups spring lettuce
1 medium tomato, cubed
3 Tbsp. Italian parsley, chopped

Instructions

If using fresh artichokes, remove as many leaves as possible. Add 4 quarts of water into a pot and bring to a boil. Add artichokes, and cook for 15 minutes. Remove from heat, drain, and cool. Make sure to use only the hearts and use a spoon to scoop out the fruit. (If using canned artichokes, strain all juice, and rinse with cold water). Place into a mixing bowl. Add Roquefort cheese, seedless Kalamata olives, red pepper, carrot, oregano, lemon rings, and salt and pepper to taste. Mix gently. Prepare the dressing. Add all dressing ingredients into a blender and mix for 1 ½ minutes on high speed. Season to taste. Place spring lettuce onto a serving tray and add salad on top. Before serving, pour dressing over the salad. Garnish with tomatoes on top and sprinkle with parsley.

Artichoke Heart with Sundried Tomatoes and Mozzarella

Ingredients

24 oz. artichokes
1 cup sundried tomatoes
3 scallion onions
1 cup fresh mozzarella, cut into strips
3 Tbsp. dill

Dressing

½ cup vinegar
½ cup oil
½ cup water
2 Tbsp. oregano
Salt and pepper
1 tsp. sugar
1 tsp. lemon zest

Garnish

2 cups fresh spinach leaves
1 tomato, sliced
2 Tbsp. Italian parsley, chopped

Instructions

Put the artichokes into a mixing bowl and add the sundried tomatoes, scallions, fresh mozzarella and dill. Mix gently. Prepare a tray with spinach leaves. Add the salad on top of the spinach. Blend the dressing ingredients in a blender for approximately 1 minute. Adjust flavor if needed. Before serving pour the dressing on the salad. To garnish place tomatoes around edge of tray and sprinkle fresh parsley.

Artichoke Hearts with Crab Meat and Sour Cream Dressing Picante

Ingredients

16 oz. artichoke hearts
12 oz. lump or backfin crab meat
2 celery stalks, chopped
1 red onion, chopped
5 crispy bacon strips, chopped

Dressing

1 ½ cups sour cream
⅛ cup mayonnaise
⅛ tsp. crushed red pepper
⅛ cup vinegar
1 Tbsp. lemon zest
Salt and pepper to taste
Dash of Old Bay Seasoning

Garnish

1 ½ cups spinach, julienned
1 lemon, wedged
1 tomato, cubed
2 Tbsp. dill, chopped

Instructions

If you are using fresh artichokes, boil for 25 to 30 minutes. Remove leaves from the artichoke and scoop out the heart of the artichoke. You can also use canned artichokes. Drain the liquid and pour the artichokes into a mixing bowl. Add crab meat, red onion, and crispy bacon. Toss gently. Prepare a tray with julienned spinach and pour salad on top. Prepare the dressing in a blender with one ice cube and blend on high speed. Before serving pour dressing over the top. Garnish with lemon wedges around the edges of the salad. Sprinkle with tomato and dill.

Artichoke Hearts with Raisins and Fresh Grapes

Ingredients

24 oz. Artichoke hearts
½ cup raisins
1 red pepper
1 Tbsp. parsley
2 Tbsp. garlic
1 tomato, cubed
Dash of hot crushed red pepper
1 cup seedless black grapes

Dressing

½ cup olive oil
½ cup lemon juice
1 Tbsp. lemon zest
Salt and pepper to taste
1 Tsp. sugar
½ cup water

Garnish

2 cups lettuce, julienned
½ cup pecans, chopped
1 orange, cut into rings

Instructions

Put the artichoke hearts into a mixing bowl. Add the rest of the ingredient; raisins, red pepper, parsley, garlic, tomatoes, crushed red pepper and black grapes. Mix gently. Prepare the dressing in a blender and blend for approximately 1 minute. Adjust flavor if needed. Prepare a tray with julienned lettuce. Pour salad on top of the lettuce and pour the dressing before serving. Sprinkle chopped pecans and put the twisted orange rings around the edge of the tray.

Avocado and Baby Spinach

Ingredients

4 avocados, cubed
1 quart of baby spinach
½ red onion, chopped
½ red pepper, cut into strips

Dressing

1 cup mayonnaise
½ cup blue cheese
½ cup half and half
½ lemon for juice
Salt and pepper to taste
1 tsp. tarragon
⅛ tsp. crushed red pepper
1 tsp. garlic, chopped

Garnish

½ cup raspberries
½ cup carrots, grated
½ cup walnuts, chopped

Instructions

Wash the avocados and cut in half. Remove the seed and scoop the fruit out with a spoon. Cut the avocado in wedges. Dress a serving tray with the whole spinach leaves and place avocado on the tray. Add the avocado and red pepper. Put all dressing ingredients in a blender and blend well. Adjust flavor if needed. Before serving pour the dressing on top. Garnish with whole raspberries, grated carrots, and sprinkle chopped walnuts over the top.

Avocado and Feta with Lemon Lime Dressing

Ingredients

4 Avocados, cubed
1 cup feta cheese, crumbled
1 lemon, cubed
1 lime, cubed
1 Tbsp. lemon zest
1 red pepper, cubed
2 scallion onions, chopped

Dressing

¼ cup olive oil
¼ cup wine vinegar
¼ cup water
Salt, pepper, and sugar to taste
⅛ cup ground peanuts
1 Tbsp. garlic

Garnish

4 lettuce leaves
1 orange, cut into rings
2 Tbsp. parsley, chopped

Instructions

Wash the avocados and cut in half. Remove the seed and scoop the fruit out of the skin. Cut the avocado into cubed. Prepare a platter with the lettuce and place the avocado on the lettuce. Add the feta cheese, lemon and lime cubes, red pepper and scallion onions. Blend all the dressing ingredients in a blender and pour over the salad before serving. Garnish with the orange rings and parsley.

Avocado and Granny Smith Apples with Parmesan Dressing

Ingredients

3 avocados, cubed
2 Granny Smith apples, julienned
½ cup parmesan, grated
½ cup blackberries
2 Tbsp. dill, chopped

Dressing

½ cup mayonnaise
½ cup sour cream
¼ cup lemon juice
¼ cup parmesan
Salt and pepper to taste
1 Tbsp. tarragon
1 Tbsp. garlic

Garnish

1 cup spinach leaves
½ cup fresh blueberries
1 Tbsp. Italian parsley

Instructions

Wash the avocados with cold water and cut in half. Remove the seed and scoop the fruit out of the skin. Cut the avocado into wedges. Peel the Granny Smith apples and cut into slices and julienne. Prepare a tray with spinach leaves and place avocado and apples on the tray. Add parmesan, blackberries, and dill. Blend all dressing ingredients in a blender. Adjust flavor if needed. Pour dressing over salad before serving. Garnish with fresh blueberries and Italian parsley.

Avocado and Melon Sweet and Sour

Ingredients

4 medium avocados
2 cups cantaloupe, cubed
1 cup pomegranate seeds

Dressing

3 limes for juice
1 Tbsp. lime zest
¼ cup olive oil
3 Tbsp. dill, chopped
Salt and pepper to taste
¼ cup fresh orange juice

Garnish

6 Romaine or iceberg lettuce leaves
1 cucumber, sliced
Dash of sweet paprika

Instructions

Wash the avocados and cut in half to remove the seed. Use a spoon to scoop the avocado out of the skin. Cut into strips. Prepare a platter with lettuce. Place avocados on the lettuce. Add the melon, and pomegranate seeds on top. Put all dressing ingredients in a blender and mix for 1 ½ minutes on high speed. Pour on salad before serving. For garnish place the cucumber rings on the salad and sprinkle paprika.

Avocado and Tropical Fruit Sweet and Sour

Ingredients

2 avocados, cubed
1 mango, cubed
1 cup pomegranate seeds
1 cup papaya, cubes
1 cup pineapple, cubes
½ cup cranberry
2 Tbsp. dill, chopped

Dressing

⅓ cup avocado oil or olive oil
⅓ cup lemon juice
⅓ cup orange juice
⅛ cup water
Salt, pepper, and sugar to taste
1 Tbsp. mint leaves, chopped
1 tsp. lemon zest
1 cube of ice

Garnish

3 cups spinach leaves
3 Tbsp. roasted sliced almonds
1 lime, thinly sliced

Instructions

Peel avocados and cut in half. Remove the seed and scoop the fruit out of the skin. Slice the avocados into cubes. Peel mango, papaya, and pineapple. Remove the skin and cut into cubes. Place into a mixing bowl. Boil the cranberries for 2 minutes and let cool. Once cooled to room temperature, add to the fruit mixture and add dill. Toss gently. Prepare the dressing in a blender and mix well. Prepare a serving tray with spinach leaves and pour the salad on top. Pour dressing before serving. Garnish with roasted sliced almonds and lime slices.

Avocado and Veggie Lemon Lime Dressing

Ingredients

4 avocados, wedged
1 carrot, grated
1 red pepper, chopped
1 scallion onion, chopped
½ cup Kalamata olives
2 Tbsp. Italian parsley
1 cucumber, cubed

Dressing

1 lime for juice
1 lemon for juice
½ cup olive oil
2 Tbsp. garlic
Salt, pepper, and sugar to taste

Garnish

2 tomatoes, cut into rings
5 lettuce leaves
2 Tbsp. parmesan

Instructions

Wash the avocado with cold water, cut in half and remove the seed. Scoop out the fruit from the skin and cut into strips. Prepare a tray with the lettuce leaves and place the avocado slices on top. Add the carrots, pepper, scallion, Kalamata olives, cucumber and parsley. Prepare dressing in a blender and mix for 1 minute. Adjust flavor if needed. Before serving pour dressing on salad. Garnish with tomatoes and sprinkle parmesan.

Avocado and Wild Rice Dates Spicy

Ingredients

3 medium avocados, cubed
1 ½ cups wild rice
1 medium red pepper, roasted
½ cup sundried tomatoes, chopped
2 scallion onions, chopped
¾ cup dates, chopped
2 Tbsp. chives, chopped

Dressing

½ cup olive oil
½ cup balsamic vinegar
¼ cup water
1 Tbsp. garlic, chopped
1 small tomato, chopped
½ tsp. hot crushed red pepper
Salt, pepper, and sugar to taste

Garnish

3 cups spring lettuce
2 Tbsp. parsley, chopped
1 small red apple, cut into rings

Instructions

Place 4 cups of water into a pot and bring to a boil. Add 1 ½ cups wild rice and stir Bring to a boil, reduce heat to a medium simmer, cover and cook for 25 to 30 minutes. Remove from heat. Mix with a long fork and let cool. Place into a mixing bowl. Wash avocados, cut lengthwise, remove seeds and scoop fruit out. Cut into cubes and add to rice. Add roasted red pepper, sundried tomatoes, scallion onions, dates, and chives. Mix gently. Prepare the dressing. Add all dressing ingredients into a blender and mix for 1 ½ minutes on high speed. Season to taste. Place spring lettuce onto a serving tray and add salad on top. Before serving, pour dressing over the salad. Garnish with apple rings around the salad and sprinkle with parsley.

Avocado and Wild Rice Picante

Ingredients

3 medium avocados, peeled and cubed
1 cup cooked wild rice
1 Roma tomato, cubed
2 scallion onions, chopped
1 medium carrot, grated
1 tsp. garlic, chopped
Salt and pepper to taste

Dressing

½ tsp. crushed red pepper
¼ cup olive oil
½ cup wine vinegar
3 Tbsp. Parmesan
1 lime for juice
1 Tbsp. Grated lime zest
Salt to taste
½ tsp. Saffron

Garnish

2 medium tomatoes, sliced
3 Tbsp. parsley

Instructions

Wash the avocados, cut in half and remove the seed. Take a spoon and remove the avocado from the skin. Cut into large cubes and put in a mixing bowl. Add the rest of the ingredients to the avocado. Pour the wild rice into the avocado. Prepare the serving tray with put the salad on the tray. Blend dressing ingredients in the blender and pour over before serving. Cover the bottom of the tray with the spinach leaves. Pour salad on the tray. Put the tomato rings around the tray and sprinkle with parsley.

Avocado on Toast with Lemon and Persimmon Dressing

Ingredients

4 medium avocado, chopped
¼ cup red onion, chopped
1 small red pepper, chopped
1 Tbsp. fresh rosemary, chopped
1 small seedless cucumber, chopped
1 persimmon, chopped
3 Tbsp. grated parmesan
Salt and pepper to taste
8 3-inch plain round toast

Dressing

¼ cup fresh lemon juice
¼ cup olive oil
¼ cup water
1 tsp. garlic, chopped
1 small persimmon, chopped
Salt, pepper, and sugar to taste

Garnish

6 Romaine lettuce leaves
2 Roma tomatoes, cubed
2 Tbsp. Italian parsley, chopped

Instructions

Wash avocados, cut in half lengthwise, remove seeds, and scoop the fruit out. Cut avocado into cubes and place into a mixing bowl. Add red onion, red pepper, rosemary, seedless cucumber, persimmon, grated parmesan, and salt and pepper. Season to taste. Mix gently. Prepare the dressing. Add all dressing ingredients into a blender and mix for 45 seconds on high speed. Season to taste. Place bread (white or whole wheat cut into 3-inch round pieces) into the oven. Toast until golden brown. Place Romaine lettuce onto a serving tray and add toast on top. Evenly add salad mixture to each toast. Before serving, pour dressing over the toast. Garnish by sprinkling tomatoes and parsley over top.

Avocado with Cranberry and Ham Red Pepper Dressing

Ingredients

4 avocados
4 oz. fresh cranberry
6oz. Prosciutto, chopped
4oz. white sharp cheddar cheese, grated

Dressing

1 red pepper, roasted or fried
1 green pepper, fried
½ cup mayonnaise
½ cup sour cream
1 tbsp. garlic, chopped
1 lemon for juice
3 Tbsp. olive oil
⅛ cup vinegar
¼ cup white cheddar cheese, grated
Salt and pepper to taste

Garnish

2 tomatoes, sliced
¾ cup red cabbage, grated
2 Tbsp. parsley

Instructions

Wash the avocados and cut in half. Remove the seed and scoop the fruit out of the skin. Cut the avocado into long strips. Prepare a serving tray with grated cabbage and put the avocado strips on top. Cook the cranberries for 1 minute. After they cool, put them on top of the avocado slices. Add prosciutto and sprinkle cheddar cheese. Blend all dressing ingredients and pour over the salad before serving. Garnish with tomato slices around the salad. Sprinkle with red cabbage and parsley.

Avocado with Smoked White Fish and Roasted Red Pepper Dressing

Ingredients

3 avocados, cubed
10 oz. smoked white fish
¼ cup red onion
1 tsp. Capers
2 Tbsp. dill
1 pickle, chopped

Dressing

¼ cup olive oil
¼ cup red wine vinegar
¼ cup water
1 tsp. garlic
Salt, pepper, and sugar to taste
1 roasted red pepper
1 lime, grated
Dash of hot crushed red pepper

Garnish

3 cups spring lettuce
2 persimmon, sliced
2 Tbsp. parmesan

Instructions

Wash avocados and cut in half lengthwise. Separate the halves and remove the seed. Scoop fruit out with a spoon and cut into cubes. Prepare a tray with the lettuce and place avocado slices on top. Sprinkle white fish over avocados. Add red onion, capers, dill, and pickle. Blend dressing ingredients in a blender and pour dressing over the salad. Garnish with persimmon and parmesan.

Avocado with Tahini Sesame Dressing

Ingredients

4 avocados, cut into strips
1 red pepper, chopped
1 small cucumber, cubed
2 scallion onions, chopped
1 carrot, grated

Dressing

¾ cup tahini
¼ cup lemon juice
2 Tbsp. garlic
¼ cup water
1 Tbsp. lemon zest
Salt and white pepper to taste
½ Tbsp. cumin

Garnish

5 lettuce leaves
3 Tbsp. parsley
3 Tbsp. sesame seeds
1 lemon, cut into rings

Instructions

Wash the avocados and cut long lengthwise. Remove the seed and scoop the fruit out with a spoon. Put on a cutting board and cut into strips. Prepare a serving platter with the lettuce. Set the avocado on the lettuce and add the rest of the ingredients, pepper, cucumber, scallion and carrots. Blend all dressing ingredients for 2 ½ to 3 minutes on high speed. Dressing should not be watery or thick, but a consistency between the two. Pour the dressing on salad before serving. Garnish with parsley, sesame seeds and place lemon wedges around the tray.

Baby Spinach with Raspberry Cream Dressing

Ingredients

12 oz. fresh baby spinach
4 hard-boiled eggs, cut into rings
1 small red pepper, cut into thin rings
1 large lime, cubed

Dressing

1 cup fresh raspberries
¼ cup mayonnaise
½ cup sour cream
¼ cup raspberry vinegar
⅛ cup half and half
Salt and pepper to taste
1 Tbsp. tarragon

Garnish

½ cup red cabbage, shredded
1 orange, cut into rings
½ cup blackberries

Instructions

Wash the spinach and strain. Put the spinach on a serving tray or salad bowl. Add hard-boiled eggs around the outside. Add onion slices and lime cubes. Prepare the dressing in a blender and mix well for 1 minute. Adjust flavor as needed. Before serving pour dressing on salad and finish with a garnish. In the center of the spinach put the twisted orange slices. Sprinkle blackberries.

Baby Corn with Granny Smith Apples and Lemon Dressing

Ingredients

24 oz. baby corn
2 medium Granny Smith apples, julienned
1 medium red pepper, sliced thin
1 small carrot, grated

Dressing

½ cup fresh lemon juice
½ cup olive oil
¼ cup Kalamata olives
1 small jalapeños, chopped
½ cup sour cream
1 Tbsp. garlic, chopped
Salt and pepper to taste

Garnish

6-8 corn husks
2 medium limes, sliced and twisted
2 Tbsp. dill, chopped

Instructions

Wash the corn and boil for approximately 20 minutes. Strain and let cool. You can use canned baby corn as well. Drain all the liquid from the corn and put into a mixing bowl. Add the granny smith apple, red onion, pepper and carrots. Toss gently. To prepare a serving tray with corn husks. Pour salad over the corn husks. To make the dressing blend all ingredients in the blender. Adjust the flavor and pour on salad before serving. To garnish put the twisted lime slices around the edge of the salad and sprinkle chopped dill on top.

Baby Tomatoes Cooked Kale and Cheddar Cheese

Ingredients

10 oz. cherry tomatoes
16 oz. fresh kale
10 oz. cheddar cheese, grated
1 small red onion, cut into rings
1 tsp. garlic

Dressing

½ cup mayonnaise
1 cup sour cream
¼ cup fresh lemon juice
1 Tbsp. lemon zest
3 Tbsp. olive oil
1 Tbsp. curry powder
Salt and pepper to taste

Garnish

2 cups red cabbage
1 carrot, grated
2 Tbsp. parsley

Instructions

Wash the tomatoes and put into a mixing bowl. Boil water and cook kale for approximately 3 to 4 minutes. Remove from the stove and strain. Let cool and chop. Add kale to tomatoes. Add cheddar cheese, onion and garlic. Toss gently. Prepare a platter with the red cabbage. Pour salad on cabbage. Blend all ingredients in a blender for 1 ½ minutes. Adjust flavor if needed. Pour dressing on the salad , Garnish with shredded carrot across the center of the salad and sprinkle parsley.

Breaded Zucchini with Roasted Red Pepper Dressing

Ingredients

5 zucchini, wedged
2 red peppers, fried
1 red onion, cut into rings
4 Tbsp. Italian parsley
1 cup white flour
3 eggs, beaten
1 cup breadcrumbs
1 cup oil

Dressing

½ cup vinegar
¼ cup olive oil
¼ cup water
¼ cup cheddar cheese
2 Tbsp. garlic
Salt and pepper to taste
1 lemon for juice

Garnish

2 cups spinach leaves
2 tomatoes, cut into rings
½ cup carrots, shredded

Instructions

Wash the zucchini. Cut top and bottom off and cut in half. Then slice into strips. Prepare the flour beaten eggs and bread crumbs in separate bowls. Dip zucchini in flour egg then breadcrumbs. Heat oil in pan and fry until golden brown. Remove from oil and put on a paper towel. In the same oil fry the red pepper strips. Remove from oil and place on paper towel. Prepare the serving tray with spinach leaves. Lay zucchini on it and then the red pepper strips. Add the onion, and parsley. Blend dressing ingredients and blend well. Adjust flavor if needed. Before serving pour dressing on salad. Garnish with tomato rings and grated carrots.

Beet Salad with Anchovies and Sour Cream

Ingredients

5 medium beets, cooked
4 oz. anchovies
1 large pear, cut into thin slices
1 ½ cups sour cream
Salt and pepper to taste
3 Tbsp. vinegar
3 Tbsp. olive oil

Garnish

1 ½ cup lettuce
2 hard-boiled eggs, wedges
1 Tbsp. fresh rosemary, chopped

Instructions

Boil the beets for 35 to 40 minutes. Cool under cold water. Peel and cut into thin slices. Transfer to a mixing bowl and add chopped anchovies. Add pears, sour cream, salt and pepper, vinegar and oil. Toss gently. Prepare a tray with julienned lettuce. Add salad on top. Garnish with the hardboiled eggs around the salad and sprinkle with rosemary.

Broccoli and Egg with Avocado Cream Dressing

Ingredients

20 oz. broccoli spears
5 eggs, boiled
½ cup cherry tomatoes
½ cup cheddar cheese, shredded

Dressing

2 avocados
½ cup mayonnaise
½ cup sour cream
¼ cup olive oil
1 Tbsp. garlic, chopped
Salt and pepper to taste
3 Tbsp. half and half

Garnish

4 lettuce leaves
1 lemon, sliced and twisted

Instructions

Wash the broccoli and cut 1 ½ inches to 2 inches off the stem. Boil the broccoli for approximately 2 to 3 ½ minutes. Strain the broccoli and let it cool to room temperature. Chop coarsely and put in a mixing bowl. Add eggs, tomatoes, and cheddar cheese. Lay the lettuce leaves on a serving tray. Pour salad over lettuce. Pour dressing on salad before serving. Garnish with the twisted lemon rings.

Broccoli and Persimmon with Herb Parmesan Dressing

Ingredients

4 large stalks of broccoli
3 medium persimmon, cubed
1 medium Granny Smith apple, julienned
1 medium yellow pepper, sliced thin

Dressing

⅓ cup olive oil or avocado oil
⅓ cup balsamic vinegar
⅓ cup water
1 Tbsp. sugar
Salt and pepper to taste
2 Tbsp. parmesan
1 Tbsp. garlic, chopped
1 Tbsp. mint leaves, chopped
1 Tbsp. rosemary
Dash of crushed red pepper

Garnish

1 ½ cups spinach leaves
1 tomato, halved
½ cup fresh walnuts

Instructions

Wash broccoli and cut 2 inches of the stem off. Boil for approximately 5 minutes. Remove from stove and pour into strainer. Let cool. Add cubed persimmon, granny smith apple and yellow pepper. Toss gently. Prepare a serving tray with spinach leaves then put salad on top. Put all ingredients of dressing into the blender for approximately 50 seconds. Before serving, pour dressing on top. To garnish place the slices of tomato around the edges of the tray and sprinkle walnuts on top.

Broccoli and Smoked Ham with Parmesan Cream Dressing

Ingredients

20 oz. broccoli florets
10 oz. smoked ham, julienned
½ cup parmesan, shredded
1 red pepper, julienned
1 scallion onion, chopped

Dressing

1 ¼ cup mayonnaise
½ cup half and half
¼ cup vinegar
½ cup parmesan
1 Tbsp. garlic
1 Tbsp. rosemary
Salt and pepper to taste

Garnish

4 red cabbage leaves
6 pineapple slices
2 Tbsp. dill, chopped

Instructions

Wash the broccoli and boil it for approximately 2½ to 3 minutes. Strain it and let cool to room temperature. Transfer the broccoli to a mixing bowl and add the ham, red pepper, and scallion. Add all dressing ingredients in a blender and mix well. Adjust flavor as needed. Place cabbage leaves on a serving tray and pour salad over the cabbage. Pour dressing on just before serving. Garnish with the pineapple slices and chopped dill.

Vegetables | 33

Broccoli with Shrimp, Walnuts and Picante Cream Dressing

Ingredients

16 oz. fresh broccoli florets
12 oz. baby shrimp, cooked and peeled
½ cup pecans, chopped
1 red pepper, chopped
3 Tbsp. Italian parsley, chopped

Dressing

Touch of Old Bay Seasoning
¾ cup mayonnaise
¾ cup sour cream
1 jalapeños, chopped
¼ cup lemon juice
1 Tbsp. tarragon
Salt to taste
1 tsp. garlic, chopped

Garnish

6 lettuce leaves
6 strawberries, halved
2 Tbsp. Italian parsley, chopped

Instructions

Wash the broccoli and boil it in water for approximately 2 ½ to 3 minutes. Remove from the stove and strain. Let it cool to room temperature. Boil shrimp and then peel it. Put the broccoli and the shrimp in a mixing bowl and add pecans, red pepper, parsley. Mix gently. Prepare dressing in a blender. Blend on high speed for 1 minute. Lay the lettuce leaves on a serving tray and pour the salad over the lettuce. Pour dressing over the salad. Garnish with strawberry halves and sprinkle parsley.

Broccoli with Smoked Turkey and Mango Dressing

Ingredients

16 oz. broccoli florets
8 oz. smoked turkey, julienned
¼ cup red onion, chopped
1 red pepper, cut into strips
2 Tbsp. Italian parsley

Dressing

1 mango
¼ cup mayonnaise
¼ cup ketchup
¼ cup sour cream
1 tsp. garlic, chopped
⅛ cup lemon juice
Salt and pepper to taste

Garnish

3 red cabbage leaves
2 Tbsp. parsley
½ cup walnuts, chopped

Instructions

Boil broccoli florets for 2 ½ minutes. Strain and cool to room temperature. Place broccoli into a mixing bowl. Add smoked turkey, red pepper, red onion, and Italian parsley. Prepare dressing in a blender and mix until blended well. Prepare a serving tray with the red cabbage leaves and add the salad on the tray. Pour dressing over salad before serving. Garnish with parsley and chopped walnuts.

Broccoli with Tomato, Basil and Blue Cheese Dressing

Ingredients

20 oz. Broccoli
1 Granny Smith apple, julienned
2 tomatoes, wedged
1 red onion, chopped
¾ cup blue cheese, crumbled

Dressing

¼ cup olive oil
¼ cup vinegar
¼ cup water
½ cup sour cream
½ cup Kalamata olives
1 Tbsp. garlic
Salt, pepper, and sugar to taste

Garnish

1 quart spinach leaves
¼ cup peanuts ground, unsalted
1 red pepper, julienned

Instructions

Boil broccoli for 3 to 3½ minutes. Strain and let cool. Cut 2 inches off of the stem. Cut the broccoli into large chunks and transfer to a mixing bowl. Add apple, tomatoes and blue cheese. Stir gently. Prepare a tray with the spinach leaves and pour salad on top of the spinach. Blend all dressing ingredients on high speed. Adjust flavor as needed. Pour dressing over salad before serving. Garnish with ground peanuts and red pepper.

Brussel Sprouts and Fruit with Lemon Olive Dressing

Ingredients

24 oz. fresh Brussel sprouts, cooked
3 red plums, thinly wedged
3 scallion onions, chopped
1 carrot, coarsely grated
1 Granny Smith apple, julienned
½ cup seedless Kalamata olives
1 cup raspberries

Dressing

⅓ cup olive oil
⅓ cup lemon juice
¼ cup water
Salt and pepper to taste
1 Tbsp. garlic, chopped
½ cup sour cream

Garnish

3 red cabbage leaves
2 Tbsp. dill, chopped
Dash of sweet paprika

Instructions

Wash brussels sprouts, boil for approximately 15 to 20 minutes. Remove and let cool. Put into a mixing bowl and add the rest of the ingredients; plums, scallion, carrots, apple, kalamata olives and raspberries. Toss gently. Prepare a serving tray with the green cabbage leaves. Pour salad on top. Blend the ingredients for 45 seconds and adjust flavor. Pour over salad before serving. Garnish with dill and sweet paprika.

Brussel Sprouts with Fruit and Kalamata Lemon Dressing

Ingredients

20 oz. fresh Brussel sprouts
1 cup spinach, julienned
1 medium red pepper, roasted and chopped
1 medium lime with skin, cut into rings
1 small red onion, cut into thin rings
1 Tbsp. fresh tarragon, chopped
1 tsp. lemon skin, grated
1 small Granny Smith apple, julienned
1 plum, cut into small cubes

Dressing

¼ cup fresh lemon juice
⅓ cup olive oil
⅓ cup water
½ cup seedless Kalamata olives
1 tsp. jalapeños, chopped
Salt, pepper, and sugar to taste

Garnish

2 cup red cabbage, julienned
2 Tbsp. parsley chopped
1 medium tomato, small cubes
¼ cup walnuts, coarsely chopped
2 Tbsp. grated parmesan cheese

Instructions

Place 3 quarts of water into a pot and bring to a boil. Add Brussel sprouts, place a lid covering ¾ of the top, and cook 20 to 25 minutes. Remove from heat, rinse with cold water, strain, and place into a mixing bowl. Add spinach, roasted red pepper, lime, red onion, tarragon, lemon skin, Granny Smith apple, and plum. Mix gently. Prepare the dressing. Add all dressing ingredients into a blender and mix for 45 seconds on high speed. Season to taste. Add dressing to salad and mix gently. Place red cabbage onto a serving tray and add salad on top. Garnish with tomato rings around the tray. Sprinkle with parsley, tomatoes, walnuts, and parmesan.

Carrot and Fruit with Honey Sour Dressing

Ingredients

3 medium carrot, cooked and sliced
2 red plums, wedged
1 pear, julienned
1 apple, julienned
1 cup seedless black grapes

Dressing

½ cup honey
2 lemons for juice
1 tsp. lemon zest
1 Tbsp. sugar
Salt and pepper to taste
3 Tbsp. dill, chopped
2 Tbsp. mustard
¼ cup olive oil

Garnish

5 lettuce leaves
4 Tbsp. walnuts, chopped
1 lemon, wedged

Instructions

Wash the fruits and carrots. Peel the carrots and boil for 6 to 7 minutes. Strain and let cool. Slice into rings and put into a mixing bowl. Add plums, pears and apples and grapes. Toss gently. Prepare the dressing in a blender for 1 ½ to 2 minutes. Adjust flavor if needed. Prepare a tray with lettuce leaves. Pour salad on tray. Before serving add the dressing. Finish with garnish. Sprinkle walnuts on top. Add lemon wedges around the salad.

Carrot and Hard Boiled Eggs with Mayonnaise Base

Ingredients

4 carrots, cooked
4 hard-boiled eggs, grated
2 scallion onions, chopped
1 red pepper, chopped
1 cup fresh spinach, julienned

Dressing

1 cup mayonnaise
1 lemon for juice
1 Tbsp. fresh oregano
Salt and pepper to taste
1 tsp. garlic
3 Tbsp. sour cream

Garnish

3 red cabbage leaves
2 Tbsp. dill
1 lemon, wedged

Instructions

Peel the carrots and cut the top and bottom off. Boil for 5 to 7 minutes. Cool and cut into rings. Transfer to a mixing bowl. Add other ingredients an mix gently. Prepare dressing in a blender and mix well. Adjust flavor if needed. Put the red cabbage leaves on a tray and pour salad on top. Pour dressing over the top. Garnish with lemon wedges and dill.

Carrot and Pineapple with Honey Mustard Raisin Dressing

Ingredients

4 large carrots, peeled, cooked and chopped
2 cups pineapple, cubes
½ red onion, chopped
1 Tbsp. fresh rosemary, chopped

Dressing

¼ cup olive oil
½ cup honey
¼ cup mustard
Salt and pepper to taste
¼ cup raisins
1 lemon for juice
1 tsp. lemon skin, grated

Garnish

2 cups fresh spinach leaves
1 orange, cut into rings
1 Tbsp. parsley, chopped

Instructions

Peel the carrot cut the top and bottom and boil for 5 to 7 minutes. Remove from the water. Cool and cut into rings. Transfer to a mixing bowl and add pineapple, onion and rosemary. Prepare the dressing in a blender until well mixed. Adjust flavor if needed. Before serving prepare a serving tray or salad bowl with spinach leaves. Pour salad on top of the spinach. Right before serving pour dressing on. Garnish with the orange rings and sprinkle chopped parsley.

Vegetables

Cauliflower with Feta Cheese and Cream of Tomato Rosemary Dressing

Ingredients

1 cauliflower, florets
1 cup sharp cheddar cheese, shredded
½ cup red onion, thinly sliced
1 tomato, cubed

Dressing

1 cup mayonnaise
½ cup sour cream
½ cup tomato juice
2 Tbsp. rosemary
1 lemon for juice
1 tsp. lemon zest
Salt, pepper, and sugar to taste
1 Tbsp. garlic

Garnish

6 lettuce leaves, julienned
2 Tbsp. parsley, chopped
1 lemon, wedged
¼ cup breadcrumbs, browned

Instructions

Wash the cauliflower and boil for approximately 45 minutes. Remove from the stove and pour in a strainer. Let cool. Transfer to a mixing bowl and add red onion and tomato. Prepare a serving tray with julienned lettuce. Blend dressing ingredients until well blended. Pour salad over the tray. Pour dressing before serving. Garnish with parsley lemon wedges and breadcrumbs.

Cauliflower with Parmesan and Herb Dressing

Ingredients

1 cauliflower, cooked
1 red pepper, chopped
½ cup parmesan, grated
2 scallion onions, chopped
1 Tbsp. oregano

Dressing

1 ¼ cup mayonnaise
¼ cup half and half
⅛ cup lemon juice
1 Tbsp. garlic
¼ cup parmesan, grated
½ cup onion, chopped
Salt and pepper to taste

Garnish

5 lettuce leaves
3 Tbsp. dill, chopped
6 grapefruit, sliced
½ cup roasted pecans, chopped

Instructions

Wash the cauliflower and break it into florets. Boil the cauliflower for 5 to 6 minutes. Put into a strainer and let cool. Put in a mixing bowl and add parmesan, red pepper, scallion onion, and oregano. Toss gently. Blend all dressing ingredients for 1 to 1 ½ minutes. Adjust flavor if needed. Lay the lettuce leaves on a tray and put salad on top. Pour dressing over the salad before serving. Garnish with dill, and pecans. Place grapefruit slices around the salad.

Cauliflower with Olive Oil and Feta Dressing

Ingredients

1 cauliflower
¾ cup feta cheese, crumbled
½ cup seedless Kalamata olives

Dressing

½ cup olive oil
½ cup white vinegar
½ cup water
2 Tbsp. garlic, chopped
1 Tbsp. oregano
Salt, pepper, and sugar to taste
½ cup feta cheese
1 Tbsp. dill, chopped
1 Tbsp. jalapeños, chopped

Garnish

1 ½ cup red cabbage, julienned
3 Tbsp. parsley, chopped
1 cup watermelon, cubed

Instructions

Wash the cauliflower and break it into big pieces. Boil the cauliflower for 5 to 6 minutes. Put it into a trainer and let it cool. Transfer it to a mixing bowl and add feta cheese and Kalamata olives. Blend all dressing ingredients on high speed for 1 ½ minutes. Adjust flavor if needed. Before serving put the red cabbage on a tray and pour salad over top. Pour dressing on before serving. Garnish with chopped parsley and watermelon.

Cherry Tomatoes, Blue Cheese and Feta with Poppy Seeds

Ingredients

16 oz. cherry tomatoes
10 oz. blue cheese
4 oz. poppy seeds
3 scallion onions, chopped
2 Tbsp. garlic
3 Tbsp. dill
4 oz. feta cheese, crumbled

Dressing

¼ cup olive oil
1 Tbsp. mustard
2 Tbsp. Worchester
¼ cup red wine vinegar
¼ cup water
1 Tbsp. sugar
Salt and pepper to taste

Garnish

6 lettuce leaves, julienned
½ cup pecans, chopped
1 lemon, cut into rings

Instructions

Wash the tomatoes with cold water. Put into a mixing bowl and add the blue cheese, poppy seeds, scallion onions, garlic, dill and feta cheese. Mix lightly. Prepare a tray with the julienned lettuce. Pour the salad on to the tray. Blend all dressing ingredients and pour on salad before serving. Garnish with pecans and place lemon rings around the salad.

Cherry Tomatoes, Kalamata and Cream Cheese Dressing Picante

Ingredients

16 oz. cherry tomatoes
8 oz. seedless Kalamata olives
1 carrot, grated
1 jalapeños, chopped
4 oz. cheddar cheese, grated
2 tsp. fresh rosemary, chopped

Dressing

8 oz. cream cheese
¼ cup half and half
1 lemon for juice
⅛ cup wine vinegar
Salt and pepper to taste
1 tsp. garlic, chopped
2 Tbsp. dill, chopped

Garnish

2 cups alfalfa sprouts
2 mushrooms, thinly sliced
2 Tbsp. parsley, chopped

Instructions

Wash the tomatoes with cold water and put into a mixing bowl. Add Kalamata olives, carrots, jalapeños, cheddar cheese, and rosemary. Toss gently. Prepare a salad bowl or serving tray. Put salad on the serving tray and place alfalfa sprouts around edges of the salad. Blend all dressing ingredients for 1 to 1 ½ minutes. Pour dressing over the salad before serving. Garnish with mushrooms and chopped parsley.

Collard Greens with Sour Cream and Bacon

Ingredients

2 ½ lbs. green collards
¼ cup red onion
8 strips bacon, crunchy, chopped
¼ cup red pepper, chopped
1 Granny Smith apple, julienned
2 Tbsp. tarragon, chopped
½ cup feta cheese, crumbled

Dressing

¼ cup tarragon vinegar
¼ cup sour cream
1 tsp. lemon zest
1 Tbsp. garlic
Salt, pepper, and sugar to taste

Garnish

4 red cabbage leaves
3 oz. Pepperoni, julienned
1 lemon, sliced

Instructions

Boil 4 to 5 quarts of water and put the collars in. Cook 5 to 6 minutes. Strain and place onto a cutting board. Chop collards coarsely and place into a mixing bowl. Add onion, bacon, red pepper, apple, tarragon, and feta cheese. Toss gently. Prepare the dressing in a blender and mix for 1 minute. Adjust flavor as needed. Prepare a serving tray with red cabbage leaves and add salad on top. Pour dressing over the salad. Garnish with pepperoni and lemon slices.

Chick Peas, Poppy Seed and Cheddar Cheese with Olive Oil Dressing

Ingredients

24 oz. chick peas
1 cup sharp cheddar cheese
½ cup Kalamata olives
1 Tbsp. Jalapeños
1 medium tomato
¼ cup poppy seeds

Dressing

½ cup olive oil
½ cup balsamic
¼ cup water
1 Tbsp. garlic
1 Tbsp. oregano
3 Tbsp. honey
Salt, pepper, and sugar to taste

Garnish

2 Roma tomatoes, roasted
2 Tbsp. parsley, chopped
¼ cup raisins

Instructions

You can use dried beans. Soak in water overnight. Cook the next day an hour and a quarter. Remove from the stove and strain. Let cool. You can also use canned beans. Wash with cold water and put into a mixing bowl. Add the cheddar cheese, Kalamata, jalapeños, tomatoes and poppy seed. Blend all dressing ingredients for 1 minute. Adjust flavor. Before serving pour the salad on a salad tray and pour dressing on top. Garnish with the roasted tomatoes around the salad. Sprinkle the parsley and raisins.

Cooked Spinach with Parmesan and Sundried Tomatoes

Ingredients

2 lbs. fresh spinach, cooked
1 ½ cups sour cream
3 Tbsp. parmesan
1 cup sundried tomatoes, chopped
1 red onion, cut into rings
2 Tbsp. garlic, chopped

Dressing

2 lemons for juice
Salt and pepper to taste
½ Tbsp. nutmeg
4 Tbsp. olive oil

Garnish

1 large lime, cut into rings
1 roasted red pepper, cut into strips
1 cup croutons

Instructions

Boil spinach in water for about 2 minutes. Pour into a strainer until all liquid is gone. Put on a cutting board and chop largely. Transfer to a mixing bowl and add the sour cream, parmesan, tomatoes, onion, and garlic. Toss gently. Prepare a tray for serving. Pour salad on the tray. Mix dressing ingredients in a mixing bowl. Add the dressing to the salad before serving. Garnish with the lime rings around the salad. Put the red pepper strips along the center of the salad and sprinkle croutons.

Cooked Zucchini and Pear with Balsamic Dressing

Ingredients

4 large zucchini, cooked
1 large pear, julienned
¼ cup red onion, chopped
1 medium red pepper, chopped

Dressing

¼ cup balsamic vinegar
¼ cup olive oil
¼ cup cheddar cheese white
Salt and pepper to taste
1 Tbsp. garlic, chopped
Dash of sugar
1 small lemon for juice
1 tsp. lemon zest

Garnish

½ cup sour cream
1 lemon, wedged
2 Tbsp. parsley

Instructions

Wash the zucchini and cut the top and bottom off. Boil for 3 minutes. Remove from water and let cool. Chop the zucchini coarsely and put in a mixing bowl. Add the rest of the ingredients. Prepare a tray with lettuce. Place the salad on the lettuce. Blend dressing ingredients on high speed and pour on salad before serving. Garnish with a spoon of sour cream across the middle of the salad. Place lemon wedges around the salad on the tray and sprinkle with parsley.

Cucumber and Anchovy with Sour Cream Dressing

Ingredients

3 seedless cucumbers, sliced
6 oz. anchovies, chopped
1 beet, cooked and julienned
2 scallion onions, chopped
1 apple, julienned

Dressing

1 ½ cups sour cream
¼ cup lemon juice
1 Tbsp. garlic, chopped
Salt and pepper to taste

Garnish

2 tomatoes, wedged
1 Tbsp. tarragon
2 Tbsp. parsley

Instructions

Wash the cucumbers and slice them with the skin. Put into a mixing bowl and add the rest of the ingredients: anchovies, beets, scallion onions, and apple. Toss gently. Prepare a serving tray or salad bowl and pour the salad onto the serving tray. Blend all the dressing ingredients until well mixed. Pour dressing over the salad before serving. Garnish with the tomato wedges around the salad. Sprinkle tarragon and parsley.

Cucumber and Parmesan with Dill Dressing

Ingredients

2 cucumbers, sliced
3 Tbsp. dill, chopped
1 cup seedless black grapes
1 apple, peeled and julienned
2 scallion onions, chopped
½ cup parmesan cheese

Dressing

½ cup balsamic vinegar
½ cup olive oil
½ cup water
Salt, pepper, and sugar to taste
¾ cup parmesan, grated
1 tsp. garlic, chopped

Garnish

4 lettuce leaves
1 carrot, grated
1 lime, sliced

Instructions

Wash cucumbers and cut the top and bottom off. Slice into thin rings and place into a mixing bowl. Add dill, black grapes, apple, onion, and parmesan. Mixing gently. Prepare a tray with lettuce leaves and pour salad over the top of the lettuce. Prepare dressing ingredients in a blender and blend for 1 minute. Pour the dressing on the salad before serving. Garnish with grated carrot and lime slices.

Cucumber and Carrot Salad with Cream Cheese Dill Dressing

Ingredients

2 large seedless cucumbers, cubed
1 carrot, grated
1 red onion, sliced
2 Tbsp. dill, chopped
1 cup seedless black grapes

Dressing

1 cup cream cheese
3 Tbsp. dill, chopped
⅛ cup olive oil
½ cup half and half
1 lemon for juice
1 Tbsp. lemon skin, grated
1 Tbsp. garlic, chopped
Salt, pepper, and sugar to taste

Garnish

½ cup peanuts, chopped
1 lemon, wedged
1 cup spinach, julienned

Instructions

Wash the cucumbers and cut into cubes. Put them in a mixing bowl. Add carrots, onion, seedless grapes, and dill. Mix gently. Prepare a tray with spinach leaves and pour the salad over the spinach leaves. Put all dressing ingredients in a blender for 2 minutes. Adjust flavor if needed. Before serving pour dressing over the salad. Garnish with the chopped peanuts and place lemon wedges around the tray.

Cucumber Salad with Feta and Olive Oil Lemon Dressing

Ingredients

4 cucumbers, seedless
1 ½ cups feta cheese, crumbled
½ cup red onion, thinly sliced
2 Tbsp. dill, chopped
2 Tbsp. mint leaves, chopped
¾ cup seedless Kalamata olives

Dressing

¼ cup olive oil
¼ cup lemon juice
Salt, pepper, and sugar to taste
Dash of cumin
1 Tbsp. garlic, chopped
¼ cup water
1 Tbsp. lime zest

Garnish

3 cups lettuce, julienned
1 tomato, wedged
1 Tbsp. lemon zest
1 carrot, grated

Instructions

Wash cucumbers and cut the top and bottom off. Place into a mixing bowl. Add feta cheese, red onion, dill, mint leaves, and Kalamata olives. Blend the dressing ingredients until well mixed. Prepare a serving tray and pour the salad over top. Before serving pour the dressing over the salad. Garnish with tomato wedges around the tray and sprinkle lemon zest and grated carrots.

Cucumber Salad with Smoked Salmon and Sour Cream Dressing

Ingredients

2 large seedless Asian cucumbers, unpeeled and sliced into rings
4 oz. smoked salmon, chopped
¼ cup red onion, chopped
1 Tbsp. garlic, chopped
¼ cup red pepper, chopped

Dressing

12 oz. sour cream
1 medium lemon for juice
1 Tbsp. lemon zest
2 Tbsp. fresh dill, chopped
2 Tbsp. grated parmesan
2 Tbsp. half and half or milk
Salt and pepper to taste

Garnish

6 whole romaine lettuce leaves
2 Tbsp. pecans, chopped
1 Tbsp. fresh Italian parsley, chopped
1 medium tomato, wedged

Instructions

Wash cucumbers, cut into rings and put them in a mixing bowl. Add smoked salmon, onion, garlic and red pepper. Toss lightly. To prepare the serving tray lay the lettuce leaves on the tray. Pour salad over the top. Blend all the dressing ingredients in a blender for approximately 45 seconds. Adjust the flavor. Pour over salad just before serving. To garnish sprinkle chopped pecans and parsley. Place tomato wedges around the edge of the tray.

Cucumber with Blue Cheese and Tarragon Dressing

Ingredients

2 cucumbers
1 cup blue cheese, crumbled
1 carrot, grated
1 onion, chopped
3 Tbsp. parsley, chopped

Dressing

½ cup tarragon vinegar
½ cup olive oil
½ cup water
1 Tbsp. garlic, chopped
Salt, pepper, and sugar to taste
3 Tbsp. dill, chopped

Garnish

5 lettuce leaves
1 tomato, sliced
1 cup alfalfa sprouts

Instructions

Wash the cucumber and slice into rings. Put them in a mixing bowl. Add blue cheese, carrots, onion, and parsley. Toss gently. Prepare a platter with the lettuce leaves and add salad to the tray. Blend all dressing ingredients in a blender for 1 minute. Adjust flavor as needed. Pour dressing over salad. Garnish with the tomato slices around the salad and the alfalfa sprouts down the middle.

Cucumber with Cream Cheese and Lemon Dressing

Ingredients

5 seedless cucumbers
2 scallion onions, chopped
1 Granny Smith apple, julienned
1 Tbsp. oregano

Dressing

6 oz. cream cheese
½ cup half and half
¼ cup lemon juice
½ cup olive oil
3 Tbsp. parsley, chopped
Salt, pepper, and sugar to taste
1 tsp. garlic, chopped
2 Tbsp. sour cream
3 Tbsp. sharp cheddar cheese

Garnish

2 cups spinach leaves
1 lime, sliced
1 red pepper, chopped

Instructions

Wash cucumbers and cut the top and bottom off. Slice into thin rings. Place into a mixing bowl. Add scallion onions, apple, and oregano. Prepare the dressing in a blender and mix for 2 minutes on high speed. Adjust flavor as needed. Prepare a serving tray with spinach leaves and pour the salad over top. Pour dressing on salad before serving. Garnish with sliced lime and chopped red pepper.

Eggplant and Veggie Eggs Carrots Tomato Dressing

Ingredients

1 medium eggplant, cut into medium rings
1 cup flour
1 ½ cup vegetable or olive oil
1 medium red pepper, cut into thin strips
1 small cucumber, julienned
1 scallion onion, chopped
2 hard-boiled eggs, sliced round
1 medium carrot, finely grated

Dressing

½ cup sundried tomatoes
1 medium carrot, cooked
½ cup balsamic vinegar
¼ cup water
½ cup olive oil
Salt, pepper, and sugar to taste

Garnish

3 cups spinach, julienned
1 medium tomato, cubed
2 Tbsp. dill, chopped
1 beet, cooked and cut into thin rings

Instructions

Wash eggplant and cut into medium round slices. Dip slices into flour on both sides. Heat oil in a sauté pan. Add eggplant and cook until golden brown on both sides. Place on paper towel to drain excess oil. Place spinach onto a serving tray and evenly add eggplant slices on top. Add red pepper, cucumber, scallion onion, hard-boiled eggs, and carrots over eggplant. Prepare the dressing. Add all dressing ingredients into a blender and mix for 2 minutes on high speed. Season to taste. Pour dressing over the salad. Garnish with beet slices around the salad. Sprinkle with tomato and dill on top.

Eggplant with Feta Cheese with Oil and Vinegar Dressing

Ingredients

1 medium eggplant
½ cup olive oil
1 cup crumbled feta cheese
1 celery stalk, chopped
½ cup kalamata olives, chopped
1 small red pepper, chopped

Dressing

¼ cup olive oil
¼ cup wine vinegar
¼ cup water
1 Tbsp. sugar
Salt and pepper to taste

Garnish

6 romaine lettuce leaves
2 Tbsp. Italian parsley, chopped
3 hard-boiled eggs, wedged

Instructions

Wash the eggplant and cut the top and bottom off. Cut it into 8-10 round slices. Heat oil in a frying pan and fry the eggplant until golden brown. Remove from the pan and place on a paper towel to remove excess oil. Prepare a serving tray with lettuce leaves. Lay the eggplant slices nicely on the tray and add the rest of the ingredients; feta cheese, celery, olives, and red pepper. Blend the dressing ingredients in a blender for 45 seconds. Adjust flavor if needed. Before serving, pour the dressing on the salad. Garnish with chopped parsley and place the hard boiled egg wedges around the tray.

Eggplant with Domino Picante Dressing

Ingredients

1 medium eggplant
1 medium red pepper, chopped
1 medium cucumber
1 tomato, cubed
2 scallion onions, chopped
1 Tbsp. garlic, chopped
2 Tbsp. Italian parsley, chopped
1 small jalapeños, chopped

Dressing

½ cup olive oil
2 medium lemons for juice
Salt and pepper to taste
1 Tbsp. basil, chopped

Garnish

2 cups fresh spinach leaves
1 large lime wedge
Dash of paprika

Instructions

Wash the eggplant, poke holes with fork and place it on a tray. Bake on 400° for 35 to 40 minutes. Remove from oven put it on a plate and let the juice come out a little bit before doing anything with it. Cut down the middle across the bottom and scrape the inside out of the skin. Chop it up with a knife and put it in a mixing bowl. Add the peppers, cucumber, scallion, garlic, onion, jalapeños and parsley. Mix gently. Prepare a serving tray with fresh spinach leaves. Pour the salad on to the spinach leave. Put all the dressing ingredients into a blender or a bowl and mix it well. Adjust flavor. Pour the dressing on top of the salad before serving. To garnish put lime wedges around the salad and sprinkle the sweet paprika.

Eggplant with Spicy Sour Cream

Ingredients

1 medium eggplant
1 cup whole wheat flour
Salt and pepper to taste
1 Tbsp. fresh oregano
¾ cup vegetable oil

Dressing

1 cup sour cream
1 medium lemon for juice
1 Tbsp. garlic
2 Tbsp. dill, chopped
3 Tbsp. olive oil
½ cup shredded cheddar cheese
¼ cup half and half

Garnish

6 lettuce leaves
1 cup whole garbanzo beans
1 Tbsp. parsley, chopped
1 tomato, wedged

Instructions

Wash the eggplant, cut the top and bottom off. Cut into medium round slices. Dip them in the flour with salt, pepper and oregano and fry in hot oil until golden brown. Remove from oil and put on a paper towel. Prepare a serving tray with the romaine lettuce leaves. Place the eggplant on the lettuce. To prepare the dressing put all ingredients in the blender and blend for approximately 1 minute. Adjust flavor. Before serving pour the dressing along the top of the eggplant. Garnish with chopped parsley and the garbanzo beans on the eggplant. Place the tomato wedges around the salad on the tray.

Eggplant with Sundried Tomatoes and Sesame Dressing

Ingredients

1 eggplant, sliced and fried
¾ cup white flour
3 large eggs
1 ¼ cup bread crumbs
1 ¼ cup vegetable oil
1 cup sundried tomatoes, chopped
1 celery stick, chopped
2 Tbsp. parsley
1 avocado, cubed
1 cucumber, cubed
1 carrot, grated
1 tomato, cubed

Dressing

½ cup tahini paste
¼ cup lemon juice
½ cup water
Salt and pepper to taste 1 Tbsp. cumin
1 Tbsp. garlic

Garnish

6 romaine lettuce leaves
1 lemon sliced thin
4 bacon strips, crunchy and chopped

Instructions

Wash eggplant and cut top and bottom off. Dry with a paper towel and slice into 10 slices. Dip into the egg and then bread crumbs. Heat the oil and fry both sides until golden brown. Remove from the oil and place onto a paper towel. Prepare a serving tray with the lettuce leaves. Place the eggplant on the tray. Add sundried tomatoes, celery, parsley, avocado, cucumber, carrot, and tomato. Blend the dressing ingredients in a blender. Pour dressing over the salad. Garnish with lemon slices and sprinkle bacon and sesame seeds.

Espanol Tomato Rice Picante

Ingredients

1 ½ cups basmati rice
1 red onion, chopped
2 tomatoes, chopped
2 Tbsp. chives
3 Tbsp. Italian parsley
Salt and pepper to taste
½ Tbsp. crushed hot red pepper
¼ cup olive oil

Dressing

2 large lemons for juice
¼ cup olive oil
½ cup tomato juice
1 Tbsp. fresh tarragon
2 Tbsp. garlic
2 strips crunchy bacon

Garnish

1 cup lettuce, julienned
6 rings pineapple with skin
2 Tbsp. parsley, chopped

Instructions

Heat oil in a pot and add onion until golden brown then add tomatoes. Stir and add rice. Let heat then add boiling water. Let boil cover and reduce to a simmer. Cook 10 to 12 minutes. When it is done remove from the stove and fluff with a fork gently. Let the rice cool. Prepare a serving tray with julienned lettuce. Add the rice salad on top. Prepare dressing in a blender for 1 minute. Before serving pour dressing on the salad. Finish with a garnish. Put pineapple around the salad and sprinkle Italian parsley over top.

Fresh Asparagus with Sundried Tomatoes Picante Lemon

Ingredients

16 oz. fresh thin asparagus
8 oz. sundried tomatoes, chopped
¼ cup red onion, chopped
1 small red pepper, julienned
1 medium lemon with skin, cut into thin slices
2 Tbsp. Italian parsley
1 small Granny Smith Apple, peeled and julienned

Dressing

¼ cup olive oil
¼ cup lemon juice
¼ cup tomato juice
½ tsp. crushed hot red pepper
2 Tbsp. dry red wine
1 small tomato, chopped
Salt, pepper, and sugar to taste

Garnish

6 grape leaves, whole
1 cup croutons
2 Tbsp. parmesan, shredded

Instructions

Wash asparagus in cold water, cut off 1 inch from the bottom. Place water in a sauté pan, and bring to a boil. Add asparagus and cook for 2 minutes. Remove from heat and drain. Place grape leaves onto a serving tray and evenly add the asparagus on top. Add sundried tomatoes, red onion, red pepper, lemons slices, Italian parsley, and apples over asparagus. Prepare the dressing. Add all dressing ingredients into a blender and mix for 1 minute on high speed. Season to taste. Pour dressing over the salad. Garnish with croutons and parmesan over top.

Fried Artichokes with Sundried Tomato Dressing

Ingredients

24 oz. artichoke hearts
¾ cup bread crumbs
For frying:
½ cup flour
3 eggs, beaten
¾ cup vegetable oil
1 Tbsp. rosemary
Salt and pepper to taste

Dressing

10 oz. sundried tomatoes
½ cup olive oil
½ cup lime juice
½ cup water
1 Tbsp. sugar
1 Tbsp. rosemary, chopped
1 Tbsp. garlic, chopped
2 Tbsp. red onion
Salt and pepper to taste

Garnish

2 cups fresh spinach
1 Roma tomato, sliced into rings
4 Tbsp. pecans, chopped

Instructions

You can use fresh artichokes or canned. If you use fresh, boil them for about 20 minutes with lemon and salt. Let them cool and remove the leaves surrounding the artichoke. Put flour, beaten eggs and breadcrumbs each in a separate bowl. Heat oil in a medium pan and fry the artichokes until golden brown. Remove with a slotted spoon and place on a paper towel. To prepare a serving tray lay spinach leaves over the tray. Place artichokes on the spinach. Place all ingredients for dressing into a blender. Blend for approximately 60 seconds. Adjust flavor to a picante and add a touch of hot crushed red pepper. Before serving, pour dressing over the artichokes. Garnish the edges of the tray with the sliced tomatoes. Sprinkle with chopped pecans.

Fried Avocado with Cucumber and Brie Cheese Dressing

Ingredients

4 medium avocados, wedged
½ cup white flour
3 medium eggs
1 cup bread crumbs
Salt and pepper to taste
¾ cup vegetable oil

Dressing

6 oz. Brie cheese
¼ cup half and half or milk ¼ cup lemon juice
1 Tbsp. lemon zest
2 Tbsp. garlic
2 Tbsp. rosemary
2 Tbsp. peanuts
1 Tbsp. Worchester
Salt and pepper to taste

Garnish

5 red cabbage leaves
2 Tbsp. parsley, chopped
1 lemon sliced into rings

Instructions

Wash the avocados and cut in half long way, separate and remove the pit. Take a spoon and remove the avocado from skin. Cut the avocado into wedges, dip it in flour eggs and bread crumbs, Heat the oil in a pan and fry the avocado's until golden brown. Remove from the oil and put on a paper towel. Prepare a serving plater. Put the red cabbage leaves on the tray. Place fried avocados on it. To prepare the dressing out ingredients into a blender for 1 ½ minutes. Adjust flavor to taste. Before serving pour the dressing on the avocados. To garnish sprinkle chopped parsley and put lemon wedges around the tray.

Fried Green Pepper and Feta Cheese with Red Onion Lemon Dressing

Ingredients

4 green peppers, cut into strips
1 cup feta cheese, crumbled
1 red onion, sliced
1 tomato, cubed
1 jalapeños, chopped
½ cup oil

Dressing

½ cup lemon juice
½ cup olive oil
½ cup water
Salt, pepper, and sugar to taste
1 Tbsp. garlic, chopped

Garnish

6 lettuce leaves
1 cup red cabbage, grated
1 Tbsp. parsley, chopped

Instructions

Cut peppers in half. Wash them and cut into strips. Heat oil in a pan and fry the peppers until lightly golden brown. Put on a paper towel. Prepare a serving tray and place the lettuce leaves on it. Add the pepper strips, feta cheese, onion, tomato and jalapeños. Prepare the dressing in a blender and mix for 1 minute. Adjust flavor as needed. Pour dressing over the salad before serving. Garnish with red cabbage and sprinkle parsley.

Fried Pumpkin with Lime Blackberry Dressing

Ingredients

20 oz. fresh pumpkin
1 cup white flour
1 ½ cups bread crumbs
3 eggs, beaten
1 cup vegetable oil

Dressing

½ cup lime juice
½ cup olive oil
⅛ cup wine vinegar
¼ cup water
Salt and pepper to taste
Dash of sugar
½ cup sour blackberries

Garnish

2 cups spinach leaves
1 lemon, wedged
2 Tbsp. dill, chopped

Instructions

Wash the pumpkin and cut into strips. Dip the pumpkin in flour eggs and bread crumbs. Fry in a pan with oil until golden brown. Remove from oil and put on a paper towel. Prepare a platter with spinach leaves. Place friend pumpkin on lettuce. Prepare dressing in a blender for 1 minute on high speed. Adjust flavor if needed. Before serving pour dressing on the salad. Garnish with lemon wedges and sprinkle dill.

Fried Red Pepper Salad with Wine Vinegar and Hot Crushed Pepper

Ingredients

4 red peppers, sliced
2 cups spinach, julienned
1 onion, sliced
¼ cup raisins
½ cup oil

Dressing

¼ cup red wine vinegar
¼ cup olive oil
¼ cup water
1 tsp. crushed red pepper
Salt, pepper, and sugar to taste
Dash of sweet paprika

Garnish

1 cup green grapes
2 Tbsp. parsley, chopped

Instructions

Wash the pepper and cut into rings. Remove the seeds and wash again. Dry with a paper towel. Heat oil in a pan and fry the pepper rings until golden brown. Place the peppers on a paper towel. Prepare a tray and put all salad ingredients on the tray. Blend all dressing ingredients until well mixed. Pour dressing over the salad. Garnish with green grapes and sprinkle parsley.

Fried Squash with Sour Cream and Dill Dressing

Ingredients

5 squash, wedged
3 eggs
½ cup flour
¾ cup breadcrumbs
¾ cup vegetable or olive oil
Salt and pepper to taste

Dressing

1 ½ cups sour cream
1 lemon for juice
1 tsp. lemon zest
½ cup onion, browned
1 tsp. garlic, chopped
3 Tbsp. milk
1 Tbsp. mayonnaise
Dash of spicy red pepper
3 Tbsp. dill, chopped
Salt and pepper to taste

Garnish

5 lettuce leaves
½ cup black olives, chopped
3 Tbsp. parmesan

Instructions

Wash squash and cut the top and bottom off. Cut in half long ways and then cut into wedges. Dip wedges into the flour, egg, and then bread crumbs. Heat oil in a pan and fry the squash wedges until golden brown. Place squash on a paper towel. Prepare a serving tray with the lettuce leaves and place squash on top. Blend the dressing ingredients for approximately 1 ½ minutes. Adjust flavor if needed. Pour dressing over the squash before serving. Garnish with black olives and parmesan.

Fried Zucchini Salad with Lemon and Jalapenos Dressing

Ingredients

5 zucchini, cut into rings
1 carrot, cubed
1 red pepper, cut into strips
½ cup flour
¾ cup vegetable oil

Dressing

¼ cup lemon juice
¼ cup olive oil
¼ cup water
¼ cup swiss cheese
Salt to taste
1 Tbsp. garlic
¼ cup white wine dry

Garnish

1 ½ cups tossed salad
1 large tomato, cut into rings
3 Tbsp. fresh dill

Instructions

Wash the zucchini and cut the top and bottom off. Slice zucchini into medium sized rings. Dip the zucchini into the flour. Heat oil and fry the zucchini until it gets golden brown. Remove with a slotted spoon and put on a paper towel. Prepare a tray with the tossed salad. Place the zucchini rings on the salad and add carrots cooked and cubed, red pepper strips. Prepare dressing in a blender for 1 minute. Adjust flavor if needed. Before serving pour dressing on top. To garnish place tomato slices around the edge of the tray. Sprinkle with dill.

Garbanzo Spinach and Tomato Picante Flavor

Ingredients

24 oz. Garbanzo beans, cooked
3 cups fresh spinach leaves
2 tomatoes, cubed
1 small onion, chopped
1 carrot, grated

Dressing

⅓ cup olive oil
¼ cup lemon juice
1 tsp. cumin
2 Tbsp. garlic
1 Tbsp. lemon zest
Salt and pepper to taste

Garnish

½ cup pecans, chopped
1 small red pepper, cut into rings
1 small orange, wedged

Instructions

You can use dry garbanzo beans if you soak them over night in water and then cook for an 1 ¼ hours. If not, you can use canned beans. Wash the liquid off of the beans with cold water. Strain and put in a mixing bowl. Add the spinach, tomato, onion and carrot. Toss gently. Prepare the dressing by blending ingredients in a mixer for 1 ½ minutes on high speed. Put the salad on a tray. Add dressing before serving. Garnish with chopped pecans, red pepper rings and orange wedges between the pepper rings.

Grated Beets with Eggs and Carrots and Horseradish Mayonnaise Dressing

Ingredients

5 large beets, cooked
5 hard-boiled eggs
2 carrots, cooked and grated
2 Tbsp. dill

Dressing

¾ cup mayonnaise
3 Tbsp. horseradish
¾ cup sour cream
2 scallion onions
1 Tbsp. garlic, chopped
1 Tbsp. fresh raspberry

Garnish

3 leaves cabbage, grated
1 large lemon, cut into rings
3 Tbsp. parsley, chopped

Instructions

Cook beets for 35 to 40 minutes. Cook carrots for approximately 10 minutes. Grate the beets on a large grated and grate the carrots. Chop hardboiled egg and add all three to the bowl. Add chopped dill and mix gently. Prepare a tray with red cabbage. Blend all dressing ingredients for 1 ½ minutes. Before serving pour the dressing on the salad and finish with a garnish. Around the tray put lemon rings. Sprinkle Italian parsley.

Grated Radishes with Feta and Olives with Lime Dressing

Ingredients

20 oz. radishes, grated
1 red onion, sliced
1 ½ cups feta cheese, crumbled
1 cup Kalamata olives, chopped

Dressing

¼ cup fresh lime juice
1 Tbsp. lime zest
¼ cup olive oil
¼ cup water
1 Tbsp. garlic, chopped
1 Tbsp. oregano
Salt, pepper, and sugar to taste

Garnish

4 lettuce leaves
1 carrot, grated
1 cucumber, cut into rings

Instructions

Wash the radishes and cut the top and bottom off. Grate it into a mixing bowl and add the red onion, feta cheese and kalamata olives. Prepare a serving tray with the lettuce leaves and pour salad over the lettuce. Blend the dressing ingredients in a blender. Adjust flavor as needed. Pour the dressing over the salad before serving and garnish with cucumber slices and grated carrot.

Grated Radishes with Spinach and Fresh Mozzarella with Sour Cream and Lemon Dressing

Ingredients

16 oz. radishes, grated
1 quart of spinach leaves
1 cup fresh mozzarella, julienned
1 cup fresh raspberries

Dressing

1 cup sour cream
½ cup mayonnaise
¼ cup lemon juice
1 Tbsp. garlic
2 Tbsp. dill
Dash of hot red pepper
Salt and pepper to taste

Garnish

1 orange, wedged
½ cup whole walnuts
Dash of sweet paprika

Instructions

Wash the radishes and cut the top and bottom off. Grate them into a mixing bowl. Wash the spinach with cold water and add it to the radishes along with the mozzarella and raspberries. Blend all the dressing ingredients in a blender until well mixed. Adjust flavor if needed. Pour salad into a salad bowl or on a serving tray. Pour dressing on the salad before serving and garnish with orange wedges, walnuts and sweet paprika.

Green Asparagus and Hard Salami Kalamata Pepper Dressing

Ingredients

16 oz. fresh asparagus
8 oz. hard salami, julienned
6 oz. seedless Kalamata olives

Dressing

1 large red pepper, roasted
¼ cup olive oil
¼ cup balsamic
¼ cup water
1 Tbsp. honey
Salt, pepper, and sugar to taste

Garnish

1 ½ cups spinach leaves
5 figs, halved
1 tomato, cubed
1 Tbsp. dill, chopped

Instructions

Wash the asparagus in cold water. Cut 1 inch off the bottom. Boil asparagus with salt and lemon juice. Boil for 3 to 4 minutes. Remove and put in a strainer. Prepare the dressing in a blender for a minute and a half on high speed. Adjust flavor if needed. Prepare the platter with spinach leaves. Set the asparagus on the tray how you would like. Pour the julienned salami and Kalamata olives on top. Pour dressing on top of the asparagus. Garnish with halved figs around the edges of the tray. Sprinkle cubed tomatoes and chopped dill.

Green Asparagus with Veggie Mediterranean Lemon Dressing

Ingredients

20 oz. green thin asparagus
½ small red onion, cut into thin rings
2 Tbsp. dill, chopped
1 small tomato, cubed
1 red pepper, cut into thin strips
1 small lime with skin, cut thin
¼ cup pomegranate seeds
1 small carrot, coarsely grated

Dressing

¼ cup lemon juice
¼ cup olive oil
¼ cup water
¼ cup fresh orange juice
½ tsp. nutmeg, grated
Salt, pepper, and sugar to taste

Garnish

2 cups spinach, julienned
¼ cup raisins
3 hard-boiled eggs, cut into wedges

Instructions

Wash asparagus in cold water and cut ½ inch off bottom. Add 2 ½ quarts of water into deep sauté pan. Bring to a boil, add asparagus, and cook approximately 2 minutes. Remove from heat, strain and cool. Cut into 2 inch pieces. Place into a mixing bowl. Add red onion, dill, tomato, red pepper, lime skin, pomegranate seeds, and carrot. Mix gently. Prepare the dressing. Add all dressing ingredients into a blender and mix for 45 seconds on high speed. Season to taste. Place spinach onto a serving tray and add salad on top. Before serving, pour dressing over the salad. Garnish with hard-boiled egg wedges (face-up) around the salad and sprinkle with raisins on top.

Grated Zucchini with Fruit Cream Cheese Olive Oil Dressing

Ingredients

4 large zucchini
2 medium Granny Smith apples, julienned
2 large red plums, thinly wedged
2 scallion onions, chopped

Dressing

¾ cup cream cheese
¼ feta cheese
½ cup olive oil
¼ cup lemon juice
1 Tbsp. garlic
Salt and pepper
1 Tbsp. Worcestershire sauce

Garnish

4 lettuce leaves
½ cup pecans, chopped
2 hard-boiled egg, wedged

Instructions

Wash the zucchini, apples and plums. Peel the apples and julienne. Slice plums into thin wedges. Julienne the zucchini. Add all to a mixing bowl and add onions. Toss gently. Place lettuce leaves on a serving tray. Add salad on top. To prepare the dressing add all ingredients to the blender and blend. Adjust flavor as needed. Before serving pour the dressing on the salad. Sprinkle chopped pecans and add hard-boiled egg wedges around the salad on the tray.

Green Bean Salad with Marinated Red Pepper

Ingredients

16 oz. fresh green beans
1 red pepper, chopped
1 white onion, sliced
1 Tbsp. lemon zest, grated
1 carrot, julienned

Dressing

1 roasted red pepper
½ cup white vinegar
½ cup olive oil
2 Tbsp. fresh garlic
Salt, pepper, and sugar to taste
1 Tbsp. basil, chopped
¼ cup water

Garnish

1 beet, cooked and sliced
Dash of paprika
¼ cup walnuts

Instructions

Cut the top and bottom off of the green beans. Boil the green beans for approximately 5 minutes. Pour into a strainer and let cool to room temperature. Put green beans in a mixing bowl and add red pepper, onion, lemon zest, and carrots. Toss gently. Prepare the dressing by blending all the dressing ingredients in a blender. Adjust flavor as needed. Pour salad on a tray or salad bowl. Garnish with paprika, beet slices, and walnuts. Pour the dressing over the salad.

Green Beans with Cranberry and Honey Mustard Dressing

Ingredients

16 oz. fresh green beans
8 oz. fresh cranberries
2 red plums, wedged
1 Tbsp. dill, chopped

Dressing

¾ cup olive oil
¾ cup honey
⅛ cup yellow mustard
1 cup fresh raspberries
Salt and pepper to taste
1 lemon for juice
1 tsp. lemon zest, grated

Garnish

8 corn husks
¼ cup pecans, chopped
1 orange, cut into 8 wedges

Instructions

Cut the top and bottom off the green beans and boil them for 4-5 minutes. Remove with a strainer into a bowl and let cool to room temperature. Boil the cranberries in the same water for approximately 1 to 1 ½ minutes. Remove and let them cool. Pour cranberries into the mixing bowl with the green beans. Add red plum and dill. Toss gently. Put all the dressing ingredients into a blender and blend. Prepare a serving tray with the corn husks and pour salad over the top. Pour dressing over the salad. Garnish with chopped pecans and place orange wedges around the tray.

Green Beans with Red Pepper Olive and Lemon Dressing

Ingredients

16 oz. fresh green beans
2 red peppers, cut into strips
1 beet, cooked and julienned
1 Tbsp. lemon zest
2 Tbsp. orange skin

Dressing

¼ cup lemon juice
¼ cup olive oil
¼ cup vinegar
1 Tbsp. garlic
Salt and pepper to taste
1 Tbsp. saffron

Garnish

1 cup spinach leaves
1 orange, cubed
1 lemon, cut into rings
½ cup large walnuts

Instructions

Wash the green beans, cut the top and bottom off. Boil water and cook green beans for 4 to 5 minutes. Remove and pour into a strainer. Let cool. Transfer to mixing bowl and add peppers, beets, lemon zest and orange zest. Prepare the dressing in a blender for 1 minute. On a serving tray put spinach leaves and add salad. Pour dressing on salad before serving. Garnish with orange cubes and lemon rings. Sprinkle walnuts on center of salad.

Green Cabbage with Apples and Carrots with Marinated Rosemary

Ingredients

1 small red cabbage, grated
2 carrots, grated
1 apple, julienned
2 Tbsp. fresh rosemary

Dressing

½ cup olive oil
½ cup vinegar
¼ cup water
1 Tbsp. garlic, chopped
Dash of sugar
Salt and pepper to taste

Garnish

1 cup spinach leaves, julienned
1 orange, cut into rings
1 Tbsp. dill, chopped

Instructions

Wash the cabbage, carrots and apple. Peel the apple. Cut the cabbage in half and remove the stem. Chop the cabbage. Put in a mixing bowl, grate the carrots and add the julienned apple. Sprinkle rosemary and toss gently. Prepare the dressing in a blender and blend until mixed. Adjust flavor if needed. Place spinach leaves on a serving tray or a salad bowl. Put salad on the serving tray and pour dressing over the top. Garnish with orange rings and chopped dill.

Green Cabbage with Grapes and Plum Mayonnaise Base

Ingredients

1 small green cabbage, chopped
1 cup seedless red grapes
3 red plums, wedged
1 cup red cabbage, shredded
2 hard-boiled eggs, chopped
1 carrot, grated

Dressing

1 cup mayonnaise
¼ cup lemon juice
Salt, pepper, and sugar to taste
2 Tbsp. dill, chopped

Garnish

1 lemon, cut into rings and twisted
¼ cup raisins
4 lettuce leaves

Instructions

Wash the cabbage and the fruit. Cut the cabbage in half and remove the stem from the middle. Chop the cabbage. Put it into a mixing bowl and add grapes, plums, red cabbage, eggs and carrots. Toss gently. Place lettuce leaves on a tray and pour salad on top. Prepare the dressing in a blender and pour over salad at serving time. Garnish the salad with lemon rings and raisins.

Green Cabbage with Smoked Pastrami, Egg and Mayonnaise

Ingredients

2 quarts of green cabbage, shredded
2 hard-boiled eggs, grated
8 oz. pastrami, julienned or chopped
2 scallion onions, chopped
1 carrot, grated

Dressing

1 ¼ cup mayonnaise
2 lemon for juice
2 Tbsp. lemon zest
Salt, pepper, and sugar to taste
1 Tbsp. fresh oregano

Garnish

3 red cabbage leaves
2 Tbsp. parsley
3 Tbsp. pecans, chopped

Instructions

Wash the cabbage, cut in half and remove the stem. Grate the cabbage and put into a mixing bowl. Add the hardboiled egg, pastrami, scallion and grated carrots. Toss gently. Prepare the dressing in a blender and mix for 1 minute. Adjust flavor as needed. Prepare a tray or salad bowl with red cabbage leaves. Add the salad on top. Before serving pour the dressing on the salad. Garnish with parsley and pecans.

Grilled Tomatoes with Parmesan, Kalamata and Olive Oil Dressing Picante

Ingredients

4 Roma tomatoes, halved and grilled
¾ cup parmesan, grated
¾ cup seedless Kalamata olives

Dressing

½ cup olive oil
¼ cup lemon juice
Salt, pepper, and sugar to taste
¼ cup water
1 Tbsp. garlic, minced
⅛ tsp. crushed red pepper

Garnish

1 ½ cups spinach, julienned
1 lemon, sliced
2 Tbsp. parsley, chopped

Instructions

Cut the tomatoes in half long ways. Put them on the grill for 2 to 3 minutes. Remove from the grill and let cool. Put them on a tray with spinach. Add the parmesan, Kalamata olives. Prepare the dressing in a blender for 1 minute on high speed. Adjust flavor as needed. Before serving pour the dressing over the tomatoes. Fry the lemon slices in a sauté pan with a little olive oil until golden brown. Put the lemon slices around the salad and sprinkle parsley.

Heart of Palm with Corned Beef and Lemon Red Pepper Dressing

Ingredients

20 oz. heart of palm
1 lemon, peeled and cubed
1 green pepper, cut into strips
1 scallion onion, chopped
6 oz. smoked corned beef, julienned

Dressing

1 roasted pepper
¼ cup lemon juice
¼ cup olive oil
½ cup water
1 scallion onion, chopped
1 Tbsp. garlic, chopped
Salt, pepper, and sugar to taste
Dash of nutmeg
1 orange for juice

Garnish

5 lettuce leaves, whole
1 pear, julienned
2 Tbsp. fresh parsley

Instructions

If you have fresh heart of palm, boil for about 15 minutes. Remove from the water, let cool and then peel. You can also use canned heart of palm. Cut the heart of palm in 2 ½ to 3 inch long pieces. Put them in a mixing bowl and add lemon cubes, green pepper, scallion onion, and smoked corned beef. Mix gently. Prepare a tray with the whole lettuce leaves. Pour salad over the lettuce. Blend dressing ingredients and then pour over the salad. Garnish with the julienned pears over the salad and sprinkle fresh parsley.

Heart of Palm and Persimmon with Kalamata Olive Dressing

Ingredients

24 oz. heart of palm
3 scallion onions, chopped
1 Roma tomato, cubed
3 medium persimmon, cubed

Dressing

⅓ cup olive oil
¼ cup lemon juice
⅓ cup cold water
1 tsp. garlic, chopped
½ cup kalamata olives
Salt and pepper to taste
1 Tbsp. fresh oregano

Garnish

6 romaine lettuce leaves
1 lemon, wedged
¼ cup Italian parsley, chopped

Instructions

Fresh heart of palm preferred, but you can use canned if you would like. Dip the heart of palm into boiling water for approximately 15 minutes. Remove with slotted spoon and let cool down. Option two: if you use canned heart of palm, cut them in half approximately 2 ½ inches long. Prepare a serving tray with romaine lettuce leaves. Put the heart of palm on the lettuce and add chopped scallion, tomato, and persimmon over the top. To prepare the dressing place all the ingredients into a blender and blend for about 50 seconds. Season to taste. Before serving, pour dressing over top of the salad. Garnish by arranging lemon wedges around the tray

Julienned Carrots with Shredded Vegetable Dressing

Ingredients

3 large carrots, julienned
1 medium Granny Smith apple, julienned
3 scallion onions, chopped
2 Tbsp. garlic, chopped
1 red pepper, cut into strips
2 red plums, cubed
½ cup seedless Kalamata olives

Dressing

1 celery stalk
1 tomato
½ cup olive oil
¼ cup lemon juice
¼ cup mayonnaise
¼ cup orange juice
Salt and pepper to taste
Dash of sugar
½ tsp. mustard

Garnish

2 cooked beets, cut into rings
1 cup lettuce, chopped
2 Tbsp. parsley

Instructions

Wash the carrots and peel. Cut julienned and add to a mixing bowl. Add the apple, scallion onion, garlic, red pepper, plums and kalamata olives. Mix gently. Prepare a platter with lettuce. Pour salad on top and prepare dressing. Add all ingredients to blender for 1 ½ minutes on high speed. Adjust flavor if needed. Before serving add the dressing on the salad. Garnish with the cooked beet slices around the tray. Sprinkle the parsley.

Kale Salad with Sour Cream Dressing

Ingredients

32 oz. kale
1 medium onion, chopped
1 red pepper, chopped
3 hard-boiled egg, wedged

Dressing

1 ½ cups sour cream
¼ cup lemon juice
¼ cup olive oil
1 Tbsp. garlic, chopped
½ tsp. nutmeg
Salt and pepper
2 Tbsp. parmesan

Garnish

2 cups red cabbage, shredded
2 Tbsp. dill
1 carrot, grated

Instructions

Boil water and add the Kale for 3 to 4 minutes. Remove from stove and strain. Chop the kale and put it into a mixing bowl. Add onion, red pepper. Prepare a serving tray with the red cabbage. Add the kale on top. Blend dressing ingredients for 1 ½ minutes. Adjust flavor if needed. Before serving pour the dressing on the salad. Garnish with dill and the carrots. Place the hard-boiled egg wedges down the center of the salad.

Kohlrabi Balsamic Dressing

Ingredients

3 kohlrabi
½ cup red seedless grapes
2 Tbsp. dill, chopped
2 scallion onions, chopped
1 lemon, peeled and cubed

Dressing

¼ cup olive oil
¼ cup balsamic vinegar
¼ cup water
¼ cup orange juice
2 garlic cloves
Salt, pepper, and sugar to taste
1 Tbsp. oregano

Garnish

4 iceberg lettuce leaves
⅓ cup pecans
2 Tbsp. parsley
1 lime, sliced

Instructions

Wash kohlrabi and cut top and bottom off. Cut into rings and julienned thin. Place into a mixing bowl. Add grapes, dill, onion, and lemon. Toss the salad. Prepare dressing in a blender and mix well. Pour dressing over the salad and mix well. Prepare a serving tray with lettuce leaves. Pour salad over top. Garnish with pecans, parsley and add lime slices around the tray.

Kohlrabi Cabbage with Egg and Mayonnaise

Ingredients

4 medium kohlrabi cabbage, coarsely grated
4 hard-boiled eggs, grated
½ cup red cabbage, finely shredded
2 Tbsp. dill, chopped
½ cup dates, finely chopped
1 small carrot, coarsely grated
1 cup mayonnaise
1 medium lemon for juice
Salt, pepper, and sugar to taste

Garnish

3 cups spring lettuce
1 medium tomato, cut into rings
3 Tbsp. white sharp cheddar cheese, grated
2 Tbsp. parsley, chopped

Instructions

Wash kohlrabi, remove the top and bottom, and coarsely grate. Place into a mixing bowl. Add hardboiled eggs, red cabbage, dill, dates, carrot, mayonnaise, lemon juice, and salt, pepper and sugar to taste. Mix gently to combine well. Place spring lettuce onto a serving tray and add salad on top. Garnish with tomato rings around the tray. Sprinkle with white sharp cheddar cheese and parsley on top.

Leftover Stuffed Cabbage with Spicy Tomato Oregano Dressing

Ingredients

4 leftover stuffed cabbages, sliced into 1-½ inch thickness
2 tomatoes, cubed
½ tsp. crushed hot red pepper
1 cup fresh spinach, chopped
3 hard-boiled eggs, wedged

Dressing

½ cup mayonnaise
¾ cup sour cream
1 large lemon for juice
1 tsp. garlic, chopped
Salt and pepper to taste

Garnish

2 cups red peppers, julienned
1 lemon, wedged
2 Tbsp. poppy seeds

Instructions

Place the red peppers onto a serving tray. Add stuffed cabbage evenly onto the peppers. Add tomatoes, hot red peppers, spinach and hard-boiled eggs over the stuffed cabbage. Prepare the dressing. Add all dressing ingredients into a blender and mix for 1 minute on high speed. Season to taste. Before serving, pour dressing evenly over the salad. Garnish with lemon wedges, fruit side up, over salad and sprinkle with poppy seeds.

Leftover Stuffed Pepper Salad with Olive Oil Picante Dressing

Ingredients

4 whole stuffed peppers, cut into ½-inch rings
3 Tbsp. dill, chopped
2 scallion onions, chopped
½ cup Kalamata olives, chopped
3 mushrooms, thinly sliced
1 small jalapeños, chopped

Dressing

¼ cup lemon juice
½ cup olive juice
½ cup water
Salt, pepper, and sugar to taste
1 tsp garlic, chopped
1 tsp. lemon skin, finely grated

Garnish

6 lettuce leaves, julienned
2 Roma tomatoes, cut into thin rings
2 Tbsp. Italian parsley, chopped

Instructions

Place lettuce onto a serving tray. Add cut stuffed peppers layered like steps on top of the lettuce. Add dill, scallion onions, Kalamata olives, mushrooms, and jalapeños over the stuffed peppers. Prepare the dressing. Add all dressing ingredients into a blender and mix for 1 minute on high speed or place in a mixing bowl and stir for 3 minutes. Before serving, pour dressing over the salad. Garnish by placing a slice of tomato on each slice of stuffed pepper and sprinkle with parsley.

Marinated Beet Salad with Mustard and Honey Dressing

Ingredients

5 medium beets, cooked
1 large Granny Smith apple, julienned
2 Tbsp. dill, chopped
1 small lime, cubed
1 small onion, chopped

Dressing

¼ cup yellow mustard
½ cup olive oil
3 Tbsp. vinegar
1 Tbsp. garlic, chopped
¾ cup honey
Salt and pepper to taste
1 celery stalk, chopped

Garnish

1 cup spinach
¼ cup chopped pecans
2 Tbsp. Italian parsley, chopped

Instructions

Wash the beets with cold water. Boil beets for 35 to 40 minutes. Cool under cold water. Peel the skin and cut into thin slices. Put into a mixing bowl and add the rest of the ingredients: Granny Smith apple, dill, lime and onion. Mix gently. Prepare a tray with spinach leaves. Pour salad on top. Put all dressing ingredients in a blender and blend for 1 to 1 ½ minutes. Before serving pour dressing on the salad. Sprinkle pecans and Italian parsley on top.

Marinated Cucumber Picante Cream Dressing

Ingredients

3 medium seedless cucumbers, with skin and cut into rings
1 medium red peppers, chopped
2 Tbsp. dill, chopped
½ cup red onion, thinly sliced
2 red plums, small cubes
½ cup white cheddar cheese, shredded

Dressing

½ cup mayonnaise
½ cup sour cream
¼ cup lemon juice
1 tsp. garlic, chopped
¼ cup half & half cream
½ tsp. crushed hot red pepper
1 Tbsp. lemon skin, finely grated
Salt and black pepper to taste

Garnish

6 leaves lettuce, julienned
4 white mushrooms, thinly sliced
2 Tbsp. parsley, chopped

Instructions

Place cucumbers into a mixing bowl. Add red pepper, dill, red onion, plums, and white cheddar cheese. Mix gently. Prepare the dressing. Add all dressing ingredients into a blender and mix for 1 ½ minutes on high speed. Season to taste. Place lettuce leaves onto a serving tray and add salad. Before serving, pour dressing over the salad. Garnish with mushrooms on top and sprinkle with parsley.

Marinated Fruit, Vegetables and Feta

Ingredients

1 medium Granny Smith apple, julienned
1 cup parsley
1 pear
2 plums, wedged
1 carrot, grated
1 red pepper, strips
2 scallion onions, chopped
1 tomato, thin wedges
2 celery stalks, chopped
1 cup feta cheese
1 cucumber, sliced

Dressing

½ cup olive oil
½ cup vinegar
1 lemon for juice
1 tsp. lemon zest
Salt and pepper to taste
1 tsp. sugar
¼ cup water

Garnish

2 cups iceberg lettuce
2 cooked beets julienned

Instructions

Wash all fruits and vegetables and peel them if necessary. Cut them and put them into a mixing bowl. Put the dressing ingredients into the blender for approximately 1 minute. Adjust flavor as needed. Prepare a tray with lettuce and pour the salad on top. Put the dressing on top before serving. Place the beets around the edge of the tray and sprinkle with chopped parsley.

Marinated Okra Salad with Lime Picante Dressing

Ingredients

16 oz. okra
1 red pepper, thinly sliced 1 onion, sliced
5 mushrooms, sliced
1 carrot, grated

Dressing

½ cup tomato juice
½ cup olive oil
½ cup balsamic vinegar
1 Tbsp. garlic, chopped
2 Tbsp. tabasco
Salt, pepper, and sugar to taste

Garnish

5 lettuce leaves
1 cup cherry tomatoes, whole
2 Tbsp. Italian parsley
1 cucumber, sliced

Instructions

Boil okra for approximately 3 minutes. Pour into a strainer and let cool to room temperature. Cut the top of the okra off. Put them in a mixing bowl and add red pepper, onion, mushrooms and grated carrots. Toss gently. Prepare a tray for serving with lettuce leaves. Add the salad to the tray. Blend all dressing ingredients for 1 minute. Adjust flavor as needed. Pour the dressing over the salad before serving. Garnish with the cherry tomatoes, Italian parsley, and cucumber rings.

Mediterranean Carrot Salad with Parmesan and Picante Mayonnaise

Ingredients

6 large carrots, cooked and peeled
1 medium Granny Smith apple, julienned
½ cup walnuts, coarsely chopped

Dressing

¾ cup mayonnaise
¼ cup fresh lemon juice
2 Tbsp. Fresh rosemary
3 Tbsp. grated parmesan
¼ cup olive oil
Salt and pepper to taste
1 Tbsp. jalapeños, chopped
2 Tbsp. raisins

Garnish

4 iceberg lettuce leaves
3 Tbsp. scallion onions, chopped
Dash sweet paprika
2 Tbsp. Italian parsley, chopped

Instructions

Wash carrots with cold water, peel and boil for 7 to 8 minutes. Remove from water and let cool. Slice them into rings and place into a mixing bowl. Add apple and walnuts. Toss 2 or 3 times. Place all dressing ingredients into a blender or a mixing bowl. Stir or blend well. Adjust flavor to picante. Prepare serving tray with iceberg lettuce. Pour the salad onto the lettuce, then add the dressing. Garnish by sprinkling with scallion onions, sweet paprika and parsley.

Mediterranean Chopped Veggie and Fruit Salad with Feta, Olive Oil and Vinegar Dressing

Ingredients

1 tomato, cubed
½ red onion, chopped
1 green pepper, cubed
5 asparagus sticks, cut
1 Granny Smith apple, julienned
5 red figs, halved
1 tsp. garlic, chopped
½ cup pomegranate seeds
8 oz. feta cheese, cubed
1 Tbsp. oregano

Dressing

⅓ cup olive oil
¼ cup lemon juice
½ cup grapefruit
¼ cup orange juice
Salt, pepper, and sugar to taste
1 Tbsp. mint leaves

Garnish

6 lettuce leaves, whole
3 hard-boiled egg, wedged
1 lemon, cut into slices

Instructions

Wash all vegetables, cut as specified and place into a mixing bowl. Toss gently. Prepare a serving tray with the lettuce leaves. Blend all dressing ingredients until well mixed. Pour the salad over the tray and pour dressing on before serving. Garnish with the hard-boiled egg wedges and lemon slices.

Mountain Mushroom with Spinach Sour Cream Dressing Picante

Ingredients

16 oz. mountain mushroom, cut into strips
¼ cup olive oil
2 cups spinach, julienned
1 small red onion, cut into thin rings
1 medium red pepper, cut into thin strips
1 small lemon peeled, cut into small cubes
1 Tbsp. fresh tarragon, chopped
3 hard-boiled eggs, sliced round
4 strips crunchy bacon, chopped

Dressing

1 ½ cups sour cream
¼ cup fresh lemon juice
¼ cup half & half cream
Dash hot crushed red pepper
1 tsp. garlic, chopped
Salt and pepper to taste

Garnish

4 iceberg leaves, whole
½ cup crunchy blueberries
¼ cup white sharp cheddar cheese, grated

Instructions

Wash mushrooms, remove stem, cut into medium strips. Heat oil in a sauté pan, add mushrooms and cook 2 to 2 ½ minutes. Remove from heat, strain. Place iceberg lettuce onto a serving tray and add fried mushrooms on top. Add spinach, red onion, red pepper, lemon, tarragon, hard-boiled eggs, and bacon. Prepare the dressing. Add all dressing ingredients into a blender and mix for 1 minute on high speed. Season to taste. Before serving, pour dressing over the salad. Garnish by sprinkling blueberries and white sharp cheddar cheese on top.

Mushroom Feta and Cucumber with Dill Lemon Dressing

Ingredients

12 oz. fresh mushrooms
8 oz. feta cheese, crumbled
1 medium seedless cucumber
1 small carrot, grated
1 small pickle, chopped

Dressing

1 cup fresh spinach
3 Tbsp. dill, chopped
⅓ cup lemon juice
⅓ olive oil
⅓ cup water
Salt, pepper, and sugar to taste
1 tsp. tabasco

Garnish

1 cup green cabbage, shredded
½ cup fresh raspberries
2 hard-boiled eggs, wedged

Instructions

Wash the mushrooms with cold water, cut in half long ways with the stem. Put them into a mixing bowl and add feta cheese, cucumber, carrots and pickle. Mix gently. Prepare a serving tray with shredded green cabbage. Pour salad on top and prepare dressing. Add all ingredients into a blender on high speed for a 1 ½ minutes. Adjust flavor if needed. Before serving pour dressing on top of salad. Garnish with the raspberries. Place hard boiled-egg wedges around the edge of the tray.

Mushroom Salad with Cream of Herbs

Ingredients

16 oz. fresh baby mushrooms
1 red pepper, julienned
1 red onion, chopped
1 cucumber, cubed
10 cherry tomatoes

Dressing

1 cup mayonnaise
½ cup sour cream
1 lemon for juice
¼ cup half and half
¼ cup feta cheese
1 Tbsp. garlic
Salt and pepper to taste
Dash of crushed red pepper

Garnish

2 cups spinach leaves
1 large lemon, wedged
Dash of paprika
1 Tbsp. dill, chopped

Instructions

Put the mushrooms in a hot with cold water. Let them sit for 5 to 10 minutes. Remove them from the water and cut the stem off the mushrooms. Cut them in half. Put them in a mixing bowl and add red pepper, onion, cucumber and tomatoes. Prepare the dressing in a blender and mix for 1 minute. Adjust flavor if needed. Before serving place spinach leaves on a tray and pour salad on top. Pour dressing over the salad. Garnish with lemon wedges around the edge of the tray and sprinkle paprika.

Napa Cabbage with Grilled Tuna Marinated with Vinaigrette Oil Dressing

Ingredients

3 medium or 2 large Napa cabbage, cooked and cubed small
12 oz. grilled tuna filets, cubed
1 scallion onion, coarsely chopped
1 medium carrot, coarsely grated
1 large orange, cubed
1 cup grapefruit, cubed
⅛ cup hot crusted red pepper
2 Tbsp. dill, chopped

Dressing

½ cup wine vinaigrette
½ cup olive oil
1/cup water
1 medium tomato
1 Tbsp. garlic, chopped
Dash of Old Bay Seasoning
Salt, pepper, and sugar to taste

Garnish

2 cups spinach leaves, whole
½ cup red cranberries, chopped
¼ cup raisins
1 medium lemon, cut into rings and twisted

Instructions

Place 3 quarts of water into a pot and bring to a boil. Wash cabbage, remove top and bottoms. Add to boiling water and cook 7 to 10 minutes. Remove from heat, rinse with cold water, and drain. Cut into medium slices, then cut into small to medium cubes. Place into a mixing bowl. Add tuna, scallion onion, carrot, orange, grapefruit, hot crushed red pepper, and dill. Mix gently. Prepare the dressing. Add all dressing ingredients into a blender and mix for 1 ¼ minutes on high speed. Season to taste. Place spinach leaves onto a serving tray and add salad on top. Before serving, pour dressing over the salad. Dip cranberries into boiling water for 2 minutes, drain, and chop. Garnish with lemon twists around the tray. Sprinkle with cranberries and raisins.

Okra and Apples with Curry Picante Dressing

Ingredients

16 oz. okra
1 Granny Smith apple, julienned
1 red pepper, chopped
1 celery stalk, chopped
1 scallion onion, chopped

Dressing

½ cup balsamic vinegar
½ cup olive oil
½ cup water
¼ cup mayonnaise
¼ cup sour cream
1 tomato
1 Tbsp. garlic, chopped
2 Tbsp. dill, chopped
Salt, pepper, and sugar to taste
1 Tbsp. curry powder

Garnish

1 cup red cabbage, julienned ½ cup blueberries
1 tomato, wedged
Dash of parsley

Instructions

Boil the okra for approximately 2 to 3 minutes. Pour into a strainer and let cool. Cut the tops of the okra and place into a mixing bowl. Add red pepper, celery, and scallion. Toss gently. Prepare a tray with julienned red cabbage and pour salad on top. Blend the dressing for 1 minute. Adjust flavor as needed. Pour dressing over salad before serving. Garnish with blueberries and place tomato wedges around the salad. Sprinkle with parsley.

Okra Salad with Marinated Tomato Dressing

Ingredients

16 oz. okra
2 tomatoes, cubed
1 lemon, peeled and cubed
1 carrot, julienned
2 persimmon, sliced

Dressing

½ cup tomato juice
½ cup olive oil
½ cup wine vinegar
Salt, pepper, and sugar to taste
2 Tbsp. garlic, chopped
1 jalapeños, chopped
1 Tbsp. dill
½ cup sundried tomatoes

Garnish

2 cups lettuce, julienned
1 lime, wedged
½ cup black olives, chopped

Instructions

Wash the okra and boil them for approximately 3 minutes. Pour into a strainer and let cool. Cut the top off of the okra and put into a mixing bowl. Add tomatoes, lemon, carrot, and persimmon. Prepare a tray with julienned lettuce and pour salad over lettuce. Prepare the dressing in a blender and mix for 1 ½ minutes. Pour dressing over salad before serving. Garnish with lime wedges around the salad and sprinkle black olives.

Orzo Artichoke and Spinach with Spicy Tomato Dressing

Ingredients

2 Tbsp. vegetable oil
16 oz. orzo
12 oz. artichoke hearts, halved
1 cup spinach, julienned
1 jalapeños, chopped
1 tomato, cubed
1 scallion onion, chopped

Dressing

¾ cup olive oil
¾ cup balsamic vinegar
1 Tbsp. garlic chopped
1 lemon juiced
Salt, pepper, and sugar to taste
⅛ tsp. nutmeg
¼ cup sundried tomatoes

Garnish

5 lettuce leaves
1 lime, sliced
2 Tbsp. raisins
1 Tbsp. parsley

Instructions

Heat oil in a pot on the stove and add orzo. Stir and cook until golden brown. Add 2 ¼ cups water into the pot and reduce to a simmer. Cook 8 to 10 minutes. Remove from heat, mix with a fork and let it cool. Place into a mixing bowl. Add artichokes, spinach, jalapeños, tomato, and scallion onions. Toss gently. Prepare the dressing in a blender and mix on high speed. Prepare a serving tray with lettuce leaves and pour the salad on top. Add dressing over the salad. Garnish with lime slices, raisins, and parsley.

Pea Salad with Shredded Vegetables and Kalamata Dressing

Ingredients

20 oz. fresh peas or frozen
1 medium carrot, grated
2 scallion onions, chopped
1 red pepper, julienned
4 medium radishes, cut into rings

Dressing

⅓ cup olive oil
⅓ balsamic vinegar
⅓ water
1 Tbsp. oregano
½ cup Kalamata olives
Salt and pepper to taste
1 tsp. garlic

Garnish

2 cups spinach, julienned
1 tomato, wedged
2 Tbsp. parsley, chopped

Instructions

Wash the fresh peas, put into a pot and boil for 45 minutes. Pour into a strainer and then into a mixing bowl. Add the carrots, scallion, pepper, and radishes. Mix gently. Prepare a platter or salad bowl with the julienned spinach leaves. Pour the salad on top. Blend all dressing ingredients in a blender. Adjust flavor as needed. Before serving pour the dressing on the salad. Finish with the tomato wedges around the tray. Sprinkle chopped parsley.

Pea Salad with Tomato, Mozzarella and Tarragon Dressing

Ingredients

16 oz. peas cooked, fresh or frozen
2 tomatoes, cubed
4 oz. mozzarella, julienned
2 Tbsp. tarragon, chopped
1 small red pepper, chopped
2 Tbsp. garlic, chopped

Dressing

¼ cup olive oil
¼ cup tarragon vinegar
1 large lemon for juice
1 tsp. sugar
Salt and pepper to taste
¼ cup water

Garnish

½ cup sundried tomatoes, chopped
3 Tbsp. dill, chopped
1 lemon, wedged

Instructions

Boil the peas for 5 minutes. Put into a strainer and let cool. Pour into a mixing bowl and add tomato, mozzarella, tarragon, onion and garlic. Mix gently. Prepare a salad bowl or tray for serving. Pour the salad on the platter. Put all ingredients into a blender and mix for 1 ½ minutes. Adjust flavor if needed. Before serving pour dressing on top. To garnish put sundried tomatoes across the salad and lemon wedges around the edge of the tray.

Pearl Onion with Blue Cheese Dressing and Rosemary

Ingredients

16 oz. pearl onions
10 oz. blue cheese
2 Tbsp. rosemary
3 Tbsp. cilantro, chopped
1 Granny Smith apple, cubed
1 small carrot, grated
1 cup sour white grapes

Dressing

¼ cup olive oil
½ cup ricotta cheese
¼ cup lemon juice
¼ cup sesame seeds.
Salt and pepper to taste
Dash of sugar

Garnish

1 cup red cabbage, julienned
2 Tbsp. Italian parsley, chopped

Instructions

Peel the pearl onions and cut in half. Put into a mixing bowl and add the blue cheese, rosemary, cilantro, apple, carrots and grapes. Mix gently. Prepare a platter for serving. Place cabbage on tray and add salad. Blend dressing ingredients to blender and mix well for 1 ½ minutes. Adjust flavor as needed. Before serving pour dressing on salad. Garnish with chopped parsley.

Portobella Mushrooms with Egg Picante and Cumin

Ingredients

3 portobella mushrooms
½ cup vegetable oil
3 hard-boiled egg, cut in half
1 red pepper, julienned
1 Tbsp. jalapeños
1 Roma tomato, wedged

Dressing

⅓ cup olive oil
⅓ cup lemon juice
¼ cup water
2 Tbsp. garlic
2 Tbsp. rosemary
Salt and pepper to taste
Dash of sugar
Dash of cumin

Garnish

2 cups lettuce, julienned
1 carrot, coarsely grated
2 Tbsp. parsley, chopped

Instructions

Wash the mushrooms and dry with a paper towel. Heat oil in a pan. Cut the mushrooms in strips and fry in hot oil for 2 to 3 minutes. Remove from the oil and put on a paper towel. Prepare a tray with julienned lettuce. Put the mushrooms on the lettuce. Add eggs around the tray or down the center. Add the rest of the ingredients red pepper jalapeno and tomatoes. Blend dressing in a blender and pour on salad before serving. To garnish sprinkle shredded carrots and parsley over the salad.

Pearl Onion with Red Pepper and Fresh Mozzarella Picante

Ingredients

16 oz. pearl onions
2 red pepper, roasted
10 oz. fresh mozzarella, julienned
2 Tbsp. tarragon
½ Tbsp. crushed red pepper
3 Tbsp. Italian parsley
1 small cucumber, cubed

Dressing

¼ cup olive oil
¼ cup lemon juice
1 Tbsp. garlic, chopped Salt and pepper to taste

Garnish

2 tomatoes, thinly sliced
1 seedless cucumber, cut into rings
2 Tbsp. dill, chopped

Instructions

Wash the pearl onions peel and put in a mixing bowl. Add roasted red peppers: You can roasted the peppers in the oven on the stove or on the grill. Mozzarella, tarragon, crushed red pepper, parsley and cucumber. Toss gently. Pour the salad on a serving tray. Blend dressing ingredients in a blender and pour over the salad. Place sliced tomatoes around the salad. Put the cucumber sliced down the center of the salad and sprinkle chopped dill.

Pumpkin and Apple Salad with Lemon and Olive Oil

Ingredients

20 oz. fresh pumpkin
1 medium Granny Smith apple, julienned
3 Tbsp. dill, chopped
½ cup spinach leaves, julienned

Dressing

¼ cup olive oil
¼ cup lemon juice
¼ cup water
1 tsp. garlic
2 Tbsp. dill, chopped
¼ cup onion
Dash of nutmeg

Garnish

6 lettuce leaves
1 lemon, wedged
1 red beet, cooked and sliced

Instructions

Wash the 20 oz. Pumpkin with cold water. Boil for 12 to 15 minutes. Remove and put in a strainer. Bring to room temperature. Cut it into large pieces. Prepare a plater with lettuce and put the pumpkin on top. Place apples, dill and lemon on top. Blend all the dressing ingredients together and adjust flavor. Pour the dressing on top before serving. Place Beet slices around the edges of tray. Put lemon slices on the middle of the salad.

Pumpkin Salad with Sour Cream and Parmesan Dressing

Ingredients

16 oz. fresh pumpkin
2 persimmon, cubed
1 Tbsp. dill, chopped
1 tsp. lemon zest

Dressing

1 cup sour cream
¼ cup grated parmesan
⅛ cup olive oil
1 tsp. garlic
2 lemons for juice
Salt and pepper to taste
1 orange for juice
1 Tbsp. orange skin

Garnish

1 ½ cups lettuce
1 orange, cut into rings
1 Tbsp. dill, chopped

Instructions

Wash the pumpkin and boil for approximately 4 to 5 minutes. Remove and put in a strainer. Place on a cutting board and chop lightly. Put pumpkin in a mixing bowl and add the rest of the ingredients. Toss gently. Prepare a tray with lettuce. Scoop the pumpkin salad on top of the lettuce. Blend all dressing ingredients on high speed. Before serving pour dressing across the salad. Garnish with twisted orange slices. Put sour cream down the middle of the salad and sprinkle dill.

Pumpkin Patty Salad with Cream of Herb Dressing

Ingredients

20 oz. fresh pumpkin
½ cup onion, chopped
1 Tbsp. garlic, chopped
1 celery stalk, chopped
Salt and pepper to taste
½ cup bread crumbs
2 eggs
1 Tbsp. fresh parsley
1 ½ cups vegetable oil

Dressing

¾ cup mayonnaise
¼ cup sour cream
⅛ cup tarragon vinegar
3 Tbsp. olive oil
¼ cup Kalamata olives
Salt and pepper to taste
3 Tbsp. parmesan cheese
3 strips crunch bacon, chopped

Garnish

4 lettuce leaves
1 tomato, cut into rings
2 Tbsp. parsley

Instructions

Wash the pumpkin and boil for 3 to 4 minutes. Let cool and chop fine. Add to mixing bowl and add onions garlic celery salt and pepper breadcrumbs egg and parsley. Mix well and make patties out of the mixture. Heat oil in a pan and fry patties until golden brown. Remove and place on a paper towel. Prepare a tray with lettuce and place patties on lettuce. Blend dressing ingredients and adjust flavor if needed. Before serving pour dressing over salad. Garnish by placing tomato rings around the salad and sprinkle parsley.

Pumpkin with Veggie, Lemon and Cheddar Cheese Dressing

Ingredients

16 oz. pumpkin
1 carrot, grated
2 Tbsp. dill, chopped
¾ cup cheddar cheese, shredded
2 scallion onions, chopped
1 green pepper, chopped

Dressing

¼ cup lemon juice
¼ cup olive oil
Salt, pepper, and sugar to taste
1 tsp. garlic, chopped
1 lime for juice
1 tsp. lime zest

Garnish

2 cups spinach leaves
1 red pepper, chopped
1 lemon, sliced

Instructions

Make sure to remove the skin and stem from the pumpkin. Boil the pumpkin for 3 to 4 minutes. Remove the pumpkin with a strainer and let cool to room temperature. Prepare a serving tray with spinach leaves and add the cooked pumpkin on top. Add carrots, dill, shredded cheese, scallion onions, and green pepper. To prepare the dressing, blend all dressing ingredients on high speed for 1 minute. Pour dressing over the salad before serving. Garnish with chopped red pepper and lemon slices.

Radishes and Cheddar Cheese with Kalamata Dressing

Ingredients

16 oz. radishes, sliced
½ cup sharp cheddar cheese, shredded
1 scallion onion, chopped
1 carrot, grated
4 Romaine lettuce leaves, julienned
4 persimmon, cubed

Dressing

¼ cup olive oil
¼ cup vinegar
¼ cup water
½ cup seedless Kalamata olives
Salt and pepper to taste
1 Tbsp. garlic
1 Tbsp. tarragon

Garnish

2 cups red cabbage, julienned
1 cucumber, sliced
1 Tbsp. dill, chopped

Instructions

Wash the radishes and cut the top and bottom off. Slice into thin slices. Put them in a mixing bowl and add the cheddar cheese, scallions, lettuce and persimmon. Prepare a serving dish with the cabbage. Blend dressing ingredients in a blender until well mixed. Pour the salad on the serving dish. Pour dressing over salad before serving. Garnish with sliced cucumbers and chopped dill.

Radishes and Grated Swiss Cheese with Smoked Dry Herring

Ingredients

20 oz. radishes, grated
6 oz. smoked dry herring filet
1 beet, cooked
3 hard-boiled eggs grated
2 Tbsp. parsley
½ cup red cabbage, grated

Dressing

¼ cup red wine vinegar
¼ cup olive oil
¼ cup water
2 Tbsp. fresh oregano
1 Tbsp. garlic
Salt, pepper, and sugar to taste

Garnish

1 ½ cups spinach leaves
1 lemon, cut into rings
2 Tbsp. parsley, chopped

Instructions

Wash radishes with cold water and cut the top and bottom off of the radishes. Slice and put into a mixing bowl. Chop the herring filet and add it to the radishes. Add the hard-boiled eggs, parsley, and red cabbage. Grate the cooked beet and mix gently. Blend the dressing ingredients in a blender for 45 seconds. Adjust flavor if needed. Pour dressing over the salad. Prepare a serving tray with spinach leaves and pour salad over the tray. Garnish with lemon rings and sprinkle chopped parsley.

Red Beans with Sundried Tomatoes Picante

Ingredients

20 oz. red beans
1 cup sundried tomatoes
1 Tbsp. red pepper
1 red pepper, chopped
1 small onion, cut into rings
2 Tbsp. garlic chopped
1 medium pickle, cut into small cubes

Dressing

⅓ cup lemon juice
½ cup olive oil
¼ cup water
½ cup feta cheese
2 Tbsp. Worchester
Salt and pepper

Garnish

5 lettuce leaves
1 orange, cut into rings 2 Tbsp. dill

Instructions

Soak the beans overnight with cold water. Next day boil for 45 minutes. Remove from stove, strain and cool to room temperature. Add the mixing bowl and add sundried tomatoes crushed pepper, red pepper, onion, garlic and pickles. Prepare the dressing in a blender on high speed for 1 ¼ minutes. Adjust flavor if needed. Prepare a platter with lettuce. Pour salad on top of the lettuce. Pour dressing on before serving. Garnish by placing the orange rings around the salad and sprinkle with dill.

Red Cabbage Salad with Beets Cheese and Mayonnaise

Ingredients

1 small red cabbage, shredded
3 hard-boiled eggs, shredded
1 large beets, cooked and grated
1 red onion, chopped
½ cup cheddar cheese, grated
3 Tbsp. dill, chopped

Dressing

1 ½ cups mayonnaise
¼ cup red wine vinegar
1 Tbsp. garlic
¼ cup raisins
Salt, pepper, and sugar to taste

Garnish

5 lettuce leaves
1 tomato, cut into rings
1 Tbsp. lime zest

Instructions

Wash the red cabbage, cut in half and remove the stem. Grate the cabbage into a mixing bowl. Add the eggs, beets, onions, cheddar cheese and dill. Prepare the dressing in a blender and mix for 1 minute. Adjust flavor if needed. Pour on the salad and mix gently. To prepare a tray place lettuce leaves on the tray and pour salad on top. Garnish with the tomato rings around the salad and sprinkle lime zest.

Red Onion with Feta Cheese and Olive Lime Dressing

Ingredients

3 medium red onion rings
1Lb. Feta cheese crumbled
1 cup seedless kalamata olives
1 medium tomato cubed
1 lime peeled and cubed

Dressing

½ cup lime juice
½ cup olive oil
¼ cup water
Salt, pepper, and sugar to taste
1 Tbsp. garlic
1 Tbsp. oregano

Garnish

1 ½ cups spinach leaves
3 Tbsp. poppy seeds

Instructions

Peel the onion wash, cut in half and slice. Put in a mixing bowl and add feta cheese, Kalamata olives, tomatoes and lime. Put spinach on a serving tray and pour salad on top. Blend all dressing ingredients in a blender and pour over salad just before serving. Adjust flavor if needed. Garnish with poppy seeds.

Red Cabbage with Mango Papaya Apple and Mayonnaise Dressing

Ingredients

1 small red cabbage, shredded
2 large mango, chopped
1 cup papaya, cubed
2 scallion onions, chopped
1 small Granny Smith apple, peeled and julienned

Dressing

1 cup mayonnaise
2 lemons for juice
1 Tbsp. tarragon
Salt, pepper, and sugar to taste

Garnish

4 lettuce leaves
6 pineapple rings
2 Tbsp. parsley

Instructions

Wash the red cabbage, cut in half and remove the stem. Chop or grate it into a mixing bowl. Peel the mango and cut the fruit out of the skin. Chop and put in the mixing bowl. Chop the papaya and add it to the mixing bowl. Also add the onion and the julienned apple. Toss gently. Prepare the dressing in a blender and pour over the salad before serving. Place the lettuce leaves on a serving tray and pour salad over the lettuce. Place the pineapple rings around the salad and sprinkle parsley.

Roasted Portobella Mushrooms with Red Wine Dressing Picante

Ingredients

6 portobella mushrooms, cut into strips
2 green peppers, cut into strips
1 onion red, cut into rings
2 Tbsp. jalapeños, chopped
1 carrot, grated
¼ cup red wine dry

Dressing

¼ cup red wine vinegar
¼ cup olive oil
¼ cup water
¼ cup salty peanuts ground
1 Tbsp. garlic
Salt and pepper to taste
1 Tbsp. honey

Garnish

2 cups red cabbage, julienned
1 cucumber, cut into rings
1 lime, peeled and cubed

Instructions

Wash the portobellas and dry. Cut them into strips. Cut the green pepper into strips. Heat oil in a pan and add the mushrooms and peppers. Cook until golden brown. Remove from the oil and place on a paper towel. Prepare a serving dish with the red cabbage. Pour the mushroom and pepper mixture on the tray and add the onion, jalapeños, grated carrots. Prepare the dressing in a blender until well mixed. Before serving pour dressing over the salad. Garnish with cucumber rings and lime cubes.

Roasted Portobella Mushrooms with Red Pepper Picante Dressing

Ingredients

5 portobella mushrooms, cut into strips
2 red pepper, cut into strips
1 onion, cut into rings
1 Tbsp. garlic, chopped
1 cup spinach
¼ cup vegetable oil

Dressing

½ cup balsamic vinegar
½ cup olive oil
¼ cup water
½ cup chopped avocado
1 Tbsp. fresh oregano
3 Tbsp. poppy seeds
Salt, pepper, and sugar to taste
1 Tbsp. honey
1 Tbsp. mustard

Garnish

3 green peppers, cut into rings and fried
3 Tbsp. fresh parsley

Instructions

Wash the mushrooms and remove the stems. Cut them into medium sized strips. Cut the red pepper, onion and chop the garlic. Mix it all together. Heat oil in a pan and add the vegetables. Cook for a few minutes and remove with a slotted spoon. Place them on a paper towel. Put all the ingredients in a bowl and toss gently. Prepare the dressing in a blender for 1 ½ minutes on high speed. Adjust flavor as needed. Put the salad on a tray and garnish with fried green pepper rings. Sprinkle fresh parsley. Pour the dressing over the top of the salad.

Root Salad with Shrimp and Tomato, Mayonnaise Dressing

Ingredients

2 carrots, cooked
4 radishes, thinly sliced
2 celery stalks, sliced
1 scallion onion, chopped
1 parsley root, julienned
12 oz. baby shrimp, cooked
1 cucumber, sliced

Dressing

1 cup mayonnaise
½ cup ketchup
2 Tbsp. tabasco
2 Tbsp. horseradish
Salt and pepper to taste
1 Tbsp. Worchester
Dash of Old Bay Seasoning

Garnish

2 cups spinach leaves
6 slices of white onion
3 Tbsp. parsley, chopped

Instructions

Wash all vegetables and peel as needed. Cut vegetables into thin strips. Place into a mixing bowl and add shrimp. Toss gently. Prepare a serving tray with spinach leaves and pour salad over top. Prepare the dressing in a blender and mix for 1 to 1 ½ minutes. Adjust flavor as needed. Before serving pour dressing over the salad. Garnish with onion slices and sprinkle parsley.

Scallion Onion with Julienned Corned Beef Red Wine Vinegar Dressing

Ingredients

10 scallion onions, coarsely chopped
12 oz. corned beef, julienned
½ cup Kalamata olives
1 small pepper, cut into rings
1 tomato, cubed
6 oz. Swiss cheese, julienned

Dressing

¼ cup red wine vinegar
¾ cup olive oil
1 Tbsp. garlic
Salt, pepper, and sugar to taste
⅛ cup water

Garnish

1 cup red cabbage, shredded
1 red pepper, finely chopped
¼ cup pecans, chopped

Instructions

Wash the scallion onion and cut the bottoms off. Cut large pieces and put it into a mixing bowl with corned beef, kalamata olives, pepper rings and tomato cubes. Prepare a serving tray with the red cabbage. Pour salad on top. Blend dressing ingredients in a blender. Adjust flavor if needed. Pour dressing over the salad before serving. Garnish with chopped red pepper and chopped pecans.

Scallion and Feta with Basmati Rice Picante

Ingredients

1 scallion onion, coarsely chopped
2 cups feta cheese, crumbled
1 cup basmati rice
2 Tbsp. jalapeños, chopped
½ cup green olives, chopped

Dressing

½ cup olive oil
½ cup lemon juice
¼ cup coconut milk
2 Tbsp. shredded coconut
Salt to taste
1 Tbsp. garlic, chopped

Garnish

6-8 corn husks
1 persimmon, chopped
2 Tbsp. parsley
3 Tbsp. cheddar cheese

Instructions

Wash the scallion onion, and cut in half 2 to 2 ½ inches long. Put them into a mixing bowl and add feta, jalapeno, and green olives. Boil 2 cups of water and add rice. Mix it and then bring to a boil. Cover and reduce to a simmer. Cook for approximately 10 to 12 minutes. Remove from the stove and fluff with a fork. Let it cool. Add the rice to the mixing bowl and toss gently. Prepare a tray with corn husks. Pour salad on top. Blend all dressing ingredients in a blender for 1 and a half minutes. Adjust flavor. Before serving pour dressing on top. Finish with cubes of persimmon down the center of the salad, sprinkle parsley and cheese.

Spicy Carrots with Beet Olive Oil Tarragon Dressing

Ingredients

4 carrots, peeled and cooked
2 beets, cooked, julienned
3 Tbsp. Italian parsley
2 scallion onions, chopped
3 hard-boiled eggs

Dressing

¼ cup olive oil
¼ cup lemon juice
2 tsp. garlic, chopped
Salt, pepper, and sugar to taste
1 tsp. red pepper
Dash of oregano
2 Tbsp. tarragon
⅛ cup water

Garnish

1 Granny Smith apple, sliced and fried
1 tsp. lemon zest
2 Tbsp. parsley, chopped

Instructions

Peel carrots and cut the top and bottom off. Boil for 5 to 7 minutes. Remove from the water and let cool to room temperature. Cut carrots into rings and place them into a mixing bowl. Add beets, Italian parsley, scallion onions, and hard-boiled eggs. Prepare the dressing in a blender for 1 minute. Pour the salad onto a serving tray and pour dressing on top before serving. Fry Granny Smith apples in a sauté pan until light golden brown. Garnish with lemon zest and chopped parsley.

Spicy Carrots with Curry and Olive Oil Dressing

Ingredients

4 large carrots, peeled, cooked and sliced
2 mangos, cubed
2 scallion onions, chopped
2 Tbsp. garlic
3 Tbsp. Italian parsley
1 Tbsp. Rosemary, chopped

Dressing

½ cup olive oil
½ cup tarragon
½ cup water
1 tsp. yellow mustard
Salt, pepper, and sugar to taste
1 Tbsp. curry powder

Garnish

5 lettuce leaves
1 large lime, sliced and twisted
⅛ cup raisins

Instructions

Peel and cook the carrots for 7 minutes. Remove from the stove and cool. Slice into rings and add to a mixing bowl. Add the mango, scallion onions, garlic, and parsley. Mix gently. Prepare the dressing in a blender or mixing bowl and mix for 1 minute. Adjust flavor if needed. On a serving tray put the lettuce leaves down and pour the salad on top. Garnish with the twisted lime rings and sprinkle raisins.

Spicy Eggplant with Sour Cream Avocado Dressing

Ingredients

1 medium eggplant, sliced
1 Tbsp. Jalapeños, chopped
1 red pepper, chopped
½ cup blueberries
1 cup vegetable oil
¾ cup white flour

Dressing

1 cup sour cream
1 small avocado
2 Tbsp. Worchester
1 lemon for juice
1 Tbsp. lemon zest
Salt and pepper to taste

Garnish

5 lettuce leaves
Dash of paprika
1 Tbsp. rosemary

Instructions

Wash the eggplant and cut the top and bottom off. Slice into 12 slices. Dip the eggplant slices into flour. Heat oil in a sauté pan and fry until golden brown. Place on a paper towel. Prepare a platter with lettuce leaves. Place the eggplant on the tray. Add jalapeños, red pepper, blueberries. Prepare the dressing in a blender on high speed for 1 minute. Before serving pour the dressing on the salad. To garnish sprinkle paprika and rosemary.

Spinach and Anchovy with Red Pepper Raspberry Dressing

Ingredients

5 cups fresh spinach leaves
4 oz. anchovies
1 large red pepper, cut into thin strips
1 cup fresh raspberry
1 red onion, cut into rings

Dressing

1 cup raspberry
¼ cup mayonnaise
½ cup sour cream
¼ cup fresh lemon juice
Salt and pepper to taste
Dash of sugar

Garnish

1 medium orange, cut into rings and twisted
½ cup walnuts or peanuts, chopped

Instructions

Wash the spinach leaves and strain. Cut the red pepper into thin strips. Put the spinach leaves on top of the tray. Add the anchovies, peppers, raspberry and onions. Prepare the dressing in a blender and blend for 1 ½ minutes. Adjust flavor if needed. Before serving pour dressing on salad. Garnish with twisted orange rings and sprinkle peanuts or walnuts.

Squash Salad with Tarragon Dressing

Ingredients

3 large squash, cut into strips
2 celery stalks, chopped
1 red onion, finely chopped
1 Tbsp. rosemary
½ cup sundried tomato

Dressing

¼ cup olive oil
¼ cup tarragon vinegar
¼ cup water
2 Tbsp. grated lemon zest
Salt and pepper to taste
2 tsp. garlic

Garnish

5 lettuce leaves
2 persimmon, sliced
¼ cup ground salted peanuts
1 Tbsp. dill, chopped

Instructions

Wash the squash, cut the top and bottom off. Cut long ways into strips. Heat a little oil in a pan and add the squash. Cook the squash on broil in the oven until brown. Remove from the oven. Prepare a serving tray with lettuce leaves. Lay the squash on top of the lettuce and add the celery, onion, rosemary and sundried tomatoes. Put all dressing ingredients in a blender for 1 minute. Before serving pour the dressing on the salad and garnish. Place persimmon slices around the squash and sprinkle salted peanuts and dill.

Squash Sour Cream Feta Cheese Cheddar Dressing

Ingredients

4 large squash, cut into strips
1 small onion, chopped
½ cup feta cheese, crumbled
¼ cup oil

Dressing

½ cup feta cheese
1 cup sour cream
¼ cup cheddar cheese
1 large lemon for juice
1 Tbsp. garlic
Salt and pepper to taste
¼ cup seedless Kalamata olives

Garnish

1 cup red cabbage, julienned
Dash of paprika
1 small orange, sliced and twisted

Instructions

Wash the squash and cut the top and bottom off. Cut into medium strips and put in a pan with oil. Put in the oven on broil. Cool off when removed from oven. Prepare a tray with the cabbage. Place squash on tray and add onion, feta cheese. Prepare dressing in a blender for 1 ½ minutes. Adjust flavor if needed,. Pour dressing on salad before serving. Sprinkle paprika and twisted orange rings around the tray.

Squash with Walnuts, Celery Onion and Cheese Dressing

Ingredients

4 medium squash, cut into strips
½ cup walnuts, chopped
¼ cup onion
2 tomatoes, cubed

Dressing

½ cup ricotta
½ cup cheddar cheese
½ cup sour cream
2 Tbsp. sill
2 Tbsp. garlic
1 Tbsp. jalapeños
1 lemon for juice
1 tsp. lemon skin
Salt and pepper to taste

Garnish

4 lettuce leaves
3 Tbsp. parsley, chopped
1 lime, cut into rings

Instructions

Cut the top and bottom off the squash, wash and cut into strips long ways. Put on a platter with a little bit of oil. Broil for 4 to 5 minutes. Remove and let cool. Prepare a tray with lettuce leaves. Put the squash on top and add walnuts, onion, and tomato. Blend the dressing ingredients for 1 ½ minutes on high speed. Adjust flavor if needed. Pour dressing on the salad before serving. Finish with a garnish. Sprinkle Italian parsley and place lime slices around the salad on the tray.

Stuffed Roma Tomatoes with Crab Meat and Sour Cream Lemon Dressing

Ingredients

4 Roma tomatoes, halved
12 oz. backfin crab meat
1 celery stalk, chopped
1 scallion onion, chopped

Dressing

1 ½ cups sour cream
⅛ cup lemon juice
3 Tbsp. mayonnaise
Salt and pepper to taste
Dash of Old Bay Seasoning
3 crispy bacon strips

Garnish

4 lettuce leaves
1 lemon, wedged
2 Tbsp. parsley

Instructions

Wash the tomatoes and cut in half long ways. Scoop out the inside. In a mixing bowl put the crab meat, celery and scallion. Mix well. Stuff each tomato evenly with the crab mixture. Prepare a serving tray with the whole lettuce leaves. Put the tomatoes on the tray. Blend the dressing ingredients. Before serving pour the dressing over the tomatoes. Garnish by placing a lemon wedge on the middle of each tomato. Sprinkle with parsley.

Tomato and Rosemary with Hot Pepper Dressing

Ingredients

5 tomatoes, wedged
1 jalapeños, chopped
2 Tbsp. rosemary, chopped
1 red onion, sliced
1 green pepper, sliced
½ cup dried prunes, halved

Dressing

½ cup vinegar
½ cup tomato juice
½ cup olive oil
1 Tbsp. garlic, chopped
1 scallion onion
Salt, pepper, and sugar to taste
1 lemon for juice

Garnish

4 lettuce leaves
2 Tbsp. parsley, chopped
3 Tbsp. peanuts, browned

Instructions

Wash the tomatoes and cut in half. Cut 5 wedges out of each half. Put them into a mixing bowl and add, jalapeños, rosemary, red onion, green pepper and dried prunes. Toss gently. Blend the dressing ingredients for 1 minute. Adjust flavor as needed. Prepare a serving tray with the lettuce leaves. Put salad over the lettuce and pour dressing. Garnish with parsley and ground peanuts.

Tomato and Feta with Garden Cream Dressing

Ingredients

5 tomatoes, halved
1 cup feta cheese, crumbled
2 Tbsp. oregano, chopped
2 scallion onions, chopped
1 pear, julienned

Dressing

1 cup mayonnaise
¼ cup red wine vinegar
¼ cup half and half
2 Tbsp. garlic, chopped
1 carrot, grated
1 red pepper
1 cucumber
Salt, pepper, and sugar to taste

Garnish

5 lettuce leaves
1 lime, sliced
2 Tbsp. parsley, chopped

Instructions

Wash the tomatoes and cut them in half. Slice them in half again. Put them into a mixing bowl and add feta cheese, oregano, and scallion onions. Toss gently. Prepare a serving tray with lettuce and pour salad on top of the lettuce. Prepare dressing in a blender and blend for 1 ½ minutes. Adjust flavor if needed. Before serving pour the dressing over the salad. Garnish with the lemon slices around the tray. Sprinkle parsley.

Tomato Mozzarella with Balsamic Dressing

Ingredients

5 tomatoes, wedged
1 cup mozzarella, julienned
2 Tbsp. oregano, chopped
3 figs, red or yellow, sliced

Dressing

½ cup balsamic vinegar
½ cup olive oil
½ cup water
Salt, pepper, and sugar to taste
2 Tbsp. garlic, chopped
1 lime for juice 1 tsp. lime zest

Garnish

1 ½ cups spinach leaves
1 lime, sliced
1 Tbsp. lime zest

Instructions

Wash the tomatoes and cut into wedges. Prepare a tray with fresh spinach. Place the tomatoes on the tray. Sprinkle fresh oregano and add fig slices. Prepare the dressing in a blender for 45 seconds to 1 minute. Adjust flavor if needed. Before serving pour the dressing over salad. Garnish with twisted lime slices around the tray and sprinkle lime zest.

Tomato Picante with Sour Cream and Lemon Dressing

Ingredients

5 medium tomatoes, wedged
1 small onion, sliced into rings
4 Tbsp. parsley chopped
2 Tbsp. rosemary
1 green pepper, cut into strips

Dressing

1 ½ cups sour cream
1 lemon for juice
1 Tbsp. lemon zest
2 Tbsp. grated parmesan
1 Tbsp. garlic, chopped
Salt and pepper to taste

Garnish

2 cups fresh spinach leaves
1 scallion, chopped
1 large lime, cut into rings

Instructions

Wash the vegetables, cut the tomatoes into wedges and put them in a mixing bowl. Add the onion, parsley, rosemary and red pepper and mix gently. Prepare a tray with the spinach leaves, put the salad on top. Blend dressing ingredients in a blender for 1 minute and adjust flavor if needed. Pour dressing just before serving. Garnish with scallion onions and place lemon wedges around the edge of the tray.

Tomato Salad with Tahini Dressing Picante

Ingredients

5-6 medium tomatoes, wedged
1 cup fresh spinach, julienned
½ red onion, sliced thin

Dressing

1 cup Tahini paste-Sesame
½ cup water
¼ cup fresh lemon juice
2 Tbsp. olive oil
Salt and pepper to taste
2 Tbsp. garlic, chopped

Garnish

6 Romaine lettuce leaves
¼ cup dry sesame seeds
2 Tbsp. Italian parsley
1 medium lemon, wedged

Instructions

Wash tomatoes with cold water, remove the top of the tomato. Cut it in half and then into thin wedges. Put them into a bowl and add spinach leaves and onion. Toss twice gently. Prepare a serving tray put the lettuce on the tray then pour the salad on. Prepare the dressing by blending the ingredients in a blender, mix on high speed. It should be a light creamy consistency. Before serving, pour dressing over the salad. To garnish sprinkle sesame seeds, parsley and place lemon wedges around the tray.

Tomato, Spinach and Turkey with Lemon Dressing

Ingredients

4 tomatoes, cubed
2 cups spinach, julienned
1 scallion onion, sliced
1 red pepper, cut into strips
6 oz. smoked turkey, julienned

Dressing

½ cup olive oil
½ cup lemon juice
½ cup water
¼ cup dry white wine
Salt, pepper, and sugar to taste
1 Tbsp. garlic, minced
1 Tbsp. basil, chopped
1 carrot, grated

Garnish

½ cup pecans
1 orange, wedged
Dash of paprika

Instructions

Wash the tomatoes and spinach. Cut the tomatoes in half and slice into cubed. Put them in a mixing bowl with the spinach leaves. Add scallion onion, red pepper, and smoked turkey. Toss gently. Prepare the dressing in a blender and mix for 1 minute. Adjust flavor if needed. Pour salad on tray and pour dressing over the top. Garnish with orange wedges, pecans, and sprinkle paprika.

Tomatoes and Cucumber with Humus Tahini Dressing Spicy

Ingredients

3 medium to large tomatoes, thinly wedged
1 large seedless cucumber with skin, cut into rings
2 scallion onions, chopped
12 oz. garbanzo beans, cooked
3 Tbsp. Italian parsley, chopped
2 Tbsp. jalapeños, chopped
½ cup seedless Kalamata olives

Dressing

¼ cup tahini, paste
10 oz. garbanzo beans
¼ cup fresh lemon juice
1 Tbsp. garlic, chopped
½ cup olive oil
¾ cup water
Dash of cumin
Salt and garlic to taste

Garnish

5 lettuce leaves, whole
1 large lemon, wedged
1 small lime, wedged
Dash of paprika

Instructions

Wash tomatoes and cucumber. Cut tomatoes in half and then cut into thin wedges. Place into a mixing bowl. Cut cucumber into rings and add to the tomatoes. Add scallion onions, garbanzo beans, Italian parsley, jalapeños, and Kalamata olives. Mix gently. If using canned garbanzo beans, drain, and rinse with cold water. Prepare the dressing. Add all dressing ingredients into a blender and mix for 3 minutes on high speed. Dressing consistency should be light and creamy. If it is too thick, add lemon juice and water to thin. Season to taste. Place lettuce onto a serving tray and add salad on top. Before serving, pour dressing over the salad. Garnish with lemon wedges around the tray. Place lime wedges on the center of the salad and sprinkle with paprika.

Vegetable Root Salad with Balsamic Dressing

Ingredients

3 medium carrots, julienned
2 celery stalks, julienned
2 parsley root, julienned
5 radishes, julienned
3 Tbsp. dill, chopped
3 Tbsp. Italian parsley, chopped
2 medium beets, cooked and julienned
1 Granny Smith apple, julienned
½ cup baby corn

Dressing

⅓ cup balsamic vinegar
⅓ cup olive oil
⅓ cup water
1 Tbsp. sugar
Salt and pepper to taste
1 Tbsp. rosemary

Garnish

1 ½ cup red cabbage, julienned
1 cup cherry tomatoes
1 lemon, wedged

Instructions

Wash all the vegetables, cut them as specified and put into a mixing bowl. Prepare the dressing in a blender and blend for approximately 1 ½ minutes. Adjust flavor if needed and pour it into the salad. Mix gently. Put the julienned cabbage on a serving tray and pour the salad on top. Garnish with cherry tomatoes and place lemon wedges around the tray.

Wax Beans with Tomato Picante

Ingredients

1 ½ lbs. fresh wax beans
2 medium tomatoes, cubed
1 medium green pepper, chopped
1 small red onion, thinly sliced
1 Tbsp. garlic
1 Tbsp. jalapeños
3 Tbsp. Italian parsley
1 small carrot, grated

Dressing

½ cup olive oil
½ cup balsamic vinegar
Salt and pepper
Dash of sugar
¼ cup water

Garnish

1 cup green grapes
1 cup spinach, julienned
1 red pepper, cut into strips

Instructions

Cut the top and bottom of the wax beans. Boil for approximately 4 to 5 minutes. Pour into a strainer and let them cool off. Transfer to a mixing bowl and add the rest of the ingredient; tomatoes, pepper, onion, garlic, jalapeños, parsley and carrots. Mix gently. Prepare a tray with the julienned spinach and add the salad on top. Blend dressing ingredients in a blender. Adjust flavor and add to salad before serving. To garnish pour the green grapes on top and spread the red pepper slices over the salad.

Wax Beans, Granny Smith and Sour Cream Dressing

Ingredients

20 oz. wax beans
2 apples, julienned
3 scallions, chopped
1 medium carrot, coarsely grated
3 Tbsp. fresh rosemary

Dressing

1 ½ cups sour cream
2 lemons for juice
1 Tbsp. Lemon zest, grated
½ cup black olives
Salt and pepper to taste
1 tsp. garlic, chopped

Garnish

½ cup walnuts, chopped
6 Romaine lettuce leaves
1 large lime, sliced
2 Tbsp. parsley, chopped

Instructions

Cut the top and bottom off of the wax beans and wash with cold water. Boil the beans for about 4 to 5 minutes. Remove from the stove and strain. Let cool to room temperature. Put them into a mixing bowl and add apple, scallion, carrots and rosemary and mix gently. Prepare the dressing in a blender and blend for 1 ½ minutes. Adjust flavor as needed. Put the lettuce leaves on a tray and pour the salad on top. Pour dressing over salad before serving. Garnish with chopped walnuts. Place lime slices around the tray and sprinkle chopped parsley.

White Asparagus Granny Smith and Cheddar Cheese Dressing

Ingredients

16 oz. asparagus
2 medium Granny Smith apples, julienned
1 carrot, grated ¼ cup raisins

Dressing

½ cup cheddar cheese
¼ cup mayonnaise
¼ cup sour cream
¼ cup half and half
¼ cup lemon juice
2 Tbsp. basil
Salt and pepper to taste
1 Tbsp. garlic

Garnish

1 cup red cabbage
2 Tbsp. dill
2 small persimmon, cut into rings

Instructions

Wash the asparagus with cold water and cut 1 to 1 ½ inch off the stem. Boil the asparagus in water for 4 minutes. Put into a strainer to cool. Prepare a tray with the julienned red cabbage. Lay the asparagus on the tray. Blend all dressing ingredients for 1 minute on high speed. Adjust the flavor if needed. Before serving add the Granny Smith apple, grated carrots and raisins on top. Pour dressing over salad. Sprinkle chopped dill and place the persimmon around the tray.

White Asparagus with Grilled Chicken Tarragon Dressing

Ingredients

20 oz. white asparagus, cooked
12 oz. grilled or broiled chicken, cut into strips
1 small tomato, cubed
1 scallion onion, chopped
2 Tbsp. cilantro, coarsely chopped 1 small carrot, coarsely grated
¼ cup Kalamata olives, chopped

Dressing

¼ cup tarragon vinegar
¼ cup olive oil
¼ cup sundried tomatoes, chopped
2 garlic cloves, chopped
1 tsp. fresh tarragon chopped
3 Tbsp. cold water
Dash of crushed hot red pepper
Salt, pepper, and sugar to taste

Garnish

2 cups spring lettuce
1 lime, wedged
¼ cup feta, small cubes
1 Tbsp. dill, chopped

Instructions

Wash asparagus and cut 1 inch off the bottom. Place 1 ½ quarts of water into a large sauté pan and bring to a boil. Add asparagus and cook for 5 minutes. Remove from heat, strain, and let cool to room temperature. Place spring lettuce onto a serving tray and evenly add asparagus on top. Add chicken, tomatoes, scallion onion, cilantro, carrots, and Kalamata olives over asparagus. Prepare the dressing. Add all dressing ingredients into a blender and mix for 1 ½ minutes on high speed. Season to taste. Before serving, pour dressing over the salad. Garnish with lime wedges (faceup) around the tray. Sprinkle with feta and dill over top.

White Asparagus with Spinach and Sundried Tomato Dressing

Ingredients

20 oz. white asparagus
1 cup spinach, julienned
1 small red pepper, chopped
1 scallion onion, chopped
1 small tomato, cubed
2 hard-boiled egg, cut into rings

Dressing

⅓ cup lemon juice
⅓ cup olive oil
⅓ cup water
½ cup sundried tomatoed
1 tsp. lemon skin, grated
1 tsp. caraway powder
1 Tbsp. honey
1 tsp. yellow mustard
⅛ tsp. dried crushed hot red pepper
Salt, pepper, and sugar to taste

Garnish

4 lettuce leaves, whole
1 lemon, cut into rings
1 Tbsp. parmesan cheese
1 Tbsp. sliced roasted almonds

Instructions

Place 3 quarts of water into a deep sauté pan. Bring to boil and add 2 Tbsp. lemon juice. Add asparagus to the boiling water and cook for approximately 3 minutes. Remove from heat, strain, and let cool. Remove approximately 1 inch off the bottoms of the asparagus. Cut each asparagus stalk into 3 pieces and place into a mixing bowl. Add spinach, red pepper, scallion onion, tomato, and hard-boiled eggs. Mix gently. Prepare the dressing. Add all dressing ingredients into a blender and mix for 1 ½ minutes on high speed. Season to taste. Place lettuce leaves onto a serving tray and add salad on top. Add asparagus evenly over the lettuce. Pour dressing over the salad. Garnish with lemon rings around the tray. Sprinkle with parmesan and sliced roasted al

Zucchini with Balsamic Dressing Picante

Ingredients

4 medium zucchini, cut into long wedges
1 cup white flour
3 eggs, beaten
1 ½ cups seasoned bread crumbs
1 ½ cups oil
1 medium tomato, cubed
3 Tbsp. dill, chopped
1 medium green pepper, finely chopped
½ small onion, chopped
2 persimmon, cubed

Dressing

⅓ cup olive oil
⅓ cup balsamic vinegar
¼ cup water
1 Tbsp. garlic, chopped
1 tsp. mint leaves, chopped
1 tsp. jalapeños, chopped
Salt and sugar to taste

Garnish

3 cups spring lettuce
1 lemon, wedged
3 Tbsp. grated parmesan cheese

Instructions

Wash zucchini and cut off top and bottom. Cut in half lengthwise, cut into strips, and cut in half. Prepare three plates: 1 with flour, 1 with beaten eggs, and 1 with bread crumbs. Dip each zucchini piece into flour, eggs, then bread crumbs. In a sauté pan, heat vegetable oil, and add zucchini slices. Cook until light golden brown. Remove from oil, place on paper towel to drain excess oil. Prepare the dressing. Add all dressing ingredients into a blender and mix for 1 ½ minutes on high speed. Season to taste. Place spring lettuce onto a serving tray and add zucchini, tomato, dill, green pepper, onion, and persimmon on top. Before serving, pour dressing over the salad. Garnish with lemon wedges around the tray (face up) and sprinkle with parmesan.

FISH & SEAFOOD

Anchovy, Egg and Kalamata with Cream Dressing

Ingredients

6 oz. anchovies, chopped
8 hard-boiled eggs, wedged
1 pickle, chopped
1 Tbsp. onion
1 celery stalk, chopped
1 carrot, cooked and cubed
2 Tbsp. dill, chopped
½ cup seedless Kalamata olives

Dressing

¾ cup mayonnaise
2 Tbsp. white vinegar
Salt and pepper to taste
2 Tbsp. pickle juice

Garnish

3 cups iceberg lettuce, julienned
2 Tbsp. parsley
Dash of paprika
1 cucumber, sliced

Instructions

Chop the anchovies and place into a mixing bowl. Add hard-boiled eggs, pickle, onion, celery, dill, and olives. Toss gently. Prepare the dressing in a blender until well mixed. Prepare a tray with julienned iceberg lettuce. Pour salad over the tray and add dressing on top. Garnish with cucumber slices. Sprinkle with parsley and paprika.

Breaded Flounder with Avocado Picante Dressing

Ingredients

24 oz. flounder filet, skinless
1 cup flour
3 eggs, beaten
1 ¼ cup bread crumbs
1 ½ cups vegetable oil
1 large avocado, cubed
1 roasted red pepper, julienned
2 Tbsp. Italian parsley

Dressing

¾ cup mayonnaise
¼ cup ketchup
2 Tbsp. tabasco
1 lemon for juice
Salt and pepper to taste
2 Tbsp. half and half
1 tsp. garlic, chopped
1 tomato, chopped
1 Tbsp. Worchester sauce
1 Tbsp. horseradish

Garnish

3 cups spinach leaves
1 lemon, wedged
2 Tbsp. pecans
Dash of paprika
¼ cup white cheddar cheese

Instructions

Dip flounder into flour, eggs and then bread crumbs. Heat oil on the stove and then fry the flounder until golden brown. Remove and place onto a paper towel. After it cools, cut flounder into thick strips. Prepare a tray with spinach leaves and place the flounder on top. Add avocado, roasted red pepper, and Italian parsley. Blend dressing ingredients and pour over the salad before serving. Garnish with lemon wedges, sprinkle pecans, cheddar cheese, and paprika.

Breaded Mahi Mahi Fish with Mango Lemon Dressing

Ingredients

24 oz. Mahi Mahi, cubed 1 cup white flour
4 eggs, beaten
1 ¼ cup bread crumbs 1 ½ cups oil
2 scallion onions
1 red pepper, chopped 1 mango, cubed

Dressing

⅓ cup olive oil
⅓ cup fresh lemon juice
¼ cup orange juice
Salt, pepper, and sugar to taste
1 mango, fruit filet
Dash of curry powder
1 tsp. garlic, chopped

Garnish

2 cups spinach leaves
2 Tbsp. poppy seeds
1 lime, wedged
1 oz. alfalfa sprouts

Instructions

Wash the fish and pat dry with a paper towel. Cut into small cubes. Dip into the flour, eggs, then bread crumbs. Heat oil in a pan on the stove and fry the fish cubes until golden brown. Remove and place onto a paper towel. Place fish into a mixing bowl when cool. Add scallion onions, red pepper, and mango. Blend the dressing ingredients in a blender and mix well. Prepare a serving tray with the spinach leaves and pour the salad on the tray. Pour dressing over the salad. Garnish with lime wedges and alfalfa sprouts. Sprinkle with poppy seeds.

Crab and Plum Salad Cocktail Mayonnaise Dressing

Ingredients

4 medium red plums, julienned thin
16 oz. crab meat backfin or lump, no shell
1 scallion onion, chopped
1 celery stalk, chopped
5 strips of crunchy bacon, crumbled

Dressing

¾ cup mayonnaise
¼ cup ketchup
1 Tbsp. tabasco
1 medium lemon for juice
Salt and pepper to taste

Garnish

2 cups spinach, julienned
6-8 hard-boiled eggs, halved without yolks
1 Roma tomato, wedged
1 Tbsp. dill, chopped

Instructions

Wash plums, cut in half to remove seeds, and cut to thin julienned. Place into a mixing bowl. Add crabmeat, scallion onion, celery, and crunchy bacon. Mix gently. Prepare the dressing. Add all dressing ingredients into a blender and mix for 45 seconds on high speed. Season to taste. Pour into salad and stir until well combined. Place spinach onto a serving tray. Place salad mixture into the center of each egg half and place on top of the spinach. Garnish with tomatoes wedges around the tray and sprinkle with dill.

Crab Meat and Persimmon Herb Dressing

Ingredients

24 oz. crab meat, backfin or lump
2 scallion onion, chopped
6 strips crunchy bacon
1 red pepper, chopped
2 persimmon, cubed
2 Tbsp. dill, chopped

Dressing

½ cup mayonnaise
½ cup sour cream
1 lemon for juice
2 persimmon, peeled
Salt and pepper to taste
Dash of tabasco

Garnish

1 ½ cups spinach leaves
6-8 clam shells, real or artificial
1 lemon, thinly sliced
2 Tbsp. Italian parsley

Instructions

Place crab meat in a mixing bowl. Make sure there are no pieces of shell. Add scallion onions, bacon, red pepper, persimmon, and dill. Mix it well so everything is incorporated. Prepare the dressing in a blender until well mixed. Before serving, fill the clam shells equally with the salad. Make sure that each clam shell it thoroughly washed and dried. Place spinach leaves on a serving tray and add the stuffed clam shells over the spinach. Pour the dressing over each salad. Add a lemon ring over each clam and sprinkle with Italian parsley.

Crab Meat Cocktail with Fried Ham and Cream Veggie Dressing

Ingredients

24 oz. crab meat, backfin or lump
1 cucumber, chopped
1 red pepper, chopped
1 carrot, grated
1 avocado, cubed
¼ cup onion, chopped
1 Tbsp. mint leaves, chopped
1 tsp. fresh garlic, chopped
5 oz. smoked ham, chopped

Dressing

¼ cup olive oil
¼ cup red wine vinegar
¼ cup ketchup
¼ cup mayonnaise
2 Tbsp. Worchester sauce
Salt, pepper, and sugar to taste

Garnish

4 Roma tomatoes, halved
5 lettuce leaves, julienned
1 lime, wedged
1 Tbsp. parsley, chopped

Instructions

Clean the crab meat and make sure there are no shells. Break up the crab meat and place into a mixing bowl. Add cucumber, carrot, avocado, onion, mint leaves, garlic, and smoked ham. Mix well. Prepare dressing in a blender and mix for 1 minute. Adjust flavor if needed. Before serving prepare a tray with julienned lettuce. Cut the tomatoes in half and scoop the inside out. Stuff each tomato with the crab salad. Pour dressing over each tomato. Garnish by placing a lime wedge over each tomato and sprinkle with parsley.

Crab Meat, Potato and Mayonnaise Picante

Ingredients

16 oz. backfin crab meat
2 potatoes, cooked, peeled and cut
¼ cup red onion
1 Tbsp. tarragon
1 red pepper, chopped
1 celery stick chopped
¼ cup raisins
1 jalapeños, chopped

Dressing

1 ½ cups mayonnaise
1 lemon for juice
Salt and pepper to taste

Garnish

2 cups red cabbage, grated
1 orange, sliced
¼ cup swiss cheese
1 Tbsp. dill, chopped

Instructions

Clean the crab meat and make sure there are no shells. Break up the crab meat and place into a mixing bowl. Add cucumber, carrot, avocado, onion, mint leaves, garlic, and smoked ham. Mix well. Prepare dressing in a blender and mix for 1 minute. Adjust flavor if needed. Before serving prepare a tray with julienned lettuce. Cut the tomatoes in half and scoop the inside out. Stuff each tomato with the crab salad. Pour dressing over each tomato. Garnish by placing a lime wedge over each tomato and sprinkle with parsley.

Crab Meat with Shredded Vegetable Mayonnaise and Sundried Tomatoes

Ingredients

20 oz. crabmeat backfin or lump, cleaned with no shells
1 small carrot, cooked and grated
1 scallion onion, chopped
1 small red pepper, chopped
1 small cucumber, chopped
1 hard-boiled egg, grated
1 Tbsp. rosemary, chopped
5 strips crunchy bacon, chopped

Dressing

1 cup mayonnaise
½ cup sundried tomatoes
1 lemon for juice
2 Tbsp. half and half cream
Dash of Old Bay Seasoning
Salt and pepper to taste

Garnish

3 cups spring lettuce
6-8 round seasoned toast, golden brown
1 small seedless cucumber, cut into rings
Dash paprika
2 Tbsp. parsley, chopped

Instructions

Place crabmeat into a mixing bowl. Add carrot, scallion onion, red pepper, cucumber, hard-boiled egg, rosemary, and crunchy bacon. Mix gently. Prepare the dressing. Add all dressing ingredients into a blender and mix for 1 ½ minutes on high speed. Season to taste. Place spring lettuce onto a serving tray and toast on top. Add salad onto each toast. Using a spoon, add dressing over of toast. Garnish with cucumber rings around the tray. Sprinkle with paprika and parsley on top.

Escargot and Tomato with Spicy Dressing

Ingredients

16 oz. fresh escargot, broiled
¾ cup sundried tomatoes, chopped
1 green pepper, sliced
1 red pepper, sliced
2 potatoes, cooked and cubed
1 scallion onion, chopped
1 tsp. garlic, chopped
1 jalapeños, chopped

Dressing

¼ cup olive oil
¼ cup red wine vinegar
1 tomato
1 tsp. oregano
Salt, pepper, and sugar to taste
1 lemon zest
1 tsp. mustard

Garnish

2 cups red cabbage, shredded
1 tomato, sliced
2 Tbsp. Italian parsley

Instructions

Broil the escargot in a pan with a little butter for a few minutes. Pour escargot into a mixing bowl. Add sundried tomatoes, red pepper, green pepper, potatoes, scallion, garlic, and jalapeños. Mix well. Blend the dressing ingredients on high speed until well mixed. Adjust flavor as needed. Prepare a serving tray with the shredded red cabbage. Pour the salad over the cabbage and pour dressing over the salad. Garnish with tomato slices and Italian parsley.

Flounder Filet and Orzo Picante

Ingredients

16 oz. flounder filet, broiled or grilled
10 oz. orzo
1 red pepper, thin sliced
1 scallion onion, chopped
¼ cup pistachio, chopped
1 jalapeños, chopped
1 cucumber, cubed
2 Tbsp. Italian parsley

Dressing

¼ cup olive oil
¼ cup lemon juice
1 tomato
Salt, pepper, and sugar to taste
1 tsp. curry powder
⅓ cup tomato juice
1 tsp. garlic, chopped

Garnish

6 corn husks
2 Tbsp. parmesan, grated
2 Tbsp. parsley, chopped
1 tomato, sliced

Instructions

Broil the flounder filet and let it cool. Break into small pieces into a mixing bowl. Add olive oil into a pot and add the orzo. Cook until golden brown and add 2 ½ cups of boiling water. Mix it a few times and reduce to a simmer. Cook for approximately 8 to 10 minutes. Remove from the heat and fluff with a fork. Let cool and add to the flounder. Add red pepper, scallion, pistachio, jalapeños, cucumber, and parsley. Mix well. Prepare the dressing in a blender until it is well mixed. Place the corn husks on a serving tray and pour the salad on top. Pour dressing over salad. Garnish with tomato slices around the tray. Sprinkle with parmesan and parsley.

Flounder Filet Picante with Herb Dressing

Ingredients

30 oz. fresh flounder filet
2 Tbsp. dill, chopped
1 scallion onion, finely chopped
½ cup red pepper, chopped
⅛ cup raisins
6-8 champagne glasses

Dressing

½ cup mayonnaise
¾ cup sour cream
1 Tbsp. parmesan
1 lemon for juice
Dash of Old Bay Seasoning
2 Tbsp. half and half
Salt and pepper to taste
Dash of tabasco

Garnish

2 cups spinach leaves, julienned
1 lemon, cut into 6-8 wedges
Dash of paprika

Instructions

Boil the flounder in a sauté pan with lemon for 4 minutes. Remove from the water and strain. Break the fish up with your fingers and place into a mixing bowl, making sure there is no skin or bones. Add dill, scallion onions, red pepper, and raisins. Prepare the dressing in a blender and mix for 1 to 1 ½ minutes. Adjust flavor as needed. Put spinach leaves in the bottom of each champagne glass and add the fish mixture inside. Pour the dressing over each salad. Garnish by placing a lemon wedge on the top of each salad and sprinkle the paprika.

Flounder Filet with Papaya and Cream Dressing

Ingredients

24 oz. flounder filet, cooked
2 cups papaya, cubed
1 scallion onion, chopped
1 celery stalk, chopped
1 Tbsp. dill, chopped

Dressing

½ cup mayonnaise
¾ cup sour cream
3 Tbsp. ketchup
Salt and pepper to taste
Dash of Old Bay Seasoning
1 lemon for juice
½ tsp. lemon zest

Garnish

2 cups spinach leaves
4 Roma tomatoes, halved
2 Tbsp. cheddar cheese, shredded
1 Tbsp. parsley, chopped

Instructions

Put 1 ½ quarts of water in a pan on the stove and add the flounder filets. Boil for 3 to 4 minutes. Remove from the stove and place in a strainer. Bring to room temperature and break the fish apart with your hands into a mixing bowl. Add papaya, scallion onion, celery, and dill. Toss gently. Prepare the dressing in a blender and mix for 1 minute on high speed. Before serving, place spinach leaves on a serving tray. Cut the Roma tomatoes in half and scoop the inside out. Fill tomatoes with the salad and place on the tray. Pour the dressing over the tomatoes. Garnish with cheddar cheese and parsley over each tomato half.

Fresh Escargot with Wild Rice, Vegetables and Olive Oil Dressing

Ingredients

16 oz. escargot, sautéed
1 red pepper, julienned
1 zucchini, sliced
12 oz. Wild rice
1 squash, thinly sliced
2 scallion onions, chopped
1 celery stalk, chopped
1 jalapeños, chopped
½ cup corn

Dressing

½ cup olive oil
½ cup wine vinegar
1 tsp. garlic, chopped
1 tsp. lemon zest
Salt, pepper, and sugar to taste
1 tomato, chopped
Dash of cumin

Garnish

2 cups spinach, julienned
2 hard-boiled eggs, wedged
2 Tbsp. parmesan, grated

Instructions

Wash the escargot, dry with a paper towel and sauté in a pan with 3 tablespoons of oil. Remove from the stove, place onto a paper towel to remove excess oil. Place into a mixing bowl. Add 12 oz. of wild rice and place into a pot with oil. Stir every once in a while until it gets hot. Pour 20 oz. of hot water into the pot. Mix well, reduce to a simmer and cover. Cook for 20 to 25 minutes. Remove from the heat and mix with a fork. Let it cool and add to the mixing bowl with the escargot. Add red pepper, zucchini, squash, scallion onions, celery, jalapeños, and corn. Prepare the dressing in a blender and blend on high speed for 1 minute. Adjust flavor as needed. Prepare a serving tray with spinach leaves. Pour the salad on the tray and pour dressing over top. Garnish with hard boiled eggs around the tray. Sprinkle with par

Fresh Tuna Salad with Roasted Red Pepper and Wine Vinegar Dressing

Ingredients

32 oz. fresh tuna, broiled
2 red pepper, julienned
2 fresh green pepper, sliced
¼ cup red onion, chopped
1 pickle, chopped
2 Tbsp. parsley
1 Tbsp. oregano
1 tsp. garlic, chopped
½ cup seedless Kalamata olives

Dressing

½ cup red wine vinegar
½ cup olive oil
¼ cup orange juice
½ cup pineapple, chopped
Salt, pepper, and sugar to taste
1 tsp. mint leaves

Garnish

6 lettuce leaves
1 lemon, wedged
1 Roma tomato, wedged
2 Tbsp. parmesan, grated

Instructions

Place the tuna into the oven to broil or grill. Remove from the oven and let it cool. Cut into medium-sized cubes. Place into a mixing bowl. Add red pepper, green pepper, red onion, pickle, parsley, oregano, garlic, and Kalamata olives. Prepare a serving tray with the lettuce leaves. Add the salad on top of the lettuce. Pour the dressing over the salad. Finish with a garnish of tomato wedges around the tray. Place lemon wedges between the tomato wedges and sprinkle parmesan.

Fresh Tuna Salad with Spinach and Roasted Red Pepper

Ingredients

20 oz. fresh tuna filet, grilled or broiled
2 cups spinach leaves, julienned
¼ cup red onion, chopped
2 Tbsp. dill, chopped
1 tomato, cubed
1 carrot, grated

Dressing

½ cup olive oil
½ cup balsamic
1 roasted or fried red pepper
1 tsp. garlic, chopped
Salt, pepper, and sugar to taste
⅛ tsp. crushed red pepper, hot
1 nectarine, chopped

Garnish

2 cups, shredded red cabbage
2 Tbsp. Kalamata olives, chopped
2 Tbsp. parmesan
Dash of paprika

Instructions

Wash the tuna and grill or broil. Let cool and cut into small cubes. Place into a mixing bowl. Add spinach, red onion, dill, tomato, and carrot. Mix gently. Prepare the dressing in a blender. Prepare a serving tray with shredded red cabbage. Pour the salad over the tray and pour the dressing on top. Garnish with Kalamata olives, parmesan and sprinkle with paprika.

Fried Spicy Calamari with Lemon Dressing

Ingredients

20 oz. calamari, sliced
1 cup whole wheat flour
4 large eggs, beaten
2 Tbsp. sesame seeds
1 ½ cups, vegetable oil
1 roasted red pepper, chopped
1 green pepper, thinly sliced
1 tomato, cubed
2 scallion onions, chopped

Dressing

½ cup avocado oil
¼ cup lemon juice
¼ cup orange juice
1 tsp. orange skin, grated
Salt, pepper, and sugar to taste
¼ tsp. red pepper, crushed
1 tsp. Worchester

Garnish

6 corn husks
2 Tbsp. parsley
1 lemon, wedged
2 Tbsp. parmesan, grated

Instructions

Wash the calamari and cut into ¼ inch pieces. Dip pieces into the flour and then into the egg. Heat oil on the stove and fry the calamari. Remove from the oil and place onto a paper towel. Blend the dressing ingredients until well mixed. Adjust flavor as needed. Prepare a tray with the corn husks and pour the salad over the tray. Pour dressing over the salad. Garnish with lemon wedges. Sprinkle with parmesan and parsley.

Fried Oyster Salad with Lemon Picante Dressing

Ingredients

20 oz. fresh oysters
1 cup vegetable oil
½ cup white flour
3 eggs, beaten
1 cup bread crumbs
1 red pepper, julienned
2 scallion onions, chopped
1 carrot, grated
2 Tbsp. parsley, chopped
1 tsp. lemon zest
½ cup olive oil
½ cup lemon juice
½ cup water
⅛ cup orange juice
1 tsp. hot crushed red pepper
Salt, pepper, and sugar to taste
2 tsp. garlic, chopped
Dash of Old Bay Seasoning

Garnish

6-8 round toast, seasoned
½ cup sundried tomatoes
6 lettuce leaves, julienned
1 lemon, wedged
2 hard-boiled eggs, grated

Instructions

Wash the oysters with cold water and dry with a paper towel. Dip into the flour, eggs, and then bread crumbs. Fry the oysters until golden brown and remove from the oil. Place them on a paper towel. In a mixing bowl combine red pepper, scallion onions, carrot, parsley, and lemon zest. Prepare your dressing in a blender. Adjust flavor as needed. Before serving put the julienned lettuce leaves on a serving tray. Place round toast on the tray and add the salad onto each toast. Pour the dressing over each toast. Garnish with a lemon wedge on each salad. Sprinkle grated hard-boiled eggs and sundried tomatoes on top.

Herring Filet Stuffed Tomatoes with Red Wine Dressing

Ingredients

16 oz. herring filet, skinless
1 scallion onion, chopped
1 red pepper, chopped
1 celery stalk, chopped
2 Tbsp. dill
1 pickle, chopped 1 peach, chopped

Dressing

⅓ cup olive oil
⅓ cup wine vinegar
⅓ cup water
Salt, pepper, and sugar to taste
1 tsp. garlic
1 Tbsp. parmesan
⅛ tsp. crushed red pepper

Garnish

2 cups spring lettuce
4 Roma tomatoes, halved
6-8 tsp. sour cream
1 lemon, cut into 8 wedges

Instructions

Wash the herring filet and cut to 1 inch pieces. Place into a mixing bowl. Add scallion onion, red pepper, dill, pickle, and peach. Mix well. Prepare dressing in a blender on high speed for 1 minute. Prepare a tray with the spring lettuce. Cut the tomatoes in half long ways and scoop the inside out. Stuff each tomato with the salad and place onto the tray. Pour dressing over each tomato. Garnish with a teaspoon of sour cream over each tomato and place lemon wedge on top of the sour cream.

Herring Filet with Sour Cream Picante Dressing

Ingredients

16 oz. herring filet
½ cup red onion, thinly sliced
1 tsp. capers
2 celery stalks, chopped
2 potatoes, cooked and cubed
1 cucumber, sliced
1 tsp. jalapeños
1 cup spinach leaves, julienned
½ cup, blueberries

Dressing

1 cup sour cream
1 lemon for juice
1 tsp. lemon zest
1 tsp. garlic, chopped
1 Tbsp. mayonnaise
Salt and pepper to taste

Garnish

4 red cabbage leaves
1 lemon, wedged
1 Tbsp. parsley
3 hard-boiled eggs, wedged

Instructions

Soak the herring in cold water for a couple of hour prior to using. Remove from the water and dry it. Cut into 1 ½ inch thick pieces and place into a mixing bowl. Add red onion, capers, celery, cooked potatoes, cucumber, jalapeños, spinach, and blueberries. Mix well. Prepare dressing in a blender on high speed for 1 minute. Prepare a tray with the whole red cabbage leaves. Pour the salad over the tray. Pour dressing over the salad. Garnish with lemon wedges and parsley. Add hard boiled egg wedges on the middle of the salad.

Herring Filet with Vegetable and Olive Oil Dressing

Ingredients

15 oz. herring filet, marinated
1 carrot, thinly sliced
2 scallion onions, chopped
1 red pepper, sliced
1 apple, julienned
1 tsp. garlic, chopped
1 tsp. tarragon, chopped
1 lemon, thinly sliced with skin

Dressing

⅓ cup oil
⅓ cup wine vinegar
⅓ cup water
Salt, pepper, and sugar to taste
1 Tbsp. mint leaves
1 tsp. capers

Garnish

3 cups spring lettuce
2 Tbsp. parsley
¼ cup peanuts
1 tomato, wedged

Instructions

Make sure there are no bones or skin on the herring filet. Put the herring in cold water and let sit for about an hour. Strain the water out and cut into 2 inch slices. Place into a mixing bow. Add carrot, scallion onions, red pepper, apple, garlic, tarragon, and lemon. Toss gently. Prepare the dressing in a blender and mix for 1 or 2 minutes. Adjust the flavor if needed. Prepare a serving tray with the lettuce. Pour the salad over the tray. Add dressing over the salad. Garnish with tomato wedges, peanuts and parsley.

Lobster Salad with Fig Picante

Ingredients

24 oz. lobster meat, cubed
6 red figs, quartered
1 red pepper, chopped
1 scallion onion, chopped
1 cup spinach, julienned

Dressing

2 lemons for juice
¼ cup orange juice
2 garlic cloves, chopped
¼ cup olive oil
½ tsp. crushed red pepper
Salt, pepper, and sugar to taste
1 tsp. rosemary

Garnish

4 red cabbage leaves
1 lime, sliced
2 Tbsp. parsley, chopped

Instructions

If you have any leftover lobster use it. Otherwise use fresh lobster. Cook by either broiling or grilling. Cut lobster into cubes and place into a mixing bowl. Add figs, red pepper, scallion onion, and spinach. Prepare the dressing in a blender until well mixed. Adjust flavor if needed. Put red cabbage leaves on a serving tray and pour salad over the cabbage. Pour the dressing over the salad. Garnish with lime slices around the tray and sprinkle parsley.

Lobster Salad with Sundried Tomatoes and Sour Cream Dressing

Ingredients

24 oz. steamed or grilled lobster
½ cup sundried tomatoes, chopped
1 scallion onion, chopped
1 apple, julienned

Dressing

1 cup sour cream
1 lemon for juice
1 tsp. lemon zest
Salt and pepper to taste
¼ cup shredded coconut
2 Tbsp. parmesan
3 Tbsp. half and half

Garnish

3-4 tomatoes, halved
2 Tbsp. dill, chopped

Instructions

Broil the lobster meat for approximately 3 to 4 minutes. Or you can grill it. Cut lobster meat into strips and place it into a mixing bowl. Add sundried tomatoes, scallion onion, and apple. Toss gently. Blend all the dressing ingredients in a blender until well mixed. Cut tomatoes in half and scoop out the inside. Stuff tomatoes with the salad. Place 4 lettuce leaves on a serving tray. Place the stuffed tomatoes onto the tray and pour dressing over each piece. Garnish with chopped dill. You can also place round slices of oranges over each tomato. Twist the orange a little bit to give it a nice finish.

Lobster Stuffed Tomatoes with Mayonnaise

Ingredients

16 oz. lobster meat, chopped
2 celery stalks, chopped
1 scallion onion, chopped
2 garlic cloves, chopped
Salt and pepper to taste
1 cup mayonnaise
2 lemons for juice

Garnish

4 Roma tomatoes, halved
5 lettuce leaves
1 lemon, wedged
Dash of paprika
2 Tbsp. parsley

Instructions

Cut lobster meat into cubes and place into a mixing bowl. The lobster meat can be grilled or broiled, but must be cold. Add celery, scallion onion, garlic, salt and pepper, and lemon juice. Mix well. Prepare a serving tray with the lettuce leaves. Cut tomatoes in half, scoop out the inside and stuff each half with salad. Place lemon wedge on top of each tomato half. Sprinkle with paprika and parsley.

Lobster with Veggie and Fruit Cream Picante Dressing

Ingredients

20 oz. lobster meat, grilled or broiled, cut into slices
2 celery stalk, chopped
2 persimmon, cubed
1 sweet apple, julienned
1 small carrot, grated
1 small red pepper, cut into strips
2 Tbsp. dill, chopped
1 Tbsp. rosemary, chopped
4 strips of crunchy bacon, chopped

Dressing

⅓ cup olive oil
⅓ cup wine vinegar
⅓ cup water
2 garlic cloves, chopped
2 Tbsp. grated parmesan
Salt, pepper, and sugar to taste

Garnish

3 cups spinach leaves
1 large lemon, wedged
½ cup crunchy blueberries, whole

Instructions

To prepare lobster tail: use a sharp knife to make a cut on top of shell to crack. Broil or grill. As the lobster tail cooks, the shell will crack. Once cooked, remove from shell, cut into slices. Place into a mixing bowl. (Leftover lobster can be used by cutting into cubes). Add celery, persimmon, apple, carrot, red pepper, dill, rosemary, and crunchy bacon . Mix gently. Prepare the dressing. Add all dressing ingredients into a blender and mix for 1 ½ minutes on high speed. Season to taste. Place spinach leaves onto a serving tray and add salad on top. Before serving, pour dressing over the salad. Garnish with lemon wedges around the tray and sprinkle with blueberries.

Mahi Mahi Filet with Spaghetti Picante

Ingredients

16 oz. Mahi mahi, grilled, baked or broiled
12 oz. spaghetti noodles, cooked
1 tomato, cubed
¼ cup red onion, chopped
1 Tbsp. rosemary, chopped
1 tsp. garlic, chopped
3 Tbsp. parsley, chopped
1 cup spinach, julienned

Dressing

½ cup olive oil
½ cup wine vinegar
1 Tbsp. Worchester sauce
Salt, pepper, and sugar to taste
½ cup sundried tomatoes
⅛ tsp. hot crushed red pepper
Dash of Old Bay Seasoning

Garnish

1 tomato, sliced
2 Tbsp. dill, chopped
1 tsp. sweet paprika
3 Tbsp. white sharp cheddar cheese

Instructions

Wash the Mahi mahi and grill, broil or bake. Let cool and cut it into small cubes. Place into a mixing bowl. Boil water and add spaghetti noodles. Cook for approximately 12 to 13 minutes. Pour into a strainer and let it cool. Add to the mixing bowl with the mahi mahi. Add tomato, red onion, rosemary, parsley, and spinach. Mix together until everything is incorporated. Prepare the dressing in a blender and mix on high speed. Pour the salad over a serving tray and pour the dressing over it. Garnish with the tomato slices. Sprinkle with dill, sweet paprika and cheddar cheese.

Mahi Mahi with Veggie Curry and Lemon Dressing with Tahini

Ingredients

20 oz mahi mahi, grilled or broiled, cubed
1 medium seedless cucumber, cubed
1 medium Granny Smith apple, cubed
2 scallion onion, chopped
1 celery stalk, chopped
3 ¼ cups fresh pineapple, cubed

Dressing

¼ cup tahini paste
¼ cup fresh lemon juice
½ cup water
1 Tbsp. garlic, chopped
1 tsp. curry powder
Dash of Old Bay Seasoning
Salt, pepper, and sugar to taste

Garnish

6 Romaine lettuce leaves
1 tomato, cut into rings
1 small red apple, peeled and cut into rings
2 Tbsp. sesame seeds

Instructions

Place mahi mahi into a mixing bowl. Add seedless cucumber, Granny Smith apple, scallion onions, celery, fresh pineapple. Mix gently. Prepare the dressing. Add all dressing ingredients into a blender and mix for 2 minutes on high speed. Season to taste. Dressing should be light and creamy. Place Romaine lettuce onto a serving tray and add salad on top. Before serving, pour dressing over the salad. Garnish with apple rings around the tray. Sprinkle with sesame seeds and add tomato rings down the center of the salad.

Marinated Herring Fillet with Beet Olive Oil Dressing

Ingredients

12 oz. smoked herring fillet
2 large beets, cooked and julienned
1 red onion, cut into rings
4 Tbsp. Italian parsley, chopped

Dressing

¼ cup olive oil
½ cup red wine vinegar
1 lemon for juice
Salt, pepper, and sugar to taste
1 Tbsp. capers
1 Tbsp. horseradish

Garnish

3 leaves of lettuce
1 small carrot, grated
1 tomato, wedged

Instructions

Cut the herring filet to an inch and a half sliced. Put into a mixing bowl and add beets, onion and Italian parsley. Toss gently. Prepare a tray with lettuce leaves. Pour salad on top. Put all dressing ingredients in a blender and blend. Adjust flavor if needed. Before serving pour dressing on salad. Garnish with grated carrots and tomato wedges.

Marinated Spicy Shrimp Picante

Ingredients

30 oz. medium shrimp, cooked, peeled, and deveined
2 celery stalks, chopped
1 scallion onions, chopped
½ cup sundried tomatoes

Dressing

¼ cup lemon juice
¼ cup olive oil
4 Tbsp. ketchup
2 Tbsp. red dry wine
½ tsp. Old Bay Seasoning
½ tsp. hot crushed red pepper
1 tsp. lemon zest
Salt to taste
½ tsp. mustard
1 Tbsp. horseradish

Garnish

6 lettuce leaves, julienned
1 cucumber, sliced
2 Tbsp. parsley

Instructions

Cook shrimp in boiling water or steam it. Peel and devein. Place the shrimp in a mixing bowl and add celery, onion, and sundried tomatoes. Blend all the dressing ingredients for 2 minutes. Prepare a serving tray with the lettuce leaves. Add the shrimp mixture on top of the tray. Pour the dressing over the shrimp. Garnish with the cucumber slices and sprinkle parsley.

Mediterranean Fried Sardines with Red Wine Dressing

Ingredients

24 oz. fresh sardines
1 cup white flour
1 ½ cups vegetable oil
2 scallion onions, chopped
½ cup red pepper, chopped
2 Tbsp. parsley, chopped

Dressing

¼ cup red wine vinegar
¼ cup olive oil
1 lemon for juice
1 tsp. lemon zest
1 tsp. garlic, chopped
1 Tbsp. dill
Salt, pepper, and sugar to taste
⅛ tsp. crushed red pepper

Garnish

2 cups lettuce leaves, julienned
½ cup Kalamata olives, chopped
2 Tbsp. parsley, chopped

Instructions

Wash the sardines and make sure there are no scales. Cut the head off and down the middle . Clean the sardines so there is nothing inside of them. Wash them again. Place them on a paper towel and dry them as much as you can. Dip into flour and deep fry them in a pan until golden brown. Remove them and put them on a paper towel. Prepare a tray with the julienned lettuce leaves. Place the sardines on the tray and put the onions and red pepper. Prepare the dressing in a blender and blend for 1 ½ minutes. Before serving pour the dressing over the sardines. Garnish with the Kalamata olives and sprinkle parsley.

Red Snapper Cocktail with Fruit

Ingredients

20 oz. red snapper filet, broiled or grilled, skinned and deboned
2 kiwi, cut into small cubes
½ cup papaya, cubed
1 scallion onion, chopped
2 Tbsp. dill, chopped
1 small Granny Smith apple, julienned thin

Dressing

¾ cup mayonnaise
1 large lemon for juice
3 Tbsp. half and half cream
1 small Roma, chopped
3 Tbsp. ketchup
3 garlic cloves, chopped
Salt and pepper to taste

Garnish

6-8 4 oz. wide mouth champagne glasses
2 cup spring lettuce
1 lemon cut into 8 wedges
8 mint leaves, whole

Instructions

Break red snapper into small pieces, making sure there is no skin or bones. Place into mixing bowl. (Leftover snapper can also be used). Add kiwi, papaya, scallion onion, dill, and Granny Smith apple. Mix gently. Prepare the dressing. Add all dressing ingredients into a blender and mix for 45 seconds on high speed. Season to taste. Place champagne glasses onto a serving tray. Add spring lettuce to each glass. Scoop salad evenly into each of the glasses. Using a spoon, evenly pour dressing over the salad. Garnish with a lemon wedge on the side of each glass. Place mint leaf into the center of each.

Red Snapper Filet with Avocado Persimmon Sour Picante

Ingredients

24 oz. red snapper filet, broiled or grilled
2 avocados, cubed
2 persimmon, cubed
3 Tbsp. red onion, chopped
1 red pepper, chopped
1 Tbsp. mint leaves
1 celery stalk, chopped

Dressing

¾ cup mayonnaise
1 large lemon, juiced
2 Tbsp. parmesan
1 Tbsp. tabasco
1 tsp. garlic
Salt and pepper to taste
Old Bay Seasoning to taste
3 Tbsp. sour cream

Garnish

6 lettuce leaves
1 tomato, halved
1 Tbsp. parsley

Instructions

Grill or broil the red snapper. Remove from the heat and let cool. Break the filet up into smaller pieces with your hands. Place into a mixing bowl. Add avocado, persimmon, red onion, red pepper, mint leaves, and celery. Prepare the dressing in a blender and mix on high speed for 1 minute. Prepare a serving tray with the lettuce leaves. Pour the salad over the tray and pour dressing over the top. Garnish with tomato halves and sprinkle with parsley.

Salmon Filet with Spicy Mango Tahini Dressing

Ingredients

24 oz. salmon filet, grilled or broiled
2 mango, cubed
2 Tbsp. dill, chopped
2 scallion onions, chopped

Dressing

¼ cup tahini paste
½ cup water
¼ cup lemon juice
1 tsp. jalapeños
Salt and pepper to taste
1 tsp. curry powder
1 tsp. garlic

Garnish

8 lettuce leaves, julienned
1 lemon, wedged
3 Tbsp. parsley

Instructions

Grill or broil the salmon filet. Break apart with your fingers into large chunks and place into a mixing bowl. Add mango, dill, and scallion onion. Prepare dressing in a blender and mix for 2 to 3 minutes on high speed. Adjust flavor as needed. Before serving , place lettuce onto a serving tray and add salad on top. Pour dressing over the salad before serving. Garnish with lemon wedges and parsley.

Salmon Fish Filet with Marinated Mango

Ingredients

24 oz. fresh salmon filet
1 large mango, peeled and cubed
1 scallion onion, chopped
1 Tbsp. rosemary
1 tsp. lemon zest

Dressing

¼ cup olive oil
1 mango
1 lemon for juice
¼ cup water
1 tsp. garlic, chopped
Dash of crushed red pepper
Salt, pepper, and sugar to taste
1 orange for juice

Garnish

5 lettuce leaves, whole
3 hard-boiled eggs, wedged
2 Tbsp. parsley, chopped
1 tomato, sliced

Instructions

Bake or broil the salmon filet. Break up the salmon and put it into a mixing bowl. Add mango, scallion onion, rosemary, and lemon zest. Toss gently. Prepare the dressing in a blender for 1 ½ minutes. Adjust flavor as needed. Before serving prepare a tray with lettuce leaves. Place the salad onto the tray and pour the dressing over top. Garnish with hard-boiled eggs across the center of the salad. Place tomato slices around the tray and sprinkle with parsley.

Salmon Salad with Fruit, Veggies and Cream of Lemon Dill Dressing

Ingredients

20 oz. salmon fish filet, broiled or grilled
1 Granny Smith apple, julienned
1 plum, cubed
1 carrot, grated
1 cucumber, cubed
1 persimmon, cubed
1 Tbsp. dill, chopped

Dressing

¾ cup sour cream
¼ cup mayonnaise
¼ cup lemon juice
2 Tbsp. dill, chopped
3 Tbsp. half and half
Salt and pepper to taste
1 plum, shredded
1 tsp. garlic, chopped

Garnish

8 corn husks
1 lime, sliced
¼ cup red pepper, chopped
3 Tbsp. parmesan, grated

Instructions

Rinse fish with water and pat dry with a paper towel. Grill or broil the fish, let it cool and break it apart into large pieces. Place into a mixing bowl. Add apple, plum, carrot, cucumber, persimmon, and dill. Toss gently. Prepare the dressing in a blender. Mix for 1 ½ minutes. Adjust flavor as needed. Prepare a serving tray with corn husks and add salad on top. Pour the dressing over the salad before serving. Garnish with lime slices around the tray. Sprinkle with red pepper strips and parmesan.

Salmon Salad with Honey Chambord Dressing

Ingredients

24 oz. salmon filets, broiled or grilled
1 medium red pepper, julienned
1 small red onion, chopped
2 Tbsp. dill, chopped
1 tsp. lemon skin, finely grated
½ cup chopped walnuts
1 garlic clove, chopped

Dressing

¼ cup honey
¼ cup Chambord liquor
¼ cup olive oil
3 Tbsp. fresh lemon juice
4 Tbsp. water
Salt, pepper, and sugar to taste

Garnish

6 Romaine lettuce leaves
8 fried orange rings
½ cup sour cream
2 Tbsp. dill, chopped

Instructions

Break up the salmon filets with your fingers and place into a mixing bowl. (Leftover salmon may be substituted). Add red pepper, red onion, dill, lemon skin, walnuts, and garlic. Mix gently. Prepare the dressing. Add all dressing ingredients into a blender and mix for 1 ½ minutes on high speed. Season to taste. Place Romaine lettuce onto a serving tray and add salad on top. Before serving, pour dressing over the salad. Garnish with fried orange rings around the tray. Place sour cream across the center of the salad, smoothing to the edges. Sprinkle dill on top.

Salmon with Vegetable and Cream Dressing

Ingredients

30. oz fresh salmon filet
1 red pepper, julienned
¼ cup red onion, chopped
1 Tbsp. dill, chopped
1 celery stalk, chopped
1 Granny Smith apple, julienned

Dressing

1 cup sour cream
½ cup sundried tomatoes, chopped
¼ cup white vinegar
2 Tbsp. mayonnaise
1 tsp. garlic, chopped
Salt and pepper to taste
Dash of crushed red pepper
1 tsp. oregano
1 carrot, shredded
1 celery stalk, chopped

Garnish

5-6 lettuce leaves
1 tomato, wedged
2 Tbsp. parsley
1 Tbsp. parmesan

Instructions

Broil the salmon for 6 minutes. Remove from broiler and let cool to room temperature. Break apart with your hands into a mixing bowl. Add red pepper, red onion, dill, celery, and apple. Toss gently. Prepare a serving tray with lettuce leaves. Pour salad over the tray. Prepare the dressing in a blender until well mixed, Adjust flavor if needed. Garnish with tomato wedges around the tray and sprinkle parmesan and parsley.

Salmon with Potatoes Fruit and Vegetables

Ingredients

16 oz. fresh salmon, broiled and cubed
4 red skinned potatoes, cubed
1 apple, julienned
1 nectarine, cubed
1 scallion onion, chopped
2 carrots, grated
1 Tbsp. dill, chopped
1 celery stalk, chopped
3 strips crispy bacon, chopped

Dressing

⅓ cup mayonnaise
⅔ cup sour cream
⅛ cup lemon juice
Salt and pepper to taste
2 Tbsp. peanuts, chopped
1 tsp. garlic
2 Tbsp. olive oil
1 pickle, chopped

Garnish

5 lettuce leaves, whole
1 orange, sliced
3 hard-boiled eggs, wedged

Instructions

Wash the salmon. Broil in the oven or cook on the grill. Boil the potatoes, let cool and cut into cubes. Break the salmon apart and place into a mixing bowl. Add potatoes, apple, nectarine, scallion onion, carrots, dill, celery, and crunchy bacon pieces. Toss salad well. Prepare the dressing in a blender for 1 minute on high speed. Adjust flavor as needed. Prepare a serving tray with the lettuce leaves and pour the salad over the tray. Pour dressing over the salad. Garnish with orange slices around the salad. Add hard-boiled eggs down the center of the salad.

Seafood Cocktail with Cocktail Dressing

Ingredients

10 oz med shrimp, steamed, peeled tail removed, and deveined
8 oz. backfin crabmeat with no shells
8 oz baked salmon or flounder filets
2 persimmon, cubed
1 small Granny Smith apple, julienned thin
1 large plum, cut int small cubes
1 Tbsp. fresh rosemary, chopped

Dressing

½ cup ketchup
½ cup mayonnaise
3 Tbsp. tabasco
2 Tbsp. Worchester sauce
1 Tbsp. horseradish
1 small lemon for juice
1 Tbsp. garlic, chopped
Salt, pepper, and sugar to taste

Garnish

6-8 4 oz. wide mouth champagne glasses
2 cup spinach leaves
1 lemon, cut into 8 wedges
2 Tbsp. parsley, chopped

Instructions

Place shrimp into a mixing bowl. Crumble the crabmeat and salmon and add to mixing bowl. Add persimmon, Granny Smith apple, plum, and rosemary. Mix gently. Prepare the dressing. Add all dressing ingredients into a blender and mix for 2 minutes on high speed. Season to taste. Place champagne glasses onto a serving tray. Add spinach to each glass. Scoop the salad evenly into each of the glasses. Using a spoon, evenly pour dressing over the salad. Garnish with a lemon wedge on the side of each glass and sprinkle with parsley.

Shark Meat Salad with Curry and Sundried Tomato Dressing

Ingredients

16 oz. shark meat, filet grilled or broiled
10 oz. broccoli, steamed
¾ cup sundried tomatoes, whole
1 scallion onion
1 cucumber, sliced
1 tsp. garlic
1 tsp. Mint
1 plum, wedged

Dressing

⅓ cup olive oil
⅓ cup red wine vinegar
⅓ cup tomato juice
1 lemon for juice
1 tsp. curry powder
Salt, pepper, and sugar to taste
1 tsp. jalapeños

Garnish

2 cups spring lettuce
1 red pepper, chopped
2 Tbsp. pistachio, chopped
2 Tbsp. parmesan

Instructions

Wash the shark meat and dry it. Grill or broil it. Remove and cut into small cubes. Place into a mixing bowl. Steam the broccoli florets. Strain and add the to mixing bowl. Add sundried tomatoes, scallion onion, cucumber, garlic, mint, and plum wedges. Mix the salad. Prepare the dressing ingredients in a blender on high speed for 1 minutes. Prepare a serving tray with the spring lettuce. Pour the salad over the tray and add dressing. Garnish with red pepper. Sprinkle with pistachios and parmesan cheese.

Shark Meat Salad with Red Wine Dressing Picante

Ingredients

24 oz. shark meat filet, grilled or broiled, cubed
1 roasted red pepper, sliced
1 green pepper roasted, sliced
¼ cup onion, chopped
3 Tbsp. dill, chopped
1 cup white rice, cooked

Dressing

¼ cup water
⅓ cup olive oil
⅓ cup white wine vinegar
½ tsp. crushed red pepper
1 Granny smith apple
Salt, pepper, and sugar to taste
1 tsp. garlic, chopped
Dash of cumin

Garnish

6 lettuce leaves, whole
1 lemon, sliced
2 Tbsp. parmesan
1 Tbsp. poppy seeds

Instructions

Wash the shark filets, dry with a paper towel and grill or broil in the oven. Remove and let cool. Cut into cubes and place into a mixing bowl. Add red pepper, green pepper, onion, dill, and cooked white rice. Prepare the dressing in a blender and mix for 1 ½ minutes. Adjust flavor as needed. Prepare a tray with the lettuce leaves. Pour the salad over the tray. Pour the dressing over salad. Garnish with lemon slices, sprinkle parmesan and poppy seeds.

Shrimp and Sundried Tomatoes Picante

Ingredients

32 oz. shrimp, cooked, peeled and deveined
½ cup sundried tomatoes, chopped
1 red pepper, julienned
¼ cup red onion, chopped
1 celery stalk, chopped
1 cup spinach, julienned
2 red plums, wedged

Dressing

¼ cup olive oil
¼ cup balsamic vinegar
¼ cup water
1 tsp. garlic, chopped
Salt, pepper, and sugar to taste
Dash of cumin
Dash of Old Bay Seasoning
½ cup sundried tomatoes

Garnish

5 lettuce leaves
1 lemon, sliced
¼ cup black olives, chopped

Instructions

Put the cooked shrimp into a mixing bowl and add the sundried tomatoes, red pepper, red onion, celery, and red plums. Toss gently. Blend all the dressing ingredients. Adjust flavor as needed. Prepare a serving tray with the lettuce leaves. Pour the salad on the tray and pour dressing over salad before serving. Garnish with the lemon slices around the tray and sprinkle black olives.

Shrimp with Roasted Green Pepper and Parmesan

Ingredients

32 oz. Shrimp, cooked
1 green pepper, julienned
1 red pepper, julienned
3 Tbsp. roasted shredded coconut
1 celery stalk, chopped
1 Granny Smith apple, julienned

Dressing

1 ½ cups mayonnaise
1 tsp. Old Bay Seasoning
1 lemon for juice
3 Tbsp. Parmesan, grated
1 tsp. lemon zest

Garnish

8 corn husks
1 cup spinach leaves
1 tomato, wedged

Instructions

Cook the shrimp, peel and devein. Place the shrimp in a mixing bowl. Add green pepper, red pepper, coconut, celery, and apple. Toss gently. Prepare the dressing in a blender. Adjust flavor as needed. Put the corn husks on a serving tray and pour the salad over the tray. Pour the dressing over the shrimp. Garnish with chopped spinach and tomato wedges.

Smoked Spicy Oysters with Orzo

Ingredients

12 oz. smoked oysters
1 cup orzo
2 Tbsp. Italian parsley
1 tomato, cubed
1 scallion onion, chopped
1 jalapeños, chopped
3 Tbsp. sesame seeds
1 red pepper, chopped

Dressing

¼ cup sesame seeds
¼ cup lemon juice
½ cup sundried tomatoes
1 tomato
1 tsp. basil
2 garlic cloves
Salt, pepper, and sugar to taste

Garnish

2 cups spring lettuce
1 cucumber, sliced
1 lemon, sliced

Instructions

Place the smoked oysters into a mixing bowl. Add 1 ¾ cups of water into a pot on the stove and pour 1 cup of orzo in when the water starts to boil. Stir and reduce heat. Cover and cook for 8 10 minutes. Remove from the stove and fluff with a fork. Let cool and then pour into the mixing bowl with the oysters. Add tomato, scallion onion, jalapeños, sesame seeds, and red pepper. Prepare the dressing in a blender and mix for 1 ½-2 minutes. Before serving, prepare a serving tray with spring lettuce. Pour the salad over the tray and pour dressing on top. Garnish with cucumber and lemon slices.

Smoked White Fish with Scallion, Avocado and Olive Oil Dressing

Ingredients

24 oz. smoked white fish, filet
2 scallion onions, chopped
1 red pepper, chopped
½ cup sundried tomatoes, chopped
3 garlic cloves, chopped
2 Tbsp. dill

Dressing

⅓ cup avocado oil
¼ cup lemon juice
Salt, pepper, and sugar to taste
¼ cup water
1 tsp. Capers
1 tsp. lemon zest, grated

Garnish

2 cups spring lettuce
1 tomato, wedged
1 pickle, cubed
Dash of paprika

Instructions

Break up the white fish with your hands into a mixing bowl. Add scallion onions, red pepper, garlic, and dill. Mix gently. Prepare the dressing in a blender. Adjust flavor as needed. Prepare a tray with the spring lettuce. Add the salad onto the tray and pour dressing over the salad. Garnish with tomato wedges, pickle, and paprika.

Snow Crab Legs with a Cream Vegetable Dressing

Ingredients

20 oz. snow crab legs, steamed
10 oz. broccoli, chopped and steamed
1 scallion onion, chopped
½ cup sundried tomatoes, chopped
1 Tbsp. basil, chopped
1 celery stalk, chopped
1 red pepper, cubed
3 oz. sharp cheddar cheese

Dressing

¾ cup mayonnaise
⅓ cup sour cream
1 large lemon for juice
Salt and pepper to taste
Dash of Old Bay Seasoning
1 tsp. garlic, chopped
1 carrot, cooked
3 Tbsp. half and half

Garnish

2 cups spinach leaves
2 Tbsp. parsley
1 tomato, wedged

Instructions

Steam the snow crab legs. Cut into half inch pieces and place into a mixing bowl. Steam or boil the broccoli. Let cool and then cut into large pieces. Add sundried tomatoes, scallion onion, celery, red pepper, and cheddar cheese. Toss gently. Prepare the dressing in a blender and mix for 1 minute. Adjust flavor as needed. Prepare a serving tray with the spinach leaves. Pour the salad over the tray and pour dressing over the salad. Garnish with tomato wedges around the salad and sprinkle with parsley.

Snow Crab Legs with Fruit and Lemon

Ingredients

20 oz. snow crab legs, steamed
1 Granny Smith apple, julienned
¾ cup cherry, chopped
2 Tbsp. dill
1 lemon with skin, sliced
½ cup peaches, cubed

Dressing

¼ cup lemon juice
⅓ cup olive oil
¼ cup orange juice
Salt, pepper, and sugar to taste
1 tsp. mint leaves, chopped

Garnish

2 cups lettuce, julienned
1 lime, sliced
2 Tsp. parsley, chopped
2 Tbsp. walnuts, chopped

Instructions

Steam the snow crab legs. Once they are done, let cool and remove them from the shells. Cut meat into half inch pieces and place it into a mixing bowl. Add apple, cherries, peaches, dill, and lemon. Toss gently. Prepare a serving tray with the julienned lettuce. Prepare the dressing in a blender until well mixed. Pour the salad over the tray and pour dressing over the salad. Garnish with lime slices, parsley, and chopped walnuts.

Spicy Claw Crabmeat with Sundried Tomatoes and Cream Dressing

Ingredients

20 oz. claw crab meat
1 cup sundried tomatoes, chopped
¼ cup onion, chopped
1 roasted red pepper, sliced
1 Tbsp. tarragon, chopped
1 apple, julienned
2 garlic cloves, chopped
2 Tbsp. Italian parsley

Dressing

1 cup mayonnaise
2 Tbsp. half and half
Salt and pepper to taste
1 lemon for juice
1 tsp. lemon zest
1 tomato, chopped

Garnish

6-8 crab shells, cleaned, washed and dried
2 cups spinach leaves
1 tsp. paprika
4 oz. white cheddar cheese, shredded

Instructions

Place the crab meat into a mixing bowl and break it up with your hands into smaller pieces, making sure there are no shells. Add sundried tomatoes, onion, red pepper, tarragon, apple, garlic, and parsley. Mix well. Prepare the dressing in a blender until well mixed. Adjust flavor as needed. Before serving put the spinach leaves on a tray. Fill each crab shell with the salad and place onto the tray. Pour dressing over each salad. Garnish with paprika and shredded cheddar cheese.

Spicy Shrimp

Ingredients

32 medium – large shrimp, cooked, peeled, and deveined
2 cups spinach leaves
¼ cup roasted coconut, shredded
2 medium tomatoes, cubed
1 red pepper, roasted and cut into thin strips
¼ cup red onion, chopped
1 tsp. crushed hot red pepper
¾ cup sundried tomato strips

Dressing

½ cup olive oil
½ cup wine vinegar
½ cup water
1 tsp. garlic, chopped
Salt, pepper, and sugar to taste

Garnish

1 medium orange, cut into rings
2 Tbsp. poppy seeds
2 kiwi, cut into rings

Instructions

Place shrimp into a mixing bowl. Add spinach leaves, roasted coconut, tomatoes, roasted red pepper, red onion, crushed hot red pepper, and sundried tomatoes. Mix gently. Prepare the dressing. Add all dressing ingredients into a blender and mix for 1 minute on high speed. Season to taste. Place salad onto a serving tray and add dressing on top. Garnish with kiwi rings around the salad and sprinkle with poppy seeds.

Traditional Jewish Carp Salad with Celery Horseradish Dressing

Ingredients

24 oz. ground carp fish
1 celery stalk, chopped
1 Tbsp. garlic, chopped
2 Tbsp. parsley, chopped
½ cup bread crumbs
1 egg
Salt, pepper, and sugar to taste
1 lemon for juice
2 ½ quarts water

Dressing

¼ cup olive oil
¼ cup wine vinegar
1 tsp. lemon zest
Salt, pepper, and sugar to taste
1 lemon for juice
⅛ cup water
1 tsp. garlic, chopped
Dash of Old Bay Seasoning

Garnish

5 lettuce leaves
1 carrot, cooked and sliced
1 Tbsp. parsley, chopped
2 hard-boiled eggs, wedged

Instructions

Put the ground carp fish into a mixing bowl. Add celery, garlic, parsley, bread crumbs, and egg. Salt and pepper to taste. Boil 2 ½ quarts of water. Add lemon juice. Make round balls out of the fish mixture. Boil for 7 to 10 minutes. Remove with a spoon and bring to room temperature. Prepare a tray with the lettuce leaves. Place the carp balls on top of it. Blend all the dressing ingredients for 1 ½ minutes. Before serving pour the dressing over the carp balls. Garnish with the cooked carrots around the tray. Sprinkle parsley and Old Bay Seasoning. Cut the hard-boiled eggs into wedges and place on the tray between the carp balls.

Tuna Cocktail with Veggie and Parmesan Cream Dressing

Ingredients

24 oz. Tuna strips, sautéed
1 Granny Smith apple, julienned
1 red pepper, julienned
1 scallion onion, chopped
1 Tbsp. dill
1 cucumber, cubed
1 tomato, cubed
2 Tbsp. parsley

Dressing

⅔ cup sour cream
⅔ cup mayonnaise
1 large lemon for juice
3 Tbsp. half and half
1 tsp. garlic
2 Tbsp. parmesan cheese
Salt and pepper to taste
Dash of Old Bay Seasoning

Garnish

2 cups spinach leaves
2 hard-boiled eggs, wedged
2 Tbsp. ground peanuts
6-8 champagne glasses

Instructions

Heat ¼ cup oil in a sauté pan and add fresh tuna cubes. Cook for 4 to 5 minutes on medium heat until golden brown. Remove from the oil and place on a paper towel. Place tuna into a mixing bowl and break up into small pieces. Add apple, red pepper, scallion onion, dill, cucumber, tomato, and parsley. Prepare the dressing in a blender for 1 minute. Adjust flavor as needed. Place the lettuce leaves inside the bottom of each champagne glass and add salad on top. Pour the dressing over each salad. Garnish by placing a hardboiled egg wedge over each salad and sprinkle with peanuts.

Tuna, Fruit and Vegetables with Lemon Dressing

Ingredients

24 oz. tuna, grilled
2 red plums, cubed
½ cup blueberries
1 celery stalk, chopped
1 red pepper, cubed
1 scallion onion, chopped
1 cucumber, cubed

Dressing

¼ cup olive oil
¼ cup lemon juice
¼ cup water
Salt, pepper, and sugar to taste
1 Tbsp. dill
1 tsp. garlic, chopped
½ tsp. curry powder

Garnish

5 lettuce leaves, whole
3 hard-boiled eggs, wedged
½ cup Kalamata olives
1 tomato, sliced

Instructions

Wash the tuna filets and place cook them on the grill. Remove from the grill and let cool. Cut into small cubes and place into a mixing bowl. Add plums, blueberries, celery, red pepper, scallion onion, and cucumber. Prepare the dressing in a blender and mix for 1 minute. Adjust flavor as needed. Prepare a serving tray with lettuce leaves. Pour salad over the tray and pour dressing over the top. Garnish with the hard-boiled eggs around the tray. Place tomatoes down the middle of the salad. Sprinkle Kalamata olives over the top.

PASTA

Bow Pasta with Sundried Tomatoes and Pomegranate

Ingredients

16 oz. bow pasta dry
1 cup sundried tomatoes, cut into strips
1 medium tomato, cubed
2 Tbsp. oregano, chopped
½ cup pomegranate
1 celery stalk, chopped
3 Tbsp. Italian parsley, chopped
1 small green pepper, thinly sliced
3 oz. pepperoni, thinly sliced

Dressing

½ cup pomegranate juice
½ cup olive oil
1 large lemon for juice
¼ cup pomegranate seeds
2 Tbsp. dry red wine
¼ cup water
1 tsp. garlic, chopped
1 tsp. lemon skin, finely grated
Salt, pepper, and sugar to taste

Garnish

3 cups spring lettuce
3 Tbsp. roasted sliced almonds
1 medium seedless cucumber, cut into rings

Instructions

Place 4 quarts of water into a medium pot, bring to a boil, and add 3 Tbsp. olive oil. Add bow pasta, stir, and cook for 14 to 16 minutes, stirring occasionally. Remove from heat, rinse with cold water, and strain. Place into a mixing bowl. Add sundried tomatoes, tomato, oregano, pomegranate, celery, Italian parsley, green pepper, and pepperoni. Mix gently. Prepare the dressing. Add all dressing ingredients into a blender and mix for 2 minutes on high speed. Season to taste. Place spring lettuce onto a serving tray and add salad on top. Before serving, pour dressing over the salad. Garnish with cucumbers around the salad and sprinkle with almonds.

Cheese Tortellini with Ham and Parmesan with Red Wine Dressing

Ingredients

12-14oz. tortellini, cooked
10 oz. smoked ham, julienned
1 cup parmesan, grated
1 celery stalk, chopped
1 cucumber, sliced
1 red pepper, chopped

Dressing

¼ cup red wine vinegar
¼ cup olive oil
¼ cup water
Salt, pepper, and sugar to taste
1 Tbsp. oregano, chopped
1 tsp. garlic, chopped

Garnish

6 pineapple rings
5 lettuce leaves
Dash of paprika

Instructions

Boil water and cook tortellini for 6 to 7 minutes. Remove from the heat and run under cold water. Strain and place into a mixing bowl. Add smoked ham, parmesan, celery, cucumber, and red pepper. Blend the dressing in a blender for 1 minute. Pour the dressing on the salad and mix gently. Prepare a serving tray with lettuce leaves and pour the salad over the tray. Garnish with pineapple rings around the tray and sprinkle with paprika.

Couscous and Spicy Tomato

Ingredients

12 oz. couscous
1 cup sundried tomatoes
1 red pepper
1 scallion onion, chopped
1 cup broccoli
1 Tbsp. tarragon

Dressing

¼ cup lemon juice
¼ cup olive oil
¼ cup water
1 tsp. garlic
3 Tbsp. sesame seeds
1 Tbsp. tabasco
2 Tbsp. lime juice
Salt, pepper, and sugar to taste

Garnish

3 Tbsp. spring lettuce
1 tomato, sliced thin
2 Tbsp. Italian parsley

Instructions

Boil 3 cups of water and add couscous. Stir and bring to a boil. Reduce to simmer and cover for 10 to 12 minutes. Remove from the stove and mix it with a fork. Let cool and pour into a mixing bowl. Add sundried tomatoes, red pepper, broccoli, and tarragon. Prepare dressing in a blender and mix for 1 minute. Adjust flavor as needed. Place the spring lettuce onto a tray and add salad on top. Pour dressing over the salad. Garnish with tomato slices and Italian parsley.

Couscous Salad with Chopped Smoked Ham and Lemon Mayonnaise Dressing

Ingredients

12 oz. couscous
10 oz. smoked ham, julienned
8 oz. pomegranate seeds
1 pickle, chopped
¼ cup red onion, chopped
1 Tbsp. fresh parsley, chopped

Dressing

1 cup mayonnaise
1 lemon for juice
1 lime for juice
1 tsp. lime zest
1 tsp. garlic
Salt, pepper, and sugar to taste
2 Tbsp. oregano

Garnish

2 cups spinach leaves
1 lemon, wedged
2 Tbsp. parsley, chopped

Instructions

Heat ⅛ cup of oil in a pot and add couscous. Cook until hot and add 2 ½ cups water into the pot. Stir and bring to a boil. Cover and reduce to simmer. Cook for 7 to 8 minutes. Remove from the heat and fluff with a fork. Place into a mixing bowl Add ham, pomegranate seeds, pickle, onion, and parsley. Toss gently. Prepare the dressing in a blender for 1 ½ minutes. Adjust flavor as needed. Prepare a serving tray or salad bowl with the spinach leaves. Pour salad over the tray and add the dressing on top. Garnish with lemon wedges and sprinkle with parsley.

Couscous Salad with Domino Dressing

Ingredients

12 oz. couscous
1 carrot, shredded
½ cup red cabbage, shredded
¼ cup black olives
1 red pepper, chopped
1 scallion onion, chopped
¼ cup cheddar cheese, shredded

Dressing

¼ cup balsamic
¼ cup olive oil
½ cup sundried tomatoes
1 sour apple, chopped
1 tsp. garlic, chopped
Salt and pepper to taste

Garnish

2 cups alfalfa sprouts
¼ cup peanuts, ground
2 hard-boiled eggs, wedged

Instructions

Place ⅛ cup of oil in a pot on the stove and add couscous. Stir and cook until it lightly golden brown. Add 2 ½ cups boiling water and stir. Cover and reduce to simmer. Cook for 7 to 8 minutes. Remove from the heat, fluff it and let cool to room temperature. Place into a mixing bowl. Add carrot, red cabbage, black olives, red pepper, scallion onion, and cheddar cheese. Blend the dressing ingredients for 1 ½ minutes. Prepare a serving tray with alfalfa sprouts and pour the salad over the tray. Add dressing and garnish with hard-boiled eggs and peanuts.

Couscous with Artichoke and Garbanzo Picante

Ingredients

12 oz. Couscous
12 oz. artichokes
1 Tbsp. jalapeños
1 carrot, grated
1 Granny Smith apple
¼ cup parmesan, grated
¼ cup red onion, chopped
¾ cup garbanzo beans, cooked

Dressing

¼ cup balsamic vinegar
¼ cup olive oil
¼ cup water
Salt, pepper, and sugar to taste
¼ cup tomatoes

Garnish

4 iceberg lettuce leaves
⅓ cup Kalamata olives
1 cucumber, sliced
2 Tbsp. dill, chopped

Instructions

Boil 3 ¼ cups water and add couscous. Stir and bring to a boil again. Cover and reduce to a simmer for 10 to 12 minutes. Remove from the stove stir and add into a mixing bowl. Add artichokes, jalapeno, carrot, apple, parmesan, red onion, and garbanzo. Prepare dressing in a blender and mix well. Place lettuce leaves onto a serving tray and add salad on top. Pour dressing over the salad. Garnish with Kalamata olives and cucumber slices Sprinkle with dill.

Dumplings with Spinach and Cream of Herb Dressing

Ingredients

20 oz. Small dumplings, cooked
2 cups spinach, julienned
1 carrot, grated
6 crunchy bacon, chopped
3 red plums, wedged
¼ cup red onion, chopped
1 red pepper, sliced
2 Tbsp. oregano
2 hard-boiled eggs, sliced

Dressing

½ cup mayonnaise
⅛ cup olive oil
½ cup sour cream
1 lemon juiced
¼ cup half and half
1 oz. cream cheese
Salt and pepper to taste
1 tsp. garlic, chopped
1 tsp. lemon juice

Garnish

5 lettuce leaves
1 tomato, sliced
2 Tbsp. poppy seeds

Instructions

You can use left over dumplings from the nigh before if you have them. Place into a mixing bowl and add spinach, carrot, bacon, red plums, red onion, oregano, and hard-boiled eggs. Mix gently. Prepare the dressing in a blender. Prepare a serving tray with the lettuce leaves and add salad on top. Pour dressing over the salad. Garnish with tomato slices, poppy seeds, and parmesan.

Gluten Free Pasta with Marinated Scallops and Vegetables

Ingredients

12 oz. gluten free pasta
12 oz. bay scallops
4 Tbsp. teriyaki
1 tsp. garlic
2 Tbsp. dill
1 tsp. rosemary
1 red pepper
1 cucumber, cubed

Dressing

¾ cup avocado oil
¾ lemon juice
¾ cups water
Salt, pepper, and sugar to taste
Dash of Old Bay Seasoning
1 tsp. lemon zest
1 tomato, chopped

Garnish

3 cups spring lettuce
6 Tbsp. sour cream
2 hard-boiled eggs, grated
2 Tbsp. parsley
3 Tbsp. cheddar cheese

Instructions

Boil the pasta in 3 quarts of water for 10-12 minutes. Put the pasta under cold water to cool. Strain the pasta and put it in a mixing bowl. Sautee the bay scallops in a pan with the teriyaki and chopped garlic. Sautee for 3 to 4 minutes. Let it cool and then pour it pasta. Add dill, rosemary, red pepper, and cucumber. Blend all dressing ingredients in a blender and mix well. Prepare a serving tray with spring lettuce and add salad on top. Pour dressing over the salad. Garnish by sprinkling eggs, parsley, cheddar cheese. Add sour cream across the top of the salad.

Gluten Free Pasta with Sour Cream Dressing

Ingredients

16 oz. gluten free pasta
2 scallion onions, chopped
1 celery stalk
1 red pepper, sliced thin
½ cup Kalamata olives
½ cup parmesan
½ cup pomegranate seeds

Dressing

1 ½ cups sour cream
¼ cup lemon juice
1 tsp. garlic
¼ cup half and half
1 tsp. lemon zest
Salt and pepper to taste
1 Tbsp. rosemary

Garnish

2 cups lettuce, julienned
1 lemon, sliced
2 Tbsp. dill

Instructions

Boil pasta in 4 quarts of water. Cook for approximately 10 to 13 minutes. Cool it under cold water and strain. Pour the pasta in a mixing bowl and add the onions, celery, kalamata olives, parmesan and pomegranate seeds. Toss gently. Blend the dressing ingredients until well mixed. Prepare a serving tray with the lettuce and add salad. Pour dressing over top. Garnish with lemon slices across the tray and sprinkle dill.

Gnocchi Veggie and Fruit with Raspberry Dressing

Ingredients

20 oz. gnocchi, cooked
1 carrot, grated
1 cup spinach, chopped
1 onion, chopped
1 green pepper, cubed
1 pear, cubed
1 red apple, cubed
1 plum, cubed

Dressing

½ cup raspberries
¼ cup olive oil
¼ cup lemon juice
¼ cup orange juice
1 tsp. honey
Salt, pepper, and sugar to taste

Garnish

6 lettuce leaves
2 kiwi, peeled, sliced
½ cup raspberries
1 Tbsp. dill, chopped

Instructions

Place gnocchi into a mixing bowl. Add carrots, spinach, onion, green pepper, pear, red apple, and plum. Prepare dressing in a blender and mix well. Prepare a tray with the lettuce leaves and add salad on top.
Pour the dressing over the salad. Garnish with kiwi, raspberries and dill.

High Gluten Pasta, Broccoli and Kalamata with Lemon Dressing

Ingredients

16 oz. high gluten pasta
10 oz. broccoli florets
¾ cup Kalamata olives
1 tomato, cubed
1 carrot, grated
2 scallion onions, chopped
¼ cup raisins
2 Tbsp. cilantro

Dressing

¼ cup lemon juice
½ cup olive oil
¼ cup water
1 lime peeled
Salt, pepper, and sugar to taste
1 Tbsp. garlic

Garnish

2 cups spinach leaves
2 persimmon, sliced
1 tomato, cubed
3 Tbsp. red pepper, chopped

Instructions

Boil 3 quarts of water and add pasta. Cook 7 to 9 minutes. Remove from heat and run under cold water. Strain pasta and place into a mixing bowl. Add broccoli, Kalamata olives, tomato, carrot, scallion onions, raisins, and cilantro. Prepare the dressing in a blender for 1 minute. Pour the dressing over the salad and toss. Prepare a serving tray with the spinach leaves and pour the salad over the spinach. Garnish with the persimmon slices around the tray and tomato cubed. Sprinkle with red pepper.

Leftover Dumplings with Roasted Green Pepper Picante

Ingredients

16 oz. leftover dumplings
1 roasted green pepper, chopped
1 jalapeños, chopped
½ cup red onion
1 tomato, cubed

Dressing

½ cup olive oil
½ cup balsamic
½ cup water
Salt, pepper, and sugar to taste
1 tsp. garlic
2 Tbsp. Worchester
1 pickle, chopped

Garnish

2 cups red pepper
2 Tbsp. Italian parsley
Dash of paprika

Instructions

Place leftover dumplings into a mixing bowl and add roasted green pepper, jalapeños, red onion, and tomato. Mix together. Prepare the dressing in a blender and mix for 1 ½ minutes. Adjust flavor as needed. Prepare a tray with the red cabbage and pour the salad over the cabbage. Add dressing over the salad. Garnish with red pepper, Italian parsley, and sprinkle with paprika.

Linguine with Avocado and Pomegranate Dressing

Ingredients

12 oz. dried linguine pasta
3 medium avocados, cubed
¾ cup pomegranate seeds
2 scallion onions, chopped
2 hard-boiled eggs, grated
2 Tbsp. dill, chopped
1 tsp. garlic, chopped
½ cup fresh mozzarella cheese, julienned

Dressing

½ cup pomegranate juice
½ cup olive oil
¼ cup water
1 large lemon for juice
Salt, pepper, and sugar to taste

Garnish

2 cups spinach leaves
1 small cucumber, cut into rings
2 Tbsp. parsley, chopped
¼ cup ground unsalted peanuts

Instructions

Place 3 quarts of water into a medium pot and bring to a boil. Add linguine and cook for 12 to 15 minutes, stirring occasionally. Remove from heat, rinse with cold water, and strain. Place into a mixing bowl. Wash avocado, cut in half lengthwise and remove seeds. Scoop out the fruit, cut into cubes, and add to the linguine. Add pomegranate seeds, scallion onions, hard-boiled eggs, dill, garlic, and mozzarella. Mix gently. Prepare the dressing. Add all dressing ingredients into a blender and mix for 11 ¼ minutes on high speed. Season to taste. Place spinach leaves onto a serving tray and add salad on top. Before serving, pour dressing over the salad. Garnish with cucumber rings around the edges of the salad. Sprinkle with parsley and unsalted peanuts.

Macaroni Pasta with Avocado, Papaya Picante

Ingredients

16 oz. macaroni pasta
1 avocado, cubed
¾ cup sharp cheddar cheese
1 scallion onion, chopped
½ cup papaya, cubes
1 jalapeños, chopped
1 Tbsp. Oregano
1 carrot, grated

Dressing

½ cup olive oil
¼ cup lemon juice
½ cup sundried tomatoes
Salt, pepper, and sugar to taste
¼ cup orange juice
1 tsp. garlic
1 avocado, ripened

Garnish

1 cup red cabbage, julienned
2 hard-boiled egg, grated
2 Tbsp. parsley, chopped

Instructions

Boil 3 quarts of water on the stove and add pasta. Mix and cook for 15 minutes. Remove from heat and run cold water over the pasta. Strain and place into a mixing bowl. Add avocado, cheddar cheese, scallion, papaya, jalapeños, oregano, and carrot. Prepare the dressing in a blender and mix for 1 minute. Prepare a serving tray with the red cabbage leaves and pour the salad over the tray. Before serving, add dressing and garnish with the hard-boiled eggs. Sprinkle with parsley.

Macaroni Salad with Shrimp and Lemon Sour Cream Dressing Picante

Ingredients

14 oz. macaroni pasta
16 oz. baby shrimp, cooked
1 cup sundried tomatoes, chopped
1 scallion onion, chopped
½ cup sharp cheddar cheese, shredded
2 Tbsp. dill, chopped
1 lemon, thin sliced
1 red pepper, julienned

Dressing

1 ½ cups sour cream
¼ cup lemon juice
1 Tbsp. parmesan
⅛ tsp. red pepper
Salt and pepper to taste
Dash of Old Bay Seasoning
3 Tbsp. half and half
1 tsp. garlic

Garnish

1 cup spinach, julienned
2 hard-boiled egg, wedged
1 tomato, sliced
1 Tbsp. parmesan cheese

Instructions

Boil 3 quarts of water on the stove and add pasta. Cook for 15 to 17 minutes. Remove from the heat and strain. Run cold water over the pasta to cool and place into a mixing bowl. Add baby shrimp, scallion onion, shredded cheddar, dill, lemon, and red pepper. Prepare the dressing in a blender and mix well. Prepare a serving tray with the spinach. Pour the salad over the tray. Add dressing over the salad. Garnish with hard-boiled eggs, tomato slices and parmesan cheese.

Macaroni with Vegetables, Cheddar Cheese and Pepperoni with Mayonnaise Dressing

Ingredients

10 oz. macaroni pasta
1 red pepper, cut into strips
½ cup Italian parsley
¾ cup cheddar cheese, shredded
1 cup pepperoni, sliced
1 cucumber, cubed
1 scallion onion, chopped

Dressing

1 ¼ cup mayonnaise
¼ cup half and half cream
1 lemon for juice
1 Tbsp. garlic, chopped
Salt and pepper to taste
Dash of nutmeg

Garnish

1 cup red cabbage, julienned
¼ cup pecans
2 Tbsp. dill

Instructions

Boil 3 quarts of water and add macaroni. Cook for 10 to 12 minutes. Remove from heat and cool under cold water. Pour into a strainer, place into a mixing bowl. Add red pepper, Italian parsley, cheddar cheese, pepperoni, cucumber, and scallion onion. Prepare the dressing in a blender and mix for 1 ½ minutes. Pour the dressing into the bowl with the pasta and toss gently. Prepare a serving tray with red cabbage and pour the salad over the cabbage. Garnish with pecans and dill.

Multi Colored Pasta with Spicy Clams and Mushrooms

Ingredients

16 oz. multi-colored pasta
12 oz. clams, steamed, chopped
10 oz. roasted mushrooms, sliced
1 green pepper, julienned
2 Tbsp. dill
1 scallion onion, chopped
½ cup sundried tomatoes

Dressing

½ cup olive oil
½ cup red wine vinegar
1 Tbsp. lime zest
1 Tbsp. garlic, chopped
Salt, pepper, and sugar
½ tsp. hot red pepper
1 tsp. Worchester

Garnish

4 red cabbage leaves
3 Tbsp. parmesan, grated
2 Tbsp. parsley, chopped
2 Tbsp. pecans, chopped

Instructions

Boil 3 quarts of water in a pot and add pasta. Stir and let cook for 12 to 14 minutes. Remove from heat and cool under cold water. Strain and place into a mixing bowl. Put the clams and mushrooms into a sauté pan with a little olive oil. Cook for 4 to 5 minutes. Remove from heat, strain out the liquid and add to the mixing bowl. Add green pepper, dill, scallion onion, and sundried tomatoes. Prepare the dressing in a blender and mix for 1 minute. Prepare a tray with the red cabbage leaves and pour the dressing over the salad. Garnish with parmesan, parsley, and pecans.

Multi Color Spiral Pasta with Vegetable and Avocado Olive Oil Dressing

Ingredients

12 oz. spiral pasta, multi color
1 carrot, grated
1 cup cabbage, shredded
½ cup red pepper, chopped
1 cup, spinach leaves
4 Tbsp. parmesan, shredded
1 onion, chopped

Dressing

1 avocado
½ cup olive oil
½ cup balsamic
1 cup sour cream
⅛ tsp. crushed red pepper
Salt, pepper, and sugar to taste
1 Tbsp. garlic
1 tsp. oregano

Garnish

2 tomatoes, sliced
1 lime, wedged
2 Tbsp. Italian parsley

Instructions

Boil 2 ½ to 3 quarts of water. Add pasta and cook for 9 to 11 minutes. Remove from heat and let cool. Strain pasta and place into a mixing bowl. Add carrot, shredded cabbage, red pepper, spinach leaves, parmesan, and onion. Prepare the dressing ingredients in a blender until well mixed. Prepare a serving tray and pour the salad over the tray. Add dressing over the salad. Garnish with lemon wedges down the middle of the salad and the tomato rings around the edge of the salad. Sprinkle with Italian parsley.

Orzo and Grilled Chicken with Curry Lemon Dressing

Ingredients

12 oz. Orzo
10 oz. grilled chicken, cut into strips
1 apple, julienned
¼ cup red onion, chopped
1 celery stalk, chopped

Dressing

¼ cup olive oil
¼ cup lemon juice
1 Tbsp. curry powder
¼ cup raisins
Salt and pepper to taste and sugar
⅛ cup water

Garnish

4 lettuce leaves
6 pineapple rings
2 tsp. Italian parsley, chopped

Instructions

Boil 2 ½ cups water in a pot and add orzo. Stir and bring back to a boil. Reduce heat to simmer and cover. Cook for 10 to 15 minutes. Remove from the heat and fluff with a fork. Let cool to room temperature. Place into a mixing bowl. Add apple, red onion, and celery. Prepare the dressing in a blender and pour it over the salad in the mixing bowl. Mix salad well. Prepare a serving tray with the lettuce leaves and pour the salad over the tray. Garnish with the pineapple rings and sprinkle with Italian parsley.

Orzo and Vegetables Marinated

Ingredients

12 oz. orzo pasta
1 carrot, grated
1 tomato, cubed
1 cucumber, cubed
1 red pepper, chopped
½ cup Italian parsley
1 scallion onion

Dressing

¼ cup olive oil
¼ cup lemon juice
Salt and pepper to taste
1 tsp. garlic
1 tsp. crushed red pepper

Garnish

2 cups spinach
1 lime, sliced
Dash of paprika

Instructions

Boil 2 ½ cups of water and add the orzo. Bring to a boil and stir. Reduce to simmer and cover. Cook 12 to 15 minutes. Remove from the heat and fluff with a fork. Place into a mixing bowl. Add carrot, tomato, cucumber, red pepper, Italian parsley, and scallion onion. Mix gently. Prepare the dressing in a blender and mix well. Adjust flavor as needed. Pour the dressing over the salad in the mixing bowl and toss. Prepare a serving tray with the spinach leaves. Pour salad over the tray. Garnish with lime slices and paprika.

Orzo Salad with Avocado, Sundried Tomatoes and Oil and Vinegar Dressing

Ingredients

12 oz. orzo
1 avocado, cubed
½ cup sundried tomatoes, chopped
¼ cup red onion, chopped
1 cup spinach leaves, julienned
4 crunchy bacon strips

Dressing

½ cup sundried tomatoes
¼ cup olive oil
¼ cup wine vinegar
¼ cup water
Salt, pepper, and sugar to taste
½ cup red pepper
1 tsp. garlic

Garnish

4 lettuce leaves, whole
1 lemon, sliced
2 Tbsp. Italian parsley

Instructions

Place a pot on the stove and add 3 Tbsp. oil and pour orzo into the pot. Stir and bring the orzo to a golden brown. Add 3 cups of boiling water and reduce to simmer. Stir, cover and cook for 7-8 minutes. Remove from heat and stir with a fork. Let cool and place into a mixing bowl. Add avocado, sundried tomatoes, red onion, spinach, and bacon. Toss the salad. Prepare the dressing in a blender until well mixed. Prepare a serving tray with the lettuce leaves. Pour the salad over the tray. Add the dressing over the salad. Garnish with lemon slices and Italian parsley.

Orzo Salad with Fruit and Vegetables with Mayonnaise

Ingredients

3 Tbsp. olive oil
10 oz. orzo
1 carrot grated
1 red pepper, chopped
2 tsp. dill, chopped
1 Granny Smith apple, julienned
1 persimmon, cubed
½ cup blackberries, whole

Dressing

½ cup mayonnaise
½ cup sour cream
¼ cup lemon juice
¼ cup half and half
Salt and pepper to taste
1 tsp. lemon zest
1 tsp. garlic, chopped

Garnish

2 cups lettuce, julienned
1 orange, sliced
¼ cup pecans, chopped

Instructions

Heat the oil in a pot on the stove and add orzo. Add carrot, pepper, and dill to the orzo. Stir and let cook until golden brown. Pour 2 ½ cups of water into the pot and stir. Bring to a boil, reduce heat to simmer and cover. Cook for 7 to 9 minutes. Remove from heat and mix with a fork. Let cool and then place orzo into a mixing bowl. Add apple, persimmon, and fresh blackberries. Toss gently. Prepare the dressing in a blender and mix for 1 minute. Prepare a serving tray with the lettuce and pour the salad over the tray. Add dressing over the salad. Garnish with orange slices around the edge of the tray and sprinkle with pecans.

Orzo with Figs and Red Pepper Mayonnaise

Ingredients

12 oz. orzo
⅛ cup vegetable oil
8 figs, quartered
1 red pepper, cut into strips
2 Tbsp. dill
2 Tbsp. parmesan cheese

Dressing

¾ cup mayonnaise
3 Tbsp. red wine vinegar
⅔ cup sour cream
1 tsp. garlic, chopped
Salt and pepper to taste

Garnish

5 lettuce leaves
1 tomato, sliced
2 Tbsp. dill, chopped

Instructions

Heat oil in a pot and add the orzo. Stir and bring it to a light golden brown. Add 2 ½ cups boiling water. Stir, reduce to simmer and cover. Cook for 12 to 15 minutes. Remove from the heat and fluff with a fork. Bring to room temperature and transfer it to a mixing bowl. Add figs, red pepper, dill, and parmesan. Blend the dressing ingredients in a blender and adjust flavor as needed. Pour the dressing into the mixing bowl with the orzo and toss gently. Prepare a serving tray with the lettuce leaves and pour the salad over top of the tray. Garnish with sliced tomato and sprinkle with dill.

Orzo, Tomato and Kalamata Olives with Lemon Lime Dressing

Ingredients

12 oz. Orzo
½ cup kalamata
1 tomato, cubed
1 sweet apple, cubed
1 avocado, cubed
1 Tbsp. rosemary

Dressing

⅛ cup lime juice
⅛ cup lemon juice
¼ cup olive oil
1 tsp. garlic
Salt, pepper, and sugar to taste
¼ cup tomato juice

Garnish

4 lettuce leaves
2 Tbsp. parsley, chopped
1 orange, sliced

Instructions

Boil 3 cups of water and add orzo. Stir and reduce to simmer. Cover and let cook for 12 to 15 minutes. Remove from the heat and fluff with a fork. Let cool to room temperature and then place into a mixing bowl. Add Kalamata olives, tomatoes, sweet apple, avocado, and rosemary. Prepare the dressing in a blender and mix well. Pour the dressing in the mixing bowl with the salad and stir together. Prepare a serving tray with lettuce leaves and pour the salad on the tray. Garnish with sliced orange rings and parsley.

Pasta Spaghetti Pasta with Spicy Tomatoes

Ingredients

12 oz. dried spaghetti
2 medium tomatoes, cut into cubes
1 cup sundried tomatoes, whole
3 Tbsp. fresh oregano, chopped
1 ½ spinach leaves, julienned
2 scallion onions, coarsely chopped
1 medium carrot, coarsely grated
2 sour kiwis, cubed

Dressing

⅓ cup olive oil
⅓ cup white vinegar
⅓ cup water
⅛ tsp. hot crushed red pepper
2 Tbsp. tomato paste
1 small lemon for juice
1 tsp. lemon skin, grated
Salt and sugar to taste

Garnish

6 lettuce leaves, whole
1 medium tomato, cut into rings
3 Tbsp. fresh Italian parsley, chopped
¾ cup feta cheese, crumbled

Instructions

Place 3 ½ quarts of water into a medium pot and bring to a boil. Add spaghetti, and cook for 12 to 15 minutes, stirring occasionally. Remove from heat, rinse with cold water, and strain. Place into a mixing bowl. Add sundried tomatoes, oregano, spinach leaves, scallion onions, carrot, and kiwi. Mix gently. Prepare the dressing. Add all dressing ingredients into a blender and mix for 1 minute on high speed. Season to taste. Place lettuce onto a serving tray and add salad on top. Before serving, pour dressing over the salad. Garnish with tomato rings around the salad. Sprinkle with parsley and feta cheese.

Pasta Spinach with Sour Picante Roquefort Cheese

Ingredients

16 oz. dry spinach pasta
1 medium carrot, coarsely grated
1 cup spinach julienned
8 oz. Roquefort, crumbled
2 Tbsp. dill, chopped
1 Tbsp. fresh oregano, chopped

Dressing

1 ½ cups sour cream
¼ cup fresh lemon juice
2 Tbsp. olive oil
2 Tbsp. half & half cream
1 Tbsp. garlic, chopped
⅛ tsp. grated nutmeg
1 tsp orange skin, finely grated
Salt and pepper to taste

Garnish

6 iceberg lettuce leaves, whole
¼ cup black olive, chopped
1 tomato, cubed
3 hard-boiled egg, wedged

Instructions

Place 3 ½ quarts of water into a medium pot and bring to a boil. Add dry spinach pasta, stir, and cook for 12 to 15 minutes, stirring occasionally. Remove from heat, rinse with cold water, and strain. Place into a mixing bowl. Add carrot, spinach, Roquefort cheese, dill, and oregano. Mix gently. Prepare the dressing. Add all dressing ingredients into a blender and mix for 2 minutes on high speed. Season to taste. Place iceberg lettuce onto a serving tray and add salad on top. Before serving, pour dressing over the salad. Garnish with hard-boiled eggs around the edges of the salad. Sprinkle with black olives and tomatoes.

Penne Pasta with Grilled Salmon and Pomegranate Picante Dressing

Ingredients

16 oz. Penne pasta
12 oz. grilled or broiled salmon filet
4 oz. pomegranate seeds
½ red onion, chopped
2 Tbsp. dill
1 cucumber, chopped
1 celery stalk chopped

Dressing

¾ cup pomegranate juice
¾ cup olive oil
1 lemon for juice
Salt, pepper, and sugar to taste
1 tsp. garlic
1 tsp. rosemary
Dash of crushed hot red pepper

Garnish

2 cups spinach leaves, julienned
¼ cup pomegranate seeds
2 Tbsp. parmesan, grated

Instructions

In a pot boil 3 quarts of water and add pasta. Cook for 15 minutes. Remove from heat and run under cold water. Strain and place into a mixing bowl. Add pomegranate seeds, red onion, dill, cucumber, and celery. Grill or broil the salmon. Let cool and break apart into the mixing bowl. Toss gently. Prepare the dressing in a blender and mix for 1 minute. Prepare a serving tray with spinach leaves and pour the salad over the tray. Before serving, add dressing over the salad. garnish with pomegranate seeds and parmesan.

Ravioli and Grilled Chicken with Tomatoes Picante Dressing

Ingredients

16 oz. ravioli, dry or frozen
14 oz. chicken breast strips, grilled
1 tomato, cubed
1 Tbsp. rosemary
2 Tbsp. roasted almonds, sliced
2 Tbsp. Italian parsley
1 green pepper, julienned

Dressing

¾ cup olive oil
¾ cup tomato juice
¾ cup white vinegar
½ cup sundried tomatoes
Salt, pepper, and sugar to taste
1 Tbsp. oregano, chopped
1 Tbsp. garlic

Garnish

4 green cabbage leaves
2 Tbsp. parsley
1 lemon, wedged

Instructions

Boil 3 quarts of water and add ravioli with a little bit of oil. Cook for 7 to 10 minutes. Remove from heat and cool under cold water. Strain and place into a mixing bowl. Grill the chicken breasts, slice into strips and add to the mixing bowl. Add tomato, rosemary, almonds, parsley, and green pepper. Toss gently. Prepare the dressing in a blender and mix on high speed for 1 minute. Prepare a serving tray with green cabbage leaves and pour the salad over the tray. Add dressing over the salad. Garnish with parsley and lemon wedges.

Ravioli and Sundried Tomatoes with Lemon and Cilantro Dressing

Ingredients

14 oz. Ravioli, cooked
1 cup sundried tomatoes, whole
2 Tbsp. cilantro
1 cup feta cheese, crumbled
1 lemon, peeled and cubed
1 cucumber, chopped
¼ cup red onions, chopped

Dressing

½ cup olive oil
½ cup balsamic vinegar
½ cup water
Salt, pepper, and sugar to taste
1 tsp. garlic, chopped
Dash of nutmeg
1 Tbsp. oregano

Garnish

2 cups red cabbage, julienned
2 persimmon, sliced
½ cup Kalamata olives

Instructions

Cook the ravioli and remove from the stove. Strain and let it cool. Place into a mixing bowl. Add sundried tomatoes, cilantro, feta cheese, cucumber, and red onion. Prepare the dressing in a blender on high speed for 1 minute. Pour the dressing over the salad and toss gently. Prepare a serving tray or salad bowl with the julienned cabbage leaves. Pour the salad in the bowl or onto the tray. Garnish with persimmon and kalamata olives.

Ravioli Salad with Tomatoes Picante

Ingredients

12 oz. Ravioli, fresh or frozen, cooked
1 tomato, cubed
1 jalapeños, chopped
1 carrot, grated
2 scallion onions, chopped
½ cup Italian parsley
3 Tbsp. parmesan

Dressing

¼ cup tarragon vinegar
¼ cup olive oil
¼ cup water
2 tsp. garlic, chopped
Salt, pepper, and sugar to taste

Garnish

2 cups spinach, julienned
⅓ cup pecans
½ cup sour raspberries

Instructions

Boil the ravioli for approximately 7 minutes. Remove from the heat and strain out the water. Let cool and then place into a mixing bowl. Add tomato, jalapeños, carrot, scallion onions, parsley, and parmesan. Mix together. Prepare the dressing in a blender. Adjust flavor as needed. Pour the dressing into the mixing bowl and toss gently. Prepare a serving tray with spinach leaves and pour the salad on top. Garnish with sour raspberries and pecans.

Roasted Orzo with Snow Crab Legs with Vegetable and Curry Picante Dressing

Ingredients

2 Tbsp. vegetable oil
16 oz. orzo
12 oz. snow crab legs, steamed
1 celery stalk, chopped
1 red pepper, chopped
2 Tbsp. parsley, chopped
1 apple, julienned
1 scallion onion, chopped
1 cup spinach leaves, chopped

Dressing

¼ cup olive oil
1 lemon for juice
1 lime for juice
1 tsp. garlic
1 tsp. lemon zest
1 tsp. mint leaves
Salt, pepper, and sugar to taste
1 tsp. jalapeños, chopped
1 tsp. curry powder

Garnish

2 cups spinach leaves
1 tomato, wedged
1 Tbsp. raisins
2 Tbsp. parmesan

Instructions

Heat oil in a pot on the stove and add orzo. Stir and cook until golden brown. Add 2 ½ cups of boiling water. Stir, bring to a boil and simmer. Cover and cook for 10 to 12 minutes. Remove from heat and mix with a fork. Let cool and place into a mixing bowl. Add steamed snow crab leg meat, celery, red pepper, parsley, apple, scallion onion, and spinach. Toss gently. Prepare the dressing in a blender and mix for 2 minutes. Prepare a serving tray with the spinach leaves and pour the salad over the top. Add dressing over the salad and garnish with tomato wedges around the tray. Sprinkle with raisins and parmesan.

Shell Pasta with Veggies and Fruit Marinated

Ingredients

12 oz. pasta shells
1 carrot, grated
1 tomato, cubed
1 red pepper, chopped
1 cucumber, cubed
½ cup crunch blueberries
1 apple, julienned
1 nectarine, cubed

Dressing

¼ cup oil
¼ cup balsamic vinegar
½ cup sundried tomatoes
1 tsp. garlic
1 Tbsp. Worchester
1 tsp. mint leaves
3 Tbsp. parmesan cheese
Salt, pepper, and sugar to taste
1 Tbsp. peanuts, ground
2 Tbsp. water

Garnish

5 lettuce leaves
1 lime, sliced
1 scallion onion, chopped

Instructions

Boil water in a pot and add pasta. Cook for about 12 minutes. Remove from heat and cool under cold water. Strain and place into a mixing bowl. Add carrot, red pepper, cucumber, blueberries, apple, and nectarine. Toss gently. Prepare the dressing in a blender and adjust flavor if needed. Prepare a serving tray with the lettuce leaves and pour the salad over tray. Before serving, add dressing over the salad. Garnish with lime slices and scallion onion.

Spaghetti Cheese Nuts and Gavrilovic Salami Picante Dressing

Ingredients

16 oz. dry spaghetti
1 cup sharp cheddar cheese, grated
½ cup feta cheese
6 oz. Gavrilović salami, julienned
2 Tbsp. dill chopped
1 medium roasted red pepper, chopped
¼ cup red onion, chopped

Dressing

¼ cup olive oil
¼ cup wine vinegar
¼ cup water
1 tsp. garlic, chopped
Dash of crushed hot red pepper
Salt, pepper, and sugar to taste

Garnish

3 cups spinach leaves
2 beets, cooked and cut into rings
¼ cup chopped walnuts

Instructions

Place 4 quarts of water into a medium pot, bring to a boil, and add 2 Tbsp. olive oil. Add spaghetti, stir, and cook for 12 to 15 minutes, stirring occasionally. Remove from heat, rinse with cold water, and strain. Place into a mixing bowl. Place into a mixing bowl. Add sharp cheddar cheese, feta cheese, Gavrilović salami, dill, roasted red peppers, and red onion. Mix gently. Prepare the dressing. Add all dressing ingredients into a blender and mix for 1 minute on high speed. Season to taste. Place spinach leaves onto a serving tray and add salad on top. Before serving, pour dressing over the salad. Garnish with beet rings around the edges of the tray and sprinkle with walnuts.

Spaghetti and Crab Meat Salad with Cream of Herb Dressing

Ingredients

12 oz. spaghetti
16 oz. crab meat, backfin
1 red pepper, julienned
2 Tbsp. dill, chopped
2 Tbsp. roasted coconut
1 scallion onion, chopped
1 tomato, cubed

Dressing

¾ cup mayonnaise
¾ cup sour cream
1 lemon for juice
1 tsp. oregano, chopped
1 tsp. Old Bay Seasoning
1 tsp. garlic
Salt and pepper to taste
2 Tbsp. half and half

Garnish

5 lettuce leaves
1 lemon, sliced
2 Tbsp. parsley, chopped

Instructions

Boil 3 quarts of water and add spaghetti noodles. Cook for 12 to 15 minutes. Remove from heat and cool under cold water. Strain noodles and place into a mixing bowl. Add crab meat, red pepper, dill, roasted coconut, scallion onion, and tomato. Toss gently. Prepare dressing in a blender and mix for 1 ½ minutes. Adjust flavor as needed. Prepare a serving tray with the lettuce leaves. Pour the salad over the tray and add the dressing. Garnish with lemon slices around the salad and sprinkle with parsley.

Spinach Pasta with Avocado Sour Cream and Cheese

Ingredients

15 oz. Spinach pasta
1 avocado, cubed
1 scallion, chopped
3 hard boiled eggs, grated
½ cup sharp white cheddar cheese, grated
1 Tbsp. Garlic, chopped
1 pickle, chopped
2 Tbsp. Dill
1 cup spinach, julienned

Dressing

1 ½ cups sour cream
1 avocado
¼ cup lemon juice
2 Tbsp. Half and half
Salt and pepper to taste

Garnish

5 lettuce leaves
2 Tbsp. parsley
1 tomato, wedged
2 Tbsp. pistachio or peanuts, chopped

Instructions

Boil pasta in 3 to 4 quarts of water. Cook for approximately 10 to 12 minutes. Remove from the stove and run cold water over the pasta. Strain the water from the noodles and put them in a mixing bowl. Add the avocado, scallion, hard boiled eggs, sharp white cheddar, garlic, pickle and spinach. Toss gently. Blend the dressing ingredients in a blender until well mixed. Prepare a serving tray with the lettuce leaves and pour the salad over top. Pour the dressing over the salad. Garnish with tomato wedges placed around the edges of the tray. Sprinkle with nuts and parsley.

Spinach Pasta with Herb and Avocado Dressing

Ingredients

16 oz. Spinach pasta
3 cups cooked spinach leaves
1 scallion, chopped
1 red pepper
1 tsp. garlic
1 avocado
1 Tbsp. rosemary
1 tomato, cubed

Dressing

¾ cup sour cream
¼ cup mayonnaise
2 Tbsp. parmesan cheese
Salt and pepper to taste
1 lemon juiced
1 tsp. oregano
1 tsp. lemon zest
1 avocado
Dash of crushed red pepper

Garnish

6 lettuce leaves, julienned
1 tomato, sliced
2 hard-boiled eggs, wedged
2 Tbsp. peanuts

Instructions

Boil the pasta in 4 quarts of water and add the spinach leaves. Cook for 10 to 14 minutes. Remove from the stove and pour into a strainer. Pour into a mixing bowl. Add scallion onion, red pepper, garlic, rosemary, and tomato. Toss gently. Prepare dressing in a blender. Adjust flavor as needed. Place lettuce on a serving tray and add salad over top. Pour dressing over the salad. Garnish with tomato slices, hard-boiled eggs and sprinkle peanuts.

Spinach Pasta with Ricotta and Lemon Dressing

Ingredients

16 oz. dry spinach pasta
3 cups fresh spinach leaves
8 oz. ricotta cheese
½ cup raisins
1 medium carrot, coarsely grated
1 small Granny Smith apple peeled and julienned
½ cup sundried tomatoes, chopped
½ cup seasoned croutons

Dressing

¼ cup fresh lemon juice
½ cup olive oil
½ cup water
1 tsp. grated lemon skin
1 tsp. garlic, chopped
⅛ tsp. hot crushed red pepper
Salt, pepper, and sugar to taste

Garnish

3 cups spring lettuce
2 medium beets, cooked and julienned
3 Tbsp. grated parmesan cheese

Instructions

Place 4 quarts of water into a medium pot and bring to a boil. Add dry spinach pasta and fresh spinach leaves, stir, and cook for 10 to 13 minutes, stirring occasionally. Remove from heat, strain, and let cool. Place into a mixing bowl. Add ricotta cheese, raisins, carrot, Granny Smith apple, sundried tomatoes, and croutons. Mix gently. Prepare the dressing. Add all dressing ingredients into a blender and mix for 1 ¼ minutes on high speed. Season to taste. Place spring lettuce onto a serving tray and add salad on top. Before serving, pour dressing over the salad. Garnish with beets around the edges of the salad. Sprinkle with parmesan.

Spiral Whole Wheat Pasta with Broccoli and Shrimp with Olive Oil and Vinegar Dressing

Ingredients

12 oz. whole wheat spiral pasta
10 oz. broccoli florets
10 oz. baby shrimp, cooked
1 cup sundried tomatoes
1 red pepper, cut into strips
½ cup Italian parsley
1 scallion onion, chopped

Dressing

½ cup olive oil
½ cup vinegar
¼ cup water
1 Tbsp. garlic
¼ cup tomato juice
1 tomato, chopped
1 tsp. rosemary
Salt, pepper, and sugar to taste

Garnish

4 lettuce leaves, whole
1 cucumber, sliced
Dash of paprika

Instructions

Boil 3 quarts of water and add pasta. Cook for approximately 8 to 10 minutes. One minute before the pasta is done, add the broccoli into the water. Cook for another 1 ½ minutes or so. Remove from the heat and pour into a strainer. Run cold water over the pasta and broccoli to cool off. Place into a mixing bowl. Add cooked baby shrimp, sundried tomatoes, red pepper, Italian parsley, and scallion onion. Prepare the dressing in a blender. Prepare a serving tray with the lettuce leaves and pour the salad over the tray. Add dressing onto the salad. Garnish with cucumber slices and paprika.

Sweet Linguini Pasta with Brown Sugar and Cocoa

Ingredients

12 oz. linguini pasta
½ cup brown sugar
2 Tbsp. cocoa powder
4 oz. semi sweet chocolate, grated
¼ cup raisins
½ cup ground peanuts unsalted
½ cup seedless cherries
3 Tbsp. Kahlua
½ cup whipped cream, un-whipped
½ cup half and half

Garnish

4 lettuce leaves
8 strawberries, halved
¼ cup pecans, chopped

Instructions

Boil pasta in 3 quarts of water. Cook for 12-14 minutes. Remove from stove and let cool under cold water. Strain and place into a mixing bowl. Add brown sugar, cocoa powder, semi sweet chocolate, raisins, peanuts, cherries, Kahlua, whipped cream, and half and half. Before serving, place ice berg lettuce onto a tray and add the salad on top. Garnish with strawberries and pecans.

Tortellini, Egg and Spinach with Cream of Herb Dressing

Ingredients

14 oz. tortellini, fresh or frozen
4 hard-boiled eggs, sliced
2 cups spinach leaves
1 carrot, grated
1 scallion onion, chopped

Dressing

1 ¼ cup mayonnaise
⅛ cup wine vinegar
¼ cup sour cream
Salt and pepper to taste
1 tsp. garlic, chopped
3 Tbsp. ketchup
1 Tbsp. tabasco
1 tsp. oregano

Garnish

1 lemon, sliced
½ cup walnuts, chopped
1 cup croutons

Instructions

Boil 3 quarts of water and add tortellini. Cook for 5 to 6 minutes. Pour into a strainer and let cool. Place into a mixing bowl. Add hard-boiled eggs, spinach, carrot, and scallion onion. Prepare the dressing in a blender and mix on high speed for 1 minute. Pour the dressing over the salad and toss gently. Pour the salad onto a serving tray or salad bowl. Garnish with lemon slices, walnuts, and croutons.

Tortellini and Smoked Beets with Sundried Tomato Dressing

Ingredients

16 oz. Tortellini, fresh dry or frozen
6 oz. smoked turkey
6 oz. smoked pastrami, julienned
6 oz. hard salami, julienned
½ cup red onion, chopped
1 tomato, cubed
1 Granny Smith apple, julienned
1 red pepper, sliced thin
2 Tbsp. parsley, chopped

Dressing

⅓ cup olive oil
⅓ cup red wine vinegar
⅓ cup water
1 lemon for juice
½ cup sundried tomatoes
Salt, pepper, and sugar to taste
1 tsp. garlic
1 tsp. jalapeños

Garnish

8 corn husks
2 Tbsp. parsley
2 Tbsp. parmesan cheese

Instructions

Boil tortellini in 3 to 4 quarts of water for 5 to 7 minutes. Run the pasta under cold water and then strain. Put the pasta in a mixing bowl and add turkey, pastrami, salami, red onion, tomato, apple, red pepper and parsley. Toss gently. Blend dressing ingredients in a blender until well mixed. Prepare a serving tray with the corn husks and add salad on top. Pour dressing over salad. Garnish with parsley and parmesan cheese.

Tortellini Salad with Corned Beef, Sundried Tomatoes and Sour Cream

Ingredients

14 oz. tortellini, fresh or frozen
10 oz. smoked corned beef, julienned
1 cup sundried tomatoes, whole
1 tomato, wedged
2 scallion onions, chopped

Dressing

1 ½ cups sour cream
1 lemon
¼ cup mayonnaise
1 tsp. garlic
1 tsp. lemon zest
Salt and pepper to taste
2 Tbsp. half and half
1 Tbsp. Worchester

Garnish

5 lettuce leaves
1 tomato, wedged
2 Tbsp. Italian parsley

Instructions

Boil 3 quarts of water and add tortellini. Cook for 6 to 7 minutes. Remove from the heat and run under cold water. Strain and place into a mixing bowl. Add smoked corned beef, sundried tomatoes, tomato, and scallion onion. Blend all the dressing ingredients on high speed. Pour dressing over the tortellini salad. Toss gently. Prepare a serving tray with lettuce leaves and pour the salad over the tray. Garnish with tomato wedges and Italian parsley.

Tortellini with Cheese and Veggie Kalamata Picante

Ingredients

16 oz. tortellini dry or frozen
1 cup feta cheese, crumbled
½ cup yellow sharp cheddar cheese
½ cup seedless Kalamata olives
1 small red pepper, cut into thin strips
1 small carrot, finely grated
2 Tbsp. dill, chopped
1 small lime with skin, cut into thin rings
1 small cucumber, cut into thin rings

Dressing

½ cup olive oil
½ cup white vinegar
½ cup water
½ cup seedless Kalamata olives
1 tsp. jalapeños, chopped
1 tsp. garlic, chopped
Salt, pepper, and sugar to taste

Garnish

6–8 cornhusks
2 tomatoes, cut into rings
5 strips crunchy bacon, chopped
Dash of paprika

Instructions

Place 3 to 4 quarts of water into a medium pot and bring to a boil. Add tortellini. If using dry, cook 8 10 minutes. If using frozen, cook 5 to 6 minutes. Remove from heat, strain, and let cool. Place into a mixing bowl. Add feta cheese, yellow sharp cheddar cheese, seedless Kalamata olives, red pepper, carrot, dill, lime, and cucumber. Mix gently. Prepare the dressing. Add all dressing ingredients into a blender and mix for 2 minutes on high speed. Season to taste. Place cornhusks onto a serving tray slightly extending off the tray and add salad on top. Before serving, pour dressing over the salad. Garnish with tomato rings on top of salad. Sprinkle with crunchy bacon and paprika.

Vermicelli Pasta with Clams, Bacon and Sour Cream Parmesan Dressing

Ingredients

2 Tbsp. vegetable oil
16 oz. vermicelli
6 oz. crispy bacon, crumbled
8 oz. steamed clams
1 red pepper, cubed
1 Tbsp. dill
1 scallion onion, chopped
2 Tbsp. black olives

Dressing

1 ¼ cup sour cream
1 lemon for juice
1 tsp. garlic
Dash of crushed red pepper
Salt and pepper to taste
1 tsp. lemon zest
2 Tbsp. half and half
3 Tbsp. parmesan

Garnish

2 cups spinach leaves
3 hard-boiled eggs, wedged
1 Tbsp. parmesan
2 Tbsp. parsley, chopped

Instructions

Heat oil in a pot on the stove and add vermicelli pasta. Stir and cook until golden brown. Add 2 ½ cups of boiling water and stir. Cover and reduce to simmer. Remove from heat and mix with a fork. Let cool and then place into a mixing bowl. Add bacon, clams, red pepper, dill, scallion onion, and black olives. Toss gently. Prepare dressing in a blender and mix for 1 minute. Prepare a serving tray with the spinach leaves. Before serving, pour the salad over the tray. Add dressing over the salad and garnish with the hard-boiled egg wedges. Sprinkle with parmesan and parsley.

Vermicelli Pasta with Hard Salami and Cheddar Cheese with Cucumber Dill Dressing

Ingredients

16 oz. vermicelli pasta
12 oz. hard salami, julienned
¾ cup shredded cheddar cheese
1 green pepper, thinly sliced
2 Tbsp. dill, chopped

Dressing

1 cucumber
3 Tbsp. dill
½ cup olive oil
½ cup wine vinegar
¼ cup water
Salt, pepper, and sugar to taste
Dash of hot red pepper

Garnish

2 fried tomato rings
1 scallion onion, chopped
¼ cup peanuts, grated

Instructions

Heat 3 tablespoons of oil in a pot on the stove and add vermicelli pasta. Stir and cook until golden brown. Add 3 cups of water to the pot, stir and reduce to simmer. Cover the pot and cook for 6 to 8 minutes. Remove from the heat and mix with a fork. Let it cool and place into a mixing bowl. Add salami, cheddar cheese, green pepper, and dill. Toss gently. Prepare the dressing in a blender and mix for 1 minute. Prepare a serving tray and pour the salad over the tray. Add the dressing over the salad. Garnish with fried tomato rings, scallion onion, and sprinkle with peanuts.

Whole Wheat Pasta Spaghetti with Tomato, Parmesan and Basil Dressing

Ingredients

12 oz. whole wheat pasta
2 Tbsp. basil
2 tomatoes, cubed
1 cup shredded parmesan
½ cup olives, chopped
2 scallion onions, chopped
1 red pepper, sliced
1 cup spinach leaves, julienned

Dressing

¾ cup tomato juice
1 tomato
¼ cup olive oil
¼ cup red wine vinegar
Salt, pepper, and sugar to taste
1 Tbsp. garlic, chopped

Garnish

4 lettuce leaves
1 lime, sliced
1 green pepper, cut into strips

Instructions

Boil 3 quarts of water with a touch of olive oil. Add whole wheat pasta and stir. Boil for 8 to 10 minutes. Pour pasta into a strainer, let it cool and place into a mixing bowl. Add basil, tomatoes, shredded parmesan, olives, red pepper, and spinach leaves. Toss gently. Blend the dressing ingredients in a blender. Prepare a serving tray with the lettuce leaves and pour the salad over the tray. Add dressing over the salad. Garnish with lime slices and green pepper strips.

Basmati Rice with Fruit Oriental Picante

Ingredients

1 ½ cups basmati rice
1 medium plum, cubed
1 granny Smith apple, cubed
¼ cup pecans, chopped
2 Tbsp. dill, chopped
1 small peach, cubed
3 hard-boiled eggs, grated

Dressing

¼ cup sesame oil
¼ cup lemon juice
¼ cup water
2 Tbsp. sesame seeds
1 Tbsp. grated parmesan
3 Tbsp. water
Salt, pepper, and sugar to taste

Garnish

3 cups spring lettuce
1 medium tomato, wedged
2 Tbsp. Italian parsley, chopped

Instructions

Place 3 ½ cups water into a medium-size pot on the stove; bring to a boil. Add rice; and stir well, bringing to a boil once again. Reduce heat to simmer. Cover and cook 10-12 minutes. Remove from heat, mix with a fork to separate rice, and let it cool to room temperature. Place rice into a mixing bowl. Add plum, apple, pecans, dill, peach, and hard-boiled eggs. Mix gently. Prepare the dressing. Add all dressing ingredients into a blender or mixing bowl. If using a blender, mix on high speed for 1 minute. If mixing by hand, stir for 3 minutes. Place spring lettuce onto a serving tray and add pour salad on top. Add dressing over the salad and garnish with tomato rings. Sprinkle with parsley on top.

Basmati Rice with Grilled Salmon Lemon-Lime Dressing

Ingredients

1 ½ cups basmati rice
16 oz. grilled salmon, crumbled into large pieces
2 scallion onions, chopped
1 tsp. lemon skin, grated
1 tsp. lime skin, grated
1 Tbsp. fresh rosemary, chopped
1 medium beet, cooked and cubed

Dressing

¼ cup lemon juice
¼ cup lime juice
¼ cup olive oil
1 medium orange for juice
Dash of Old Bay Seasoning

Garnish

3 cups fresh spinach leaves, julienned
2 Tbsp. parmesan cheese
1 orange, cut into thin slices
2 Tbsp. walnuts, chopped

Instructions

Place 3 cups water into a medium-size pot on the stove and bring to a boil. Add rice, stir well and bring to a boil once again. Reduce heat to simmer, cover, and cook 8-10 minutes. Remove from heat, mix with a fork to separate rice, and let it cool to room temperature. Place rice into a mixing bowl. Add grilled salmon, scallion onions, lemon skin, lime skin, rosemary, and beets. Mix gently. Prepare the dressing. Add all dressing ingredients into a blender and mix on high speed for 1 minute. Season to taste, if needed. Place spinach leaves onto a serving tray and add salad on top. Pour dressing over the salad. Garnish by arranging orange slices around the edge of the tray. Sprinkle with parmesan cheese and walnuts on top.

Basmati with Rice Avocado Spinach and Mayonnaise Based

Ingredients

2 cups basmati rice
1 large avocado , cubed
2 cups fresh spinach, julienned
2 scallion onions, chopped
1 red pepper, cubed
1 Tbsp. fresh rosemary

Dressing

1 cup mayonnaise
½ cup sour cream
¼ cup fresh lemon juice
1 tsp. garlic, chopped
1 small pickle chopped Dash of nutmeg
Salt and pepper to taste

Garnish

2 Roma tomatoes, cut into rings
2 hard-boiled egg, cut into wedges
2 Tbsp. Italian parsley

Instructions

In a medium-size sauce pan, heat 3 Tbsp. oil. Add rice to hot oil; stir well. Cook until rice is hot. Add 4 cups boiling water; mix well and it bring to a boil. Reduce to heat to a simmer; cover and cook 8 to 10 minutes. Remove from heat. Stir with a long fork to break up rice and let cool to room temperature. Place rice into a mixing bowl and add avocado, spinach, scallions, red pepper and rosemary; mix well. Prepare dressing: Add all dressing ingredients into a blender or mixing bowl; mix 1 ½ minutes. Season to taste. Place salad on a serving platter; pour the dressing over the top. Garnish with tomato rings around the outer edge of the salad. Lay the eggs down the center and sprinkle with parsley.

Brown Rice with Shrimp and Sundried Tomatoes Picante Lemon Dressing

Ingredients

1 ½ cups brown rice
12 oz. baby shrimp
¾ cup sundried tomatoes
1 mango, cubed
1 scallion onion, chopped
3 Tbsp. Italian parsley
1 cup papaya cubes
½ cup pomegranate seeds

Dressing

¼ cup lemon juice
¼ cup olive oil
¼ cup water
Salt, pepper, and sugar to taste
1 orange for juice
1 tsp. lemon zest
1 tsp. curry powder
Dash of hot crushed red pepper

Garnish

3 cups spring lettuce
1 lime, sliced
2 hard-boiled eggs, wedged
2 Tbsp. parsley

Instructions

Boil 4 cups of water and add brown rice. Stir, bring to a boil, reduce to a simmer and cover. Cook for approximately 35 to 40 minutes. Remove from stove and mix it with a fork. Let cool to room temperature and place into a mixing bowl. Add shrimp, sundried tomatoes, scallion, mango, Italian parsley, and papaya. Toss gently. Prepare dressing in a blender for 1 ½ minutes. Adjust flavor as needed. Prepare a serving tray with the lettuce leaves and add salad on top. Pour dressing over the salad. Garnish with lime slices and hard-boiled egg wedges. Sprinkle with parsley.

Chopped Rice Salad with Apple and Raisin Curry Dressing

Ingredients

⅛ cup vegetable oil
2 cups basmati rice
1 large Granny Smith apple, julienned
½ cup raisins
1 celery stalk, chopped
½ cup red onion, chopped
1 medium mango, cubed

Dressing

¼ cup olive oil
2 tsp. curry powder
¼ cup red wine vinegar
¼ cup water
1 tsp. lime skin
1 celery stalk
Salt, pepper, and sugar to taste

Garnish

4 lettuce leaves, whole
1 medium red pepper, chopped
1 lime, wedged
2 Tbsp. fresh Italian parsley

Instructions

Heat ⅛ cup of oil in medium-size sauce pan on stove until hot. Add rice, stir and cook on high heat until golden brown. Add 4 cups boiling water. Stir and bring to a boil. Reduce heat, cover, and simmer. Cook 10 to 12 minutes. Remove from heat. Mix with long fork to break up rice. Cool and place in mixing bowl. Add Granny Smith apple, raisins, celery, red onion, and mango. Prepare the dressing. Place all ingredients into a blender or a mixing bowl. Mix 1 ½ minutes in blender. Place lettuce onto a serving platter. Mix salad and add on top of lettuce. Pour dressing over salad mix. Garnish with lime wedges on top. Sprinkle with red peppers and Italian parsley.

Brown Rice with Roasted Vegetable and Dill Dressing

Ingredients

2 cups brown rice
⅛ cup vegetable oil
1 small onion, chopped
5 mushrooms, cut into strips
4 Tbsp. parsley, chopped
1 red pepper, cubed
1 cup fresh spinach leaves, julienned

Dressing

¼ cup olive oil
¼ cup wine vinegar
½ cup sour cream
¼ cup half & half
½ cup shredded parmesan cheese
1 tsp. garlic, chopped
¼ cup fresh dill, chopped
Salt, pepper, and sugar to taste

Garnish

4 Roma or Iceberg lettuce leaves, whole
2 beets, cooked and cut into rings
3 fresh mushroom, sliced

Instructions

Place medium-size pot on stove. Add oil and heat until hot. Add brown rice and cook until rice is really hot. Add 5 cups boiling water. Stir well. Reduce to medium heat and cook 30 to 35 minutes. Remove from heat and mix with fork. Let cool until room temperature and place rice into mixing bowl. Add onions, mushrooms, parsley, peppers, and spinach. Mix well. Prepare the dressing. Add all dressing ingredients into a blender. Blend for 1 ½ minutes. Place on lettuce leaves on a serving platter and add salad on top. Pour dressing over salad. Arrange beet rings around the outer edge of the platter. Place mushroom slices down the center.

Rice Mediterranean Style Spicy

Ingredients

⅛ cup olive oil
1 ½ cup white rice
1 small onion, chopped
1 tomato, cubed
1 red pepper, chopped
1 green pepper, chopped
3 Tbsp. Italian parsley, chopped ¾ cup feta cheese, crumbled ½ cup black Kalamata olives ½ tsp. hot crushed pepper
1 small cucumber, cubed

Dressing

¼ cup olive oil
¼ cup water
1 Tbsp. garlic, chopped
¼ cup lime juice
Salt, pepper, and sugar to taste

Garnish

2 cups spinach leaves, whole 1 pear, wedged
1 Tbsp. dill, chopped

Instructions

Heat oil in a medium pot on the stove . Add rice and stir until the rice is hot. Add 3 cups boiling water to rice and stir. Cover and reduce heat to simmer. Cook 12 to 15 minutes. Remove from heat. Mix with a long fork and let cool to room temperature. Place into mixing bowl. Add onion, tomato, red pepper, green pepper, Italian parsley, feta cheese, Kalamata olives, crushed red pepper, and cucumber. Mix well. Prepare the dressing. Add dressing ingredients into blender and mix for 1 minute. Season to taste. Place spinach leaves on a serving tray. Pour dressing over top of salad. Arrange pear wedges around edges and sprinkle with dill.

Rice with Avocado and Turkey with Cream of Herb Dressing

Ingredients

1 ½ cups basmati rice
2 avocados, cubed
10 oz. roasted turkey breast, cubed
2 Tbsp. oregano
1 tomato, cubed
1 cucumber, cubed
¼ cup relish

Dressing

¾ cup mayonnaise
¼ cup lemon juice
Salt and pepper to taste
1 medium tomato
⅛ tsp. hot red pepper
1 tsp. garlic
1 Tbsp. tarragon

Garnish

3 cups spinach leaves
1 red apple, julienned
1 Tbsp. parsley, chopped

Instructions

Boil 3 cups of water, bring to a boil and add rice. Bring to a boil again, reduce to a simmer, cover and cook 12 to 14 minutes. Remove from the stove and fluff it with a fork. Let cool and pour into a mixing bowl. Add avocados, roasted turkey, oregano, tomato, cucumber, and relish. Toss gently. Prepare the dressing in a blender and blend well for 1 minute. Adjust flavor as needed. Prepare a tray with spinach leaves and add salad on top. Pour dressing over salad. Garnish with red apple and sprinkle parsley.

Rice with Shredded Vegetables and Lemon Dressing

Ingredients

1 ½ cup white rice
¼ cup pecans, chopped
1 medium carrot, coarsely grated
1 Tbsp. lemon skin, finely grated
½ cup red pepper, chopped
½ cup green pepper, chopped
1 small tomato, cubed
2 Tbsp. parsley, chopped
1 small cucumber, cubed with skin

Dressing

¼ cup lemon juice
¼ cup lime juice
½ cup olive oil
¼ cup water
1 tsp. garlic, chopped
¼ cup pecans, chopped
¼ cup fresh orange juice
Salt, pepper, and sugar to taste

Garnish

5 lettuce leaves, whole
5 red onion rings, whole
Dash of sweet paprika

Instructions

In a medium-sized pot, heat 3 Tbsp. vegetable oil. Add rice; stir and cook until rice hot. Add approximately 3 ½ cups of boiling water to the rice, mix and bring to a boil. Reduce heat to simmer and cover. Cook approximately 10-12 minutes. Remove from heat and stir with a long fork to break up the rice. Let cool to room temperature. Place rice into mixing bowl. Add pecans, carrots, lemon skin, red pepper, green pepper, tomato cubes, parsley, and cucumber cubes. Mix gently. Prepare the dressing. Place all dressing ingredients into a blender or mixing bowl. (If using a blender, blend for 1 ¼ minutes on high speed). Place lettuce leaves on a serving platter and add salad on top. Pour dressing over salad. garnish with onions rings and paprika down the center.

Tomato and Basmati Rice Fruit and Veggie with Smoked Salmon

Ingredients

2 Tbsp. tomato paste
2 cup basmati rice
2 scallion onions, chopped
1 small Granny Smith apple, julienned
1 plum, wedged
2 medium tomatoes, cubed
1 red pepper, chopped
1 Tbsp. Italian parsley
1 tsp. garlic, chopped
4 oz. smoked salmon, chopped

Dressing

¼ cup olive oil
¼ cup wine vinegar
1 small tomato, chopped
⅛ tsp. hot crushed red pepper
Salt, pepper, and sugar to taste

Garnish

6 lettuce leaves, whole
2 Tbsp. parsley, chopped
1 medium lime, cut into rings and twisted

Instructions

Heat 3 Tbsp. oil in a medium-size pot and add tomato paste. Stir well. Add 4 cups of boiling water to paste, stir. Add a dash of salt and pepper. Bring to boil; add 2 cups basmati rice. Stir, bringing to a boil. Reduce and cover a simmer for 12 to 15 minutes. Remove from heat, mix with a fork and let it cool. Place into a mixing bowl. Add scallion onions, apple, plums, tomatoes, red pepper, Italian parsley, garlic, and smoked salmon. Mix gently. Prepare the dressing . Add all dressing ingredients into a blender and mix on high speed. Place lettuce leaves onto a serving tray. Add salad on top of the lettuce. Pour dressing over the salad. Garnish by sprinkling parsley over top and arranging lime twists around the edges of the tray.

White Rice with Chick Peas and Tomatoes Cumin

Ingredients

1 ½ cup white rice
⅛ cup vegetable oil
12 oz. chick peas preserves
1 tomato, cubed
1 Tbsp. garlic, chopped
½ tsp. hot crushed red pepper
3 Tbsp. Italian parsley
1 small red pepper, chopped

Dressing

⅓ cup olive oil
½ cup tomato juice
¼ cup lemon juice
2 tsp. ground cumin
1 small tomato, chopped
1 small lime for juice
Salt and pepper to taste

Garnish

1 cup red cabbage, julienned
¼ cup black olives, chopped
2 Tbsp. dill, chopped

Instructions

In a medium-sized sauce pan, heat oil. Add rice and cook until warm. Add chick peas preserves and stir until hot. Add 3 ½ to 4 cups of boiling water and mix well. Bring to a boil, cover and reduce heat to simmer. Cook for 12 to 15 minutes. Remove from heat and mix a long fork to separate rice. Let cool until room temperature. Place rice into a mixing bowl and add tomato cubes, garlic, hot crushed red pepper, Italian parsley, and chopped red pepper. Mix well. Prepare the dressing. Add dressing ingredients into a blender or bowl. If using blender, mix on high for 1 minute. If mixing by hand, stir for 2 minutes. Place cabbage on a serving platter. Pour dressing over salad. Arrange tomato slices around the edges. Sprinkle with olives and dill.

White Rice with Curry and Mango Picante

Ingredients

2 cups long grain white rice
1 Tbsp. curry powder spicy
12 oz. roast or corned beef, julienned
2 scallion onions, chopped
1 medium mango, cubed
1 small green pepper, chopped
1 Tbsp. dill, chopped
1 tsp. garlic, chopped
1 small tomato, cubed

Dressing

¾ cup coconut oil
¾ cup vinaigrette wine
Salt, pepper, and sugar to taste
½ cup mango fruit
⅛ tsp. hot crushed red pepper
1 tsp. grated lime skin
¼ cup feta cheese

Garnish

3 cups spinach leaves, whole
1 cup pineapple, cubed
2 Tbsp. walnuts, chopped

Instructions

Heat coconut oil in a medium-size pan on the stove. Add rice and stir. Add curry powder and dash of salt. Mix well and heat thoroughly. Add approximately 5 cups of boiling water and stir well. Bring to a boil. Reduce heat to simmer and cook 15 to 20 minutes. Remove from heat, mix with a long fork to separate rice and let cool to room temperature. Pour rice mixture into a mixing bowl. Add roast or corned beef, scallion onions, mango, green pepper, dill, garlic, and tomato. Mix gently. Prepare the dressing. Add all dressing ingredients into a blender. Mix on high speed for 1 minute, season to taste if needed. Place spinach leaves onto a serving platter. Add salad on top of the leaves. Pour dressing over salad. Garnish by sprinkling pineapple cubes and chopped walnuts

Wild Rice with Beets Sour Cream Lime Dressing

Ingredients

1 ½ cup wild rice
2 medium beets, cooked
1 medium carrot, coarsely grated
2 scallion onions, chopped
1 medium tomato, cubed
1 small lemon, peeled and cubed

Dressing

1 ¼ cup sour cream
¼ cup lime juice
1 cup fresh spinach, chopped
⅛ cup olive oil
1 tsp garlic, chopped
Salt, pepper, and sugar to taste

Garnish

2 limes, fried and cut into wedges
2 Tbsp. fresh parsley
½ cup fresh crunchy blueberries

Instructions

Heat ¼ cup olive oil or vegetable oil in a medium-size pan. Add beets and sauté for 4 to 5 minutes. Add rice, stir and continue to cook until rice is hot. Add approximately 4 to 4 ¼ boiling water, stir and simmer for approximately 25 to 30 minuets on low heat. Remove heat; stir with a long fork to separate the rice and let cool. Place rice into a mixing bowl. Add grated carrots, chopped onions, tomatoes cubes, and lemon cubes. Mix well. Prepare the dressing. Add all dressing ingredients into a blender and mix for approximately 1 ½ minutes. Place salad on a serving tray. Pour dressing over all. Garnish with fried limes wedge around the edges of the platter facing up. Sprinkle with parsley and add fresh crunchy blueberries on top.

Wild Rice with Black Beans and Broiled Salmon Picante Dressing

Ingredients

1 ½ cups wild rice
10 oz. black bean preserves
10 oz. broiled salmon filets, crumbled
1 small cucumber, cubed
3 Tbsp. Italian Parsley
1 small Granny Smith apple, cubed
¼ cup raisins
1 scallion onion, chopped

Dressing

½ cup balsamic vinegar
⅓ cup olive oil
1 tsp. garlic, chopped
Dash of Old Bay Seasoning
1 small jalapeños, chopped
1 small lemon for juice
1 tsp. grated lemon skin
salt, pepper, and sugar to taste

Garnish

5 Roma lettuce leaves, julienned
1 tomato, cut into rings
Dash of paprika

Instructions

Place 4 ½ cups water into a medium-size pot on the stove and bring to a boil. Add rice and stir well, bringing to a boil once again. Reduce heat to medium simmer. Cover and cook for 20 to 25 minutes. Remove from heat, mix with a fork to separate rice and let it cool to room temperature. Place rice into a mixing bowl. Add black bean preserves, salmon, cucumber, Italian parsley, apple, raisins, and scallion onion. Mix gently. Prepare the dressing. Add all dressing ingredients into a blender and mix on high speed for 1 minute. Season to taste, if needed. Place lettuce leaves onto a serving tray and add salad on top. Pour dressing over the salad. Garnish by arranging tomato rings on the outside edge of the tray and sprinkle with paprika.

Wild Rice with Orzo Veggie and Fruit Olive Oil and Lemon Dressing

Ingredients

1 ½ cup wild rice
1 small red pepper, finely chopped
1 green pepper, chopped
1 scallion onion, chopped
1 small plum, cubed
1 small peach, cubed
1 small Granny Smith apple, julienned
2 Tbsp. parsley, chopped

Dressing

⅓ cup olive oil
⅓ cup lemon juice
¼ cup water
1 tsp. garlic, chopped
1 small lemon skin, grated
Salt, pepper, and sugar to taste

Garnish

6 lettuces, whole
2 Tbsp. mint leaves, chopped
1 lemon, cut into rings and twisted

Instructions

Heat 3 Tbsp. oil in a pot on the stove. Add rice and orzo, stir and cook until really hot. Pour 3 cups boiling water into the pot and reduce heat to a simmer. Cook 15 to 17 minutes. Remove from the stove, mix with a long fork and let cool. Pour into a mixing bowl. Add red pepper, green pepper, scallion onion, plum, peach, apple, and parsley. Mix gently. Prepare the dressing in a blender; mix for 1 ½ minutes. Prepare a serving tray with lettuce leaves and pour the salad on top. Add the dressing over the salad. Sprinkle with mint leaves on top and place twisted lemon rings around the tray.

Wild Rice with Prosciutto and Smoked Cheese Picante

Ingredients

1 ½ cups wild rice
6 oz. prosciutto
1 cup smoked cheese, julienned
1 Tbsp. tarragon
1 red pepper roasted
1 cup spinach, fresh
¼ cup red onion, chopped

Dressing

¼ cup wine vinegar
¼ cup olive oil
¼ cup water
1 tsp. lemon zest
Salt, pepper, and sugar to taste
¼ cup sundried tomatoes
1 tsp. garlic

Garnish

3 cups spring lettuce
1 lemon, sliced
1 tomato, cubed

Instructions

In a pot, boil 4 cups of water and add 1 ½ cups of rice. Bring to a boil, stir, cover and reduce to a simmer. Cook 25 to 30 minutes. Remove from the stove and fluff with a fork. Let cool to room temperature and add to a mixing bowl. Add prosciutto, tarragon, smoked cheese, red pepper, spinach, and red onion. Prepare the dressing in a blender and mix well. Line a serving tray with spring lettuce and add salad on top. Pour dressing over salad just before serving. Garnish with lemon and tomato slices around the tray.

Wild Rice with Vegetable and Spicy Dressing

Ingredients

1 ½ cup wild rice
1 medium green pepper, cubed
1 red pepper medium, cubed
½ cup white onion, chopped
2 Tbsp. Italian parsley, grated
1 medium carrot, coarsely grated

Dressing

1 tsp. cayenne
1 tsp. crushed hot red pepper
¼ cup olive oil
¼ cup lemon juice
¼ cup water
1 tsp. garlic, chopped
Salt, pepper, and sugar to taste

Garnish

1 apple, sliced into rings and fried
3 Tbsp. walnuts, chopped
1 medium tomato, small cubes

Instructions

In medium-size sauce, heat ⅛ cup of olive or vegetable oil until hot. Add rice into the hot oil and mix gently. Once rice is hot, add approximately 4 ½ cups boiling water. Stir and bring to a boil. Reduce heat, cover and cook on a medium simmer. Cook for 20 to 25 minutes. Remove from heat. Break up with long fork. Cool and add into a mixing bowl. Add green pepper, red pepper, onion, Italian parsley, and carrot. Mix gently. Prepare the dressing. Place all ingredients for the dressing into blender or mixing bowl. Mix 1 ¼ minutes. Season to taste. Before serving, place salad on platter. Arrange tomato slices around the salad and fried apple rings on center lengthwise. Sprinkle with chopped walnuts.

Wild Rice with Tahini and Vegetable Dressing

Ingredients

1 ½ cup wild rice
⅛ cup vegetable oil
1 medium red pepper, chopped
2 scallion onions, chopped
1 medium lemon, peeled and cubed
2 Tbsp. fresh parsley chopped

Dressing

¾ cup tahini paste
1 large lemon juice
½ cup water
Salt and pepper to taste
2 Tbsp. chopped garlic
2 scallion onions, chopped

Garnish

5 lettuce leaves, julienned
2 tomatoes, cut into rings
2 Tbsp. parsley, chopped

Instructions

Heat oil in a medium-size pot and add rice. Cook until rice is hot. Add 3-3 ½ cups boiling water. Stir and reduce to simmer. Cook for 20-25 minutes. Remove from heat. Mix with a fork and let it cool to room temperature. Place rice into a mixing bowl. Add red pepper, scallion onions, lemon, and parsley. Stir gently. Prepare the dressing. Add all dressing ingredients into a blender and mix on high speed for 2-2 ½ minutes. Dressing should look creamy. Season to taste with lemon, garlic, and salt if needed. Place lettuce on a serving platter. Add salad on top off lettuce and pour dressing over top. Arrange tomato rings around the edges and sprinkle with parsley.

Wild Rice with Seafood and Vegetables Spicy

Ingredients

1 ½ cups wild rice
12 oz. baby shrimped, cooked
10 oz. crab meat backfin
1 small red pepper, cut into strips
2 scallion onions, coarsely chopped
1 small carrot, coarsely grated
1 cup spinach, julienned
½ cup pomegranate seeds
1 Tbsp. fresh tarragon

Dressing

⅓ cup olive oil
⅓ cup fresh lemon juice
⅓ cup water
1 tsp. horseradish
1 tsp. garlic, chopped
Salt, pepper, and sugar to taste

Garnish

6 lettuce leaves, whole
Dash of paprika
1 medium tomato, cut into rings
2 Tbsp. Italian parsley, chopped

Instructions

Heat 2 to 3 tsp. of olive or vegetable oil in a mediumsize pot. Add rice and stir well, cooking until hot. Add approximately 4 to 4 ½ cups of boiling water into the rice. Stir well and reduce to a medium simmer. Cook 20 to 25 minutes. Remove from heat, mix with a fork and let cool to room temperature. Place into a mixing bowl. Add baby shrimp, crab meat backfin, red pepper, scallion onions, carrot, spinach, pomegranate seeds, and tarragon. Mix gently. Prepare the dressing. Add all dressing ingredients into a blender and mix on high speed for 1 to 1 ¼ minutes. Season to taste if needed. If the dressing is too strong, add small amount of water, sugar, and salt. Place lettuce leaves onto a serving tray and add salad on top. Pour dressing over the salad. Arrange tomato rings around the outside edge of the platter. Sprinkle with paprika and Ital

EGGS

Boiled Eggs with Grilled Tuna Mayonnaise Picante Dressing

Ingredients

7 hard–boiled eggs, cut into rings
10 oz. grilled or broiled fresh Tuna
1 small red pepper, chopped
1 scallion onion, chopped
1 small carrot, grated
2 Tbsp. dill, chopped
1 tsp. garlic, chopped
1 small pickle, chopped
1 ¼ cup mayonnaise
2 Tbsp. lemon juice
4 oz. sharp white cheddar cheese
½ tsp. jalapeños, chopped

Garnish

3 cups spring lettuce
1 tomato, cut into rings
2 Tbsp. parsley, chopped

Instructions

Boil eggs 7 to 10 minutes with 1 Tbsp. of salt. Remove from heat, cool under cold water, and peel shells from eggs. Cut into slices and place into a mixing bowl. Cook tuna by either grilling or broiling. Cut Into cubes and add to eggs, mixing gently. Add red pepper, scallion onion, carrot, dill, garlic, pickle, mayonnaise, lemon juice, cheddar cheese, and jalapeños. Mix gently. Season to taste. Place the spring lettuce onto a serving tray and add salad on top. Garnish with tomato rings around the salad and sprinkle with parsley.

Egg and Sundried Tomatoes on Toast Picante

Ingredients

12 eggs, boiled and chopped
1 cup sundried tomatoes, chopped
1 medium potato, cooked
1 small avocado, chopped
1 kiwi, chopped
¼ cup yellow onion, chopped
3 garlic cloves, chopped
¼ cup olive oil
¼ cup vinaigrette
⅛ tsp. crushed hot red pepper Salt and pepper to taste

Garnish

3 cups spring lettuce
2 medium tomatoes, cut into rings
8 3-inch round toast
2 Tbsp. Italian parsley, chopped

Instructions

Boil eggs in water with salt for 8 to 10 minutes. Remove from heat, rinse, and cool. Peel and chop the eggs. Place into a mixing bowl. Add sundried tomatoes, potato, avocado, kiwi, yellow onion, and garlic. Mix gently until well combined. Season to taste. Place spring lettuce onto a serving tray and add round toast on top. Using a spoon, scoop the salad onto each piece of toast. Garnish with lemon twists down the center of the salad and sprinkle with parsley.

Egg and White Fish Mayonnaise Picante

Ingredients

10 eggs, boiled and cut into rings
10 oz. smoked white fish, crumbled
¼ cup relish
1 small red pepper, chopped
1 celery stalk, chopped
1 Tbsp. dill, chopped
1 small pickle, chopped
1 small carrot, cooked and grated
¼ cup red onion, chopped

Dressing

¾ cup mayonnaise
¼ cup half & half cream
2 Tbsp. marcella wine
1 tsp. horseradish
2 garlic cloves, chopped
2 Tbsp. lemon juice

Garnish

3 cups fresh spinach, julienned
2 medium beets, cooked and julienned
1 scallion onion, chopped

Instructions

Boil eggs in water with salt for 8 to 10 minutes. Remove from heat, rinse, and cool. Peel and cut into rings. Place spinach onto a serving tray and add evenly eggs on top. Add white fish, red pepper, celery, dill, pickle, carrot, and red onion. Prepare the dressing. Add all dressing ingredients into a blender and mix for 1 to 1 ¼ minutes on high speed. Season to taste. Before serving, pour dressing over the salad. Garnish with beets around the salad and sprinkle scallion onions.

Egg Salad Avocado and Cheese Sour Cream Dill Dressing

Ingredients

8 hard-boiled eggs, sliced
1 medium avocado, cubed
¾ cup white cheddar cheese, grated
1 scallion onion, chopped
1 small red pepper, chopped
2 Tbsp. dill, chopped

Dressing

1 ¼ cups sour cream
¼ cup lemon juice fresh
1 tsp. garlic, chopped
1 tsp. lime skin, grated
Salt and pepper to taste

Garnish

6 lettuce leaves, whole
1 small cucumber, cut into rings
2 Tbsp. parsley, chopped
1 small tomato, cubed

Instructions

Boil eggs 7 to 10 minutes with 1 Tbsp. of salt. Remove from heat, cool under cold water, and peel shells from eggs. Cut into slices and place into a mixing bowl. Add avocado, white cheddar cheese, scallion onion, red pepper, and dill. Mix gently. Prepare the dressing. Place all dressing ingredients into a blender and mix on high speed for 1 minute. Season to taste. Place lettuce leaves onto a serving tray and add salad on top. Pour dressing over the salad. Garnish with cucumber rings on the edges of the tray. Sprinkle with parsley and tomato on top.

Egg Salad Ham and Bacon with Sun-Dried Tomatoes

Ingredients

7 hard-boiled eggs, cut into wedges
8 oz. honey baked ham, chopped or julienned
4 oz. crunchy bacon, chopped
½ cup sun-dried tomatoes, chopped
1 tsp. dill, chopped
1 scallion onion, chopped

Dressing

¾ cup mayonnaise
1 tsp. mustard
1 tsp. honey
¼ cup sour cream
2 tsp. garlic, chopped
1 tsp. tabasco
Salt and pepper to taste

Garnish

3 cups spinach leaves
1 tomato, cut into rings
2 Tbsp. Italian parsley, chopped
2 Tbsp. parmesan cheese, grated

Instructions

Boil eggs 7 to 10 minutes with 1 Tbsp. of salt. Remove from heat, cool under cold water, and peel shells from eggs. Cut into wedges and place into a mixing bowl. Add honey ham, crunchy bacon, sun-dried tomatoes, dill, and scallion onion. Mix gently. Prepare the dressing. Place all dressing ingredients into a blender and mix on high speed for 1 minute. Place spinach leaves onto a serving tray and add salad on top. Pour dressing over the salad. Garnish with tomato rings around the salad. Sprinkle with parsley and parmesan.

Egg Salad Hard-Boiled Egg with Roasted Red Pepper Mayo and Tomatoes

Ingredients

8 hard-boiled eggs, peeled and cut into slices
1 large red pepper, roasted and chopped
2 scallion onions, chopped
1 medium pickle, chopped
1 Tbsp. dill, chopped

Dressing

1 cup mayonnaise
½ cup ketchup
2 Tbsp. white vinegar
1 medium tomato
1 tsp. garlic, chopped
1 tsp. fresh rosemary
1 tsp. yellow mustard
Salt and pepper to taste

Garnish

5 lettuce leaves, whole
1 orange, cut into rings
3 Tbsp. ground peanuts
¼ cup grated parmesan

Instructions

Boil eggs 7 to 10 minutes with 1 Tbsp. of salt. Remove from heat, cool, and peel shells from eggs. Cut into slices. Place lettuce on a serving platter. Arrange egg slices evenly over the lettuce. Sprinkle roasted red peppers, scallion onions, pickle, and dill over the egg slices. Prepare the dressing. Add all dressing ingredients into a blender and mix on high for 1 ¼ minutes. Season to taste, if needed. Pour dressing over the center of the eggs on the platter. Garnish by arranging orange slices on the edges of the platter. Sprinkle with ground peanuts and grated parmesan.

Egg Salad with Beets and Horseradish

Ingredients

8 hard-boiled eggs, peeled and wedged
2 medium beets, cooked, peeled and coarsely grated
1 Tbsp. fresh tarragon, chopped

Dressing

½ cup mayonnaise
⅛ cup white vinegar
⅛ cup pomegranate juice
1 tsp. yellow mustard
2 Tbsp. parmesan
1 tsp. horseradish
Salt and pepper to taste

Garnish

6 lettuce leaves, julienned
1 tomato, cut into rings
2 Tbsp. parsley, chopped

Instructions

Boil eggs 7 to 10 minutes with 1 Tbsp. of salt. Remove from heat, cool, and peel shells from eggs. Cut into wedges. Prepare the dressing. Place all dressing ingredients into a blender and mix on high speed for 1 minute. Place lettuce leaves onto a serving tray and add egg wedges on top. Sprinkle beets and tarragon over wedges. Pour dressing over the salad. Garnish with tomato rings around the edges of the tray and sprinkle with parsley.

Egg Salad with Dill and Sour Cream

Ingredients

10 hard-boiled eggs, cooked, peeled and sliced
½ cup swiss cheese, grated
1 scallion onion, chopped

Dressing

1 ½ cup sour cream
2 Tbsp. dill, chopped
⅛ cup ketchup
2 tsp. tabasco sauce
1 tsp. caraway seeds Salt and pepper to taste

Garnish

2 cups fresh large spinach leaves
½ cup fresh rosemary
1 lime, cut into wedges

Instructions

Boil eggs 7 to 10 minutes with 1 Tbsp. of salt. Remove from heat and cool. Peel shells from eggs and cut into slices. Prepare the dressing. Place all dressing ingredients into a blender; mix on high speed for 1 ¼ minutes. Season to taste, if needed. Place spinach leaves onto a serving tray and add egg slices on leaves. Sprinkle swiss cheese and scallion onion on top. Pour dressing over the salad. Garnish with lime wedges around edges of tray. Sprinkle with rosemary if you prefer a sour taste.

Fried Egg Salad with Feta and Spinach Mayonnaise Dressing

Ingredients

6-8 eggs
⅛ cup olive oil
1 ½ cups fresh spinach, cooked and chopped
1 small pickle, chopped
¼ cup red onion, chopped
2 Tbsp. dill, chopped
1 medium red pepper, chopped
½ cup feta cheese, crumbled

Dressing

½ cup mayonnaise
¾ cup sour cream
½ cup feta cheese
1 large lemon for juice
Salt and pepper to taste

Garnish

5 lettuce leaves
½ cup pomegranate seeds
½ cup seasoned croutons

Instructions

Cook spinach in boiling water for a few minutes. Remove from heat, strain and chop. Place ⅛ cup of olive oil in sauté pan and fry the eggs. Remove from heat and place on a paper towel. Prepare the dressing. Place all dressing ingredients into a blender and mix on high speed for 1 minute. Season to taste, if needed. Place lettuce leaves onto a serving tray; add fried eggs evenly on top of lettuce. Sprinkle the spinach, pickle red onion, dill, red pepper, and feta cheese over each fried egg. Pour the dressing evenly over each of the fried eggs. Garnish sprinkling with pomegranate seeds and croutons.

Hard-Boiled Egg with Fried Eggplant Tahini Dressing

Ingredients

6 hard-boiled eggs
1 small eggplant, peeled and cubed
¼ cup olive oil
½ small red onion, chopped
3 Tbsp. Italian parsley
1 small red pepper, finely chopped

Dressing

½ cup tahini paste
¼ cup lemon juice
¼ cup water
1 tsp. garlic
Dash of cumin
1 small carrot, grated
1 small cucumber with skin, finely chopped
1 small pickle, chopped
2 tsp. garlic, chopped
Salt and pepper to taste

Garnish

4 iceberg lettuce leaves
½ cup garbanzo beans , cooked or preserves
1 medium tomato, chopped

Instructions

Boil eggs 7 to 10 minutes with 1 Tbsp. of salt. Remove from heat, cool, and peel shells from eggs. Chop eggs and place into a mixing bowl. Heat ¼ cup olive oil in a pan. Add eggplant cubes and cook until golden brown. Remove from heat and place onto a clean paper towel. Chop and add to eggs. Add red onion, Italian parsley, and red pepper. Mix gently. Prepare the dressing. Place all dressing ingredients into a blender and mix on high for 3 minutes. Season to a light sour taste, adding salt, pepper, and garlic if needed. Place lettuce leaves onto a serving tray. Gently add salad to the center of the lettuce. Pour dressing over the salad. Garnish with garbanzo beans on top and sprinkle with tomatoes.

Hard-Boiled Egg with Spinach Chopped Salad Cream of Herbs

Ingredients

8 hard-boiled eggs, chopped
1 cup sundried tomatoes
1 cup fresh spinach leaves, julienned
1 small carrot, cooked and grated

Dressing

1 cup mayonnaise
¼ cup vinegar
¼ cup sour cream
¼ cup half/half cream
1 tsp. fresh oregano, chopped
1 tsp. garlic, chopped
1 tsp. fresh rosemary
Salt and pepper to taste

Garnish

4 iceberg lettuce leaves, whole
1 beet, cooked, cut in half and wedged
2 Tbsp. dill, chopped

Instructions

Boil eggs 7 to 10 minutes with 1 Tbsp. of salt. Remove from heat, cool and peel shells from eggs. Cut into slices. Place lettuce onto a serving platter. Arrange egg slices evenly over the lettuce. Sprinkle sundried tomatoes, spinach leaves, and carrots over the egg slices. Prepare the dressing. Add all dressing ingredients into a blender and mix on high for 1 ½ minutes. Pour dressing over the center of the eggs on the platter. Garnish by arranging beet wedges around the edges of the platter and sprinkle with dill.

Hard-Boiled Eggs with Granny Smith Apple Feta and Tomato Mayonnaise Dressing

Ingredients

10 eggs, boiled
½ cup feta cheese, crumbled
1 tomato, finely cubed
1 Granny Smith apple, julienned
1 small pickle, finely cubed

Dressing

½ cup mayonnaise
½ cup sour cream
1 tomato, cubed
1 tsp. garlic
1 tsp. tarragon
3 Tbsp. lemon juice
Salt and black pepper to taste

Garnish

8 round toast, 3-inch diameter
2 Tbsp. parsley, chopped
1 medium pickle, sliced into thin rings

Instructions

Boil eggs 7 to 10 minutes with 1 Tbsp. of salt. Remove from heat, cool under cold water, and peel shells from eggs. Cut into slices and place into a mixing bowl. Add feta cheese, tomato, apple, and pickle. Mix gently. Prepare the dressing. Place all dressing ingredients into a blender and mix on high speed for 1 to 1 ½ minute. Pour dressing into the egg mixture and mix gently. Season to taste. Place 8 round toast onto a serving tray. Using a spoon, divide the egg salad evenly onto each toast. Garnish each toast with a slice of pickle and sprinkle with parsley.

Leftover Omelet with Veggies, Cheese, and Bacon Herb Dressing

Ingredients

6 eggs (or eggs leftover from breakfast)
⅛ cup olive oil
½ cup crunchy bacon, chopped
½ cup sharp cheddar cheese, shredded
1 small cucumber, chopped
1 tomato, finely chopped
1 Tbsp. dill, chopped
1 cup fresh spinach, julienned

Dressing

½ cup mayonnaise
¾ cup sour cream
2 Tbsp. white vinaigrette
Salt and pepper to taste

Garnish

4 Romaine lettuce leaves
½ avocado, wedged
1 small lemon, cut into rings
2 Tbsp. fresh Italian parsley, chopped

Instructions

If you have leftover eggs from breakfast, proceed to preparing the dressing without making the eggs as directed below. Place 6 eggs into a mixing bowl and beat well. Add ⅛ cup of oil olive into a pan, add bacon, sharp cheddar cheese, cucumber, tomato, dill, and spinach. Cook on low heat. When the eggs start to thicken, fold over as you would a regular omelet. Cover and simmer for 2 minutes, flip over and cover again. Cook until light golden brown and no egg liquid is in the center of the omelet. Remove from heat. Prepare the dressing. Place all dressing ingredients into a blender; mix on high speed for 1 minute. Place lettuce leaves onto a serving tray. Add omelet on top of lettuce. Pour dressing over the omelet. Garnish with avocado wedges in the center of the omelet. Place lemon rings around the edges of the tray and

Simple Egg Salad with Relish and Mayo

Ingredients

8 hard-boiled eggs, sliced
½ cup relish
¼ cup Kalamata olives, chopped
1 medium carrot, cooked and grated
¼ cup shredded parmesan cheese

Dressing

¾ cup mayonnaise
2 Tbsp. white vinegar
Dash of hot red pepper
Salt and pepper to taste

Garnish

2 cups spinach leaves
1 tomato, cut into 8 wedges
Dash of paprika

Instructions

Boil eggs 7 to 10 minutes with 1 Tbsp. of salt. Remove from heat, cool under cold water, and peel shells from eggs. Cut into slices and place into a mixing bowl. Add relish, Kalamata olives, carrots, and parmesan cheese. Prepare the dressing. Place all dressing ingredients into a mixing bowl. Mix gently with a wooden spoon until well blended. Place lettuce leaves onto a serving tray and add salad on top. Pour dressing over the salad. Garnish with tomato wedges on the salad and sprinkle a dash of paprika on top.

Spicy Egg Salad

Ingredients

10 hard-boiled egg, cut into wedges
2 medium tomatoes, cubed
1 small cucumber, cut into thin rings
2 scallion onions, chopped
5 strips crunchy bacon, chopped
2 Tbsp. Italian parsley, chopped
1 tsp. jalapeños, chopped

Dressing

¾ cup sour cream ¼ cup mayonnaise 1 lemon for juice
1 tsp. mustard
2 garlic cloves, chopped
2 Tbsp. half & half cream
1 small celery stalk, chopped Salt and pepper and to taste

Garnish

5 lettuce leaves, whole
8 3-inch round toast, golden brown 3 Tbsp. grated parmesan cheese
1 Tbsp. dill, chopped

Instructions

Boil eggs in water with salt for 8 to 10 minutes. Remove from heat, rinse, and cool. Peel and cut into wedges. Place lettuce onto a serving tray and add egg wedges on top. Add tomatoes, cucumber, scallion onions, crunchy bacon, Italian parsley, and jalapeños. Prepare the dressing. Add all dressing ingredients into a blender and mix for 1 ½ minutes on high speed. Season to taste. Before serving, pour dressing over the salad. Garnish with toast around the tray. Sprinkle with parmesan and dill.

POULTRY

Boneless Breast of Chicken with Dominos Picante Dressing

Ingredients

20 oz. boneless chicken breast
¼ cup olive oil
½ red onion, sliced thin
2 Tbsp. Italian parsley
½ cup black olives
1 medium red pepper, chopped
1 small cucumber with skin, cubed

Dressing

¾ cup mayonnaise
¼ cup lime juice
1 hard-boiled egg
1 small pickle
1 tsp. jalapeños chopped
Salt, pepper, and sugar to taste
⅛ cup pickle juice
1 tsp. garlic, chopped

Garnish

4 iceberg lettuce leaves
1 red pepper, chopped
½ cup fresh sour crunchy blueberries

Instructions

Wash chicken breast, devein and cube. Heat olive oil in sauté pan. Add chicken and cook for 5 to 6 minutes. Remove from heat, strain and place into a mixing bowl. Add red onion, Italian parsley, black olives, red pepper, and cucumber. Mix gently. Prepare the dressing. Add all dressing ingredients into a blender and mix for 1 minute. Prepare a serving tray with lettuce leaves. Add salad onto lettuce and pour dressing on top. Garnish by sprinkling red peppers and blueberries over top.

Breast of Chicken Salad Mayonnaise and Celery–Simple Chicken Salad

Ingredients

24 oz. boneless chicken breast, cooked
3 medium celery stalks, chopped

Dressing

1 ½ cups mayonnaise
1 Tbsp. fresh garlic, chopped
Salt and black pepper to taste

Garnish

6 iceberg lettuce leaves
2 Tbsp. Italian parsley, chopped
1 medium pickle, sliced into rings

Instructions

Wash the chicken breast and remove all fat. Place into a pot of water and boil for 20 to 25 minutes. Remove heat and under cold water. Break apart with your fingers or chop. Place into mixing bowl, add celery and mix well. Add mayonnaise, garlic, salt, and pepper. Add more or less mayonnaise for desired thickness of salad. Season to taste. Place iceberg leaves onto a serving tray. Using a small ice cream scoop, add salad onto the lettuce. Garnish with pickle slices around the salad and sprinkle with parsley.

Breast of Cornish Hen with Light Orange Dressing

Ingredients

20 oz. roasted Cornish hen breast, cubed
1 cup croutons
1 scallion onion, chopped
1 medium tomato, cubed
½ cup seedless Kalamata olives, whole
½ cup sundried tomatoes, chopped
1 tsp. orange skin, grated finely

Dressing

½ cup mayonnaise
½ cup sour cream
¼ cup orange juice
1 medium lemon for juice
Salt, pepper, and sugar to taste
1 tsp. garlic chopped

Garnish

1 ½ cup red cabbage, julienned
2 Tbsp. parsley
1 orange, thinly sliced

Instructions

Place Cornish hen into a mixing bowl. (Leftover hen can be used). Add croutons, scallion onions, tomatoes, Kalamata olives, sundried tomatoes, and orange skin. Mix gently. Prepare the dressing. Add all dressing ingredients into a blender and mix for 1 to 1 ¼ minutes. Season to taste. Prepare a serving tray with red cabbage and add salad on top. Pour dressing over the salad. Garnish with orange slices around the tray and sprinkle parsley.

Cornish Hen Salad with Sundried Tomatoes Picante

Ingredients

24 oz. Cornish hen, skinless, boneless and dark pieces, coarsely chopped
1 cup sundried tomato strips
1 medium tomato, cubed
6 pieces of dates, chopped
2 Tbsp. parsley, chopped

Dressing

⅓ cup balsamic vinegar
⅓ cup sesame oil
⅓ cup water
1 tsp. grated orange skin
1 tsp. garlic, chopped
Dash of nutmeg
1 tsp. jalapeños, chopped
Salt, pepper, and sugar to taste

Garnish

6 cornhusks
2 tomatoes, sliced thin and broiled
2 Tbsp. sesame seeds
Dash of paprika

Instructions

Place Cornish hen pieces into a mixing bowl. Add sundried tomatoes, tomato, dates, and parsley. Mix gently. Prepare the dressing. Add all dressing ingredients into a blender and mix for 2 minutes on high speed. Season to taste. Place cornhusk onto a serving tray and add salad on top. Before serving, pour dressing over the salad. Garnish with tomato slices around the salad. Sprinkle with sesame seeds and paprika.

Dark Pieces of Chicken with Spicy Tomato Dressing

Ingredients

7 legs of roasted chicken, deveined from the bone
1 medium red pepper, julienned
½ small red onion, cut into thin rings
2 Tbsp. fresh parsley, chopped
½ cup sundried tomatoes, chopped

Dressing

½ cup tomato juice
¼ cup olive oil
1 medium tomato, chopped
¼ cup vinaigrette tarragon
1 small pickle, chopped
1 tsp. garlic, chopped
½ tsp. hot crushed red pepper
Salt, pepper, and sugar to taste

Garnish

2 cup fresh spinach leaves
1 small orange, cut into rings and twisted
Dash of sweet paprika

Instructions

Using leftover roasted chicken legs, remove any fat and break into pieces. Place into a mixing bowl and add red pepper, red onion, parsley, and sundried tomatoes. Mix gently. Prepare the dressing. Place all dressing ingredients into a blender and mix on high speed for 1 to 1 ½ minutes. Season to taste. Place spinach leaves onto a serving tray; and add salad on top. Pour dressing over the salad. Garnish with orange twists around the edges and sprinkle with paprika.

Dark Pieces of Cornish Hen Boneless with Spicy Lime Dressing

Ingredients

20 oz. dark roasted Cornish hen
¼ cup crunchy cranberries
2 green plums, wedged
½ cup small onion, chopped
1 cup fresh mushroom, sliced

Dressing

¼ cup lime juice fresh
¼ cup olive oil
¼ cup water
¼ cup fresh orange juice
Salt, pepper, and sugar to taste
1 tsp. lime skin, finely grated
1 tsp. garlic, chopped
Dash of fresh oregano

Garnish

2 tomatoes, cut into quarters and fried
6 lettuce leaves, julienned
3 Tbsp. roasted peanuts, ground

Instructions

Remove dark meat from hen, deveining and removing all fat. Place into mixing bowl. Add crunchy cranberries, plums, onions, and mushrooms. Mix gently. Prepare the dressing. Add all dressing ingredients into a blender and mix for 1 minute. Season to taste. Pour dressing on the salad and mix gently. Prepare a serving tray with lettuce leaves and pour the salad over the lettuce. Garnish with fried tomatoes lengthwise on top of the salad and sprinkle with roasted peanuts.

Grilled Breast of Chicken with Vegetable Lemon Dressing

Ingredients

20 oz. boneless chicken breast, grilled
1 small red pepper, cut into strips
1 small carrot, julienned
1 small jalapeños, chopped
2 scallion onions, chopped
1 medium seedless cucumber, cubed

Dressing

½ cup lemon juice
½ cup olive oil
½ cup water
1 tsp. lemon skin
2 tsp. garlic, chopped
1 tsp. fresh rosemary, chopped salt,
   pepper, and sugar to taste

Garnish

2 tomatoes, cut into rings and fried
1 cup spinach, julienned
¼ cup ground peanuts

Instructions

Wash the chicken breast; removing all fat. Cut the breast lengthwise and cook on the grill. Remove, cut into strips and place Into a mixing bowl. Add red peppers, carrot, jalapeños, onion, and cucumber. Mix well. Prepare the dressing. Place all dressing ingredients into a blender and mix on high speed for 1 to 1 ¼ minutes. Season to taste. Pour dressing into the salad and mix gently. Place spinach leaves onto a serving tray and add salad on top. Garnish with fried tomato rings around the edges of the tray and sprinkle with ground peanuts.

Roasted Turkey with Potato Mayonnaise Picante

Ingredients

16 oz. roasted turkey, cubed
3 potatoes, cooked, cubed
¼ cup onion
2 celery stalks, chopped
¼ cup cranberries, chopped
2 Tbsp. parsley
1 carrot, cooked, cubed
½ cup peas, cooked
1 ¼ cup mayonnaise
1 tsp. mustard
2 garlic cloves, chopped
¼ cup pickles
Salt and pepper to taste

Garnish

6 lettuce leaves
1 tomato, sliced
2 hard-boiled egg, wedged Dash of paprika

Instructions

Slice turkey breast and potatoes into cubes. Place into a mixing bowl. Add onion, celery, cranberries, parsley, carrot, peas, mayonnaise, mustard, garlic, pickle, and salt and pepper to taste. Mix well. Prepare a serving tray with lettuce leaves and add salad on top. Garnish with tomato slices and hardboiled eggs. Sprinkle paprika.

Turkey Breast with Mango and Mayonnaise

Ingredients

20 oz. roasted turkey breast, cubed
1 large mango, cubed
2 celery stalks, finely chopped
1 scallion onion, chopped
1 Tbsp. fresh rosemary, chopped
1 small red pepper, chopped
1 ¼ cup mayonnaise
2 Tbsp. wine vinaigrette
2 garlic cloves, chopped
Salt and pepper to taste

Garnish

5 romaine lettuce leaves
¼ cup chopped pecans
2 kiwi, peeled and cut round

Instructions

Place roasted turkey breast into a mixing bowl. (Leftover turkey may be substituted). Add mango, celery, scallion onion, rosemary, red pepper, mayonnaise, wine vinaigrette, and garlic. Mix gently combining all ingredients well. Season to taste. Place romaine lettuce onto a serving tray and add salad on top. Garnish with kiwi on top of the salad and sprinkle with pecans.

Turkey Breast with Portabella Mushroom Grated Vegetable Vinaigrette Oil Dressing

Ingredients

20 oz. roasted turkey breast, cubed
2 portabella mushrooms, cut into strips
2 celery stalks, chopped
1 small red pepper, cut into strips
2 scallion onions, chopped
½ cup crunchy blueberries
5 strips of bacon, chopped
1 small carrot, coarsely grated

Dressing

⅓ cup red wine vinaigrette
⅓ cup olive oil
⅓ cup water
1 tsp. garlic, chopped
¼ cup pineapple juice
1 Tbsp. honey
Salt, pepper, and sugar to taste

Garnish

3 cups spring lettuce
1 medium orange, sliced
2 Tbsp. grated parmesan cheese
1 Tbsp. parsley, chopped

Instructions

Place roasted turkey breast into a mixing bowl. (Leftover turkey may be substituted). Add celery, red pepper, scallion onions, crunchy blueberries, bacon, and carrot. Mix gently. Add 2 Tbsp. of oil to a sauté pan and add portabella mushrooms. Cook until golden brown. Remove from heat, let cool, and add to mixing bowl. Mix gently. Prepare the dressing. Add all dressing ingredients into a blender and mix for 1 ½ minutes on high speed. Season to taste. Place spring lettuce onto a serving tray and add salad on top. Before serving, pour dressing over the salad. Garnish with orange slices around the tray. Sprinkle with parmesan cheese and parsley.

Turkey Breast with Veggie and Fruit Tarragon Dressing

Ingredients

20 oz. roasted turkey breast, cut into thin strips
1 Granny Smith apple, julienned
1 small green pepper, julienned
1 persimmon, cubed
½ cup crunchy blueberries
2 scallion onions, chopped
2 Tbsp. fresh Italian parsley, chopped

Dressing

½ cup tarragon vinaigrette ½ cup olive oil
½ cup water
1 Tbsp. garlic chopped
2 Tbsp. fresh tarragon
Salt, pepper, and sugar to taste

Garnish

4 lettuce leaves
½ cup walnuts, chopped
1 tomato, cut into rings

Instructions

Place turkey breast into a mixing bowl. Add apple, green pepper, persimmon, crunchy blueberries, scallion onions, and Italian parsley. Mix gently. Prepare the dressing. Place all ingredients for dressing into a blender and mix for 1 minute. Season to taste. Place lettuce leaves onto a serving tray. Add salad on top and pour dressing over the salad. Garnish with tomato rings around edge of tray and sprinkle with walnuts.

Turkey Legs with Spicy Curry Dressing

Ingredients

3 medium roasted turkey legs
1 medium Granny Smith apple, julienned
2 celery stalks, chopped
½ cup raisins
2 scallion onions, chopped

Dressing

2 Tbsp. curry powder
1 medium mango, peeled and cut into cubes
¼ cup wine vinaigrette
¼ cup olive oil
¼ cup water
¼ cup mango juice
1 tsp garlic, chopped
Salt, pepper, and sugar to taste

Garnish

4 pineapple rings with skin, cut in half
1 red pepper, chopped medium
2 Tbsp. sesame seeds

Instructions

Remove veins and all fat from the turkey legs. Place into mixing bowl. Add apple, celery, raisins, and scallion onions and mix gently. Prepare the dressing. Add all the dressing ingredients into a blender and mix for 1 to 1 ½ minutes. Place salad on a serving tray and pour dressing over top. Garnish with pineapple rings around the tray. Sprinkle with red pepper and sesame seeds.

BEEF & VENISON

Beef Strip with Veggie and Fruit Fig Lemon Dressing

Ingredients

16 oz. beef strip, cut thin (eye round or other beef with no fat)
2 scallion onions, coarsely chopped
2 small zucchini, cut into thin rings
1 small red pepper, cut into thin strips
3 Tbsp. dill, chopped
5 figs, halved
1 Granny Smith apple, peeled and julienned
1 small potato, cooked and cubed

Dressing

¼ cup lemon juice
¼ cup sesame oil
⅛ cup water
1 orange for juice
2 figs
2 medium garlic cloves, chopped
Salt, pepper, and sugar to taste

Garnish

3 cups spring lettuce
1 medium carrot, julienned
2 Tbsp. parsley, chopped
¼ cup white cheddar cheese, grated

Instructions

Place beef into a mixing bowl. Add scallion onions, zucchini, red pepper, dill, figs, Granny Smith apple, and potato. Mix gently. Prepare the dressing. Add all dressing ingredients into a blender and mix for 2 minutes on high speed. Season to taste. Place spring lettuce onto a serving tray and add salad on top. Before serving, pour dressing over the salad. Garnish with carrots around the tray. Sprinkle with parsley and white cheddar cheese.

Chopped Beef on Garlic Toast with Tahini Dressing Picante

Ingredients

⅛ cup olive oil
16 oz. lean ground beef
2 celery stalks, chopped
1 small onion, chopped
1 tsp. garlic, chopped
2 Tbsp. parsley, chopped
6-8 pcs. 2 ½-3 inch round toast, golden brown

Dressing

½ cup tahini paste
¼ cup lemon juice
½ cup water
1 tsp. lemon skin, grated
1 tsp. garlic, chopped
2 Tbsp. jalapeños, chopped
Salt and pepper to taste

Garnish

2 cup fresh spinach leaves
1 lemon, sliced into thin wedges
2 scallion onions, chopped
Dash of paprika

Instructions

Heat ⅛ cup olive oil in a sauté pan. Add ground beef and cook for 7-8 minutes, stirring occasionally. Be sure that the meat is thoroughly cooked. Remove from heat and pour into a strainer to drain all fat and juices from meat. Place into a mixing bowl. Add celery, onion, garlic, and parsley. Mix gently. Prepare the dressing. Add all the dressing ingredients into a blender and mix for 3 minutes on high speed. Season to taste. Place the spinach leaves onto a serving tray and add the round toast. Add salad mixture evenly onto each toast. Pour dressing over each toast. Garnish with lemon wedges around the salad. Sprinkle with onions and paprika.

Leftover American Goulash with Cheese and Herb Dressing

Ingredients

24 oz. leftover American goulash (includes pasta, ground beef, and cheese)
½ tsp. hot crushed red pepper
2 Tbsp. dill, chopped
1 scallion onion, chopped
1 small red pepper, chopped
1 small green pepper, chopped
¾ cup sharp cheddar cheese

Dressing

½ cup olive oil
½ cup red wine vinegar
½ cup water
¼ cup shredded cheddar cheese
Salt, pepper, and sugar to taste
1 tsp. garlic, chopped
1 Tbsp. ketchup

Garnish

5 lettuce leaves, whole
2 tomatoes, cut into rings and fried
2 Tbsp. parsley, chopped
Dash of paprika

Instructions

Place goulash into a mixing bowl. Add hot crushed red pepper, dill, scallion onion, red pepper, green pepper, and yellow sharp cheddar cheese. Mix gently. Prepare the dressing. Place all dressing ingredients into a blender and mix for 1 minute on high speed. Season to taste. Place lettuce leaves onto a serving tray and add salad. Before serving, pour dressing over the salad. Garnish with tomato rings lengthwise onto the salad. Sprinkle with parsley and paprika.

Leftover Beef Schnitzel with Tarragon Wine Dressing

Ingredients

24 oz. leftover beef schnitzel, cut into thin strips
1 roasted green pepper, chopped
2 scallion onions, coarsely chopped
1 medium tomato, cubed
1 tsp. fresh tarragon, chopped

Dressing

½ cup sesame seeds tahini
¼ cup tarragon vinegar
½ cup water
½ lemon for juice
1 tsp. garlic, chopped

Garnish

5 iceberg lettuce leaves
1 lemon, wedged
2 Tbsp. parsley, chopped

Instructions

Place beef schnitzel strips onto a serving platter. Lay the lettuce leaves on top of the beef strips. Add roasted green pepper, scallion onions, tomatoes, and tarragon. Prepare the dressing. Add all dressing ingredients into a blender and mix for 2 ½ minute on high speed. Season to taste with salt, pepper, and garlic as needed. Pour dressing over the salad. Garnish with the lemon wedges around the edges of the salad and sprinkle with parsley.

Leftover Hungarian Beef Spicy with Tomatoes and Basil

Ingredients

24 oz. leftover Hungarian goulash, cubed
1 tsp. basil, chopped
1 green pepper, julienned
¼ cup onion, chopped
3 Tbsp. parsley, chopped
⅛ tsp. crushed hot red pepper

Dressing

½ cup olive oil
½ cup crushed tomatoes
¼ cup lemon juice
¼ cup tomato juice
⅛ tsp. crushed hot red pepper
1 Tbsp. garlic, chopped
Salt, pepper, and sugar to taste

Garnish

2 cups red cabbage, julienned
1 small red pepper, chopped
1 scallion onion, chopped

Instructions

Place Hungarian goulash into a mixing bowl. Add basil, green pepper, onion, parsley, and crushed hot red pepper. Mix gently. Prepare the dressing. Add all dressing ingredients into a blender and mix for 2 minutes on high speed. Season to taste. Prepare a serving tray with the red cabbage and add salad on top. Pour dressing over the salad. Garnish by sprinkling red pepper and scallion onions on top.

Leftover Meatballs with Tomatoes Red Pepper Spicy Dressing

Ingredients

20 oz. leftover cooked meatballs, quartered
2 medium tomatoes, cubed
1 medium red pepper, thinly sliced
1 medium jalapeños, chopped
2 Tbsp. fresh parsley, chopped
½ small red onion, thinly sliced

Dressing

¼ cup olive oil
¼ cup lemon juice
¼ cup water
¼ cup tomato juice
1 Tbsp. garlic, chopped
1 tsp. fresh oregano, chopped
Salt, pepper, and sugar to taste

Garnish

2 cups spinach leaves, whole
½ cup walnuts, chopped
¼ cup black olives, chopped
1 lime, cut into rings and twisted

Instructions

Place meatballs into a mixing bowl. Add tomatoes, red peppers, jalapeños, parsley, and red onion. Prepare the dressing. Add all dressing ingredients into a blender and mix for 1 ¼ minutes on high speed. Season to taste. Pour dressing into the mixing bowl with the salad. Mix gently. Place spinach leaves onto a serving tray and add salad. Garnish by sprinkling walnuts and black olives on top. Place lime twists around the edges of the tray.

Nonfat Roast Beef with Spicy Vegetable Dressing

Ingredients

24 oz. roast beef leftovers, cubed
1 large roasted red pepper, cubed
½ cup Kalamata olives
½ cup pomegranate seeds
2 Tbsp. fresh rosemary, chopped

Dressing

½ cup avocado
½ cup mango
¼ cup olive oil
¼ cup wine vinegar
¼ cup pickle juice
½ tsp. hot crushed red pepper
1 tsp. garlic, chopped
Salt, pepper, and sugar to taste

Garnish

2 cups large fresh spinach leaves
¼ cup poppy seeds
2 hard-boiled eggs, wedged

Instructions

Remove fat from roast beef. (Leftover beef can be used). Place roast beef into mixing bowl. Add roasted red pepper, Kalamata olives, pomegranate seeds, and rosemary. Mix gently. Prepare the dressing. Add all dressing ingredients into a blender and mix for 1 ½ minute on high speed. Season to taste. Prepare a serving tray with spinach leaves and add salad on top. Pour dressing over the salad. Garnish by sprinkling with poppy seeds and place egg wedges face-up on top of the salad.

Roasted Eye Round Beef with Sour Fruit Oil Vinegar Dressing

Ingredients

24 oz. leftover eye round beef, cubed
1 pear, julienned
1 Granny smith Apple, julienned
1 medium persimmon, cubed
1 red plum, wedged
1 scallion onion, chopped
½ cup fresh raspberries, crunchy

Dressing

½ cup lemon juice
½ cup olive oil
¼ cup water
1 tsp. garlic, chopped
Salt, pepper, and sugar to taste

Garnish

4 lettuce leaves
5 small mushrooms, sliced
2 Tbsp. dill, chopped

Instructions

If using fresh beef, trim fat; cook and cut into cubes. Place into mixing bowl. Add pear, Granny Smith apple, persimmon, red plum, scallion onion, and rosemary. Mix gently. Prepare the dressing. Add all dressing ingredients into a blender and mix for 1 ½ minutes on high speed. Season to taste. Prepare a serving tray with lettuce leaves and add salad on top. Pour dressing over the salad. Garnish with sliced mushrooms on top on the salad and sprinkle with dill.

Roasted Venison with Shredded Vegetables and Balsamic Picante Dressing

Ingredients

20 oz. Venison cut into small cubes (leftover can be used)
2 Tbsp. fresh rosemary, chopped
1 green pepper, cut into strips
1 zucchini, cut into rings
½ cup red cabbage, shredded
1 small carrot, coarsely grated
½ cup small red onion, thinly sliced
½ cup fresh mozzarella, julienned

Dressing

½ cup balsamic vinegar
½ cup olive oil
½ cup water
1 Tbsp. garlic, chopped
1 Tbsp. fresh jalapeños, chopped
Salt, pepper, and sugar to taste

Garnish

1 cup fresh spinach, chopped 1 cup croutons
2 Tbsp. chopped parsley
1 orange, cut into rings

Instructions

Place venison into a mixing bowl. Add rosemary, green pepper, zucchini, red cabbage, carrot, red onion, and mozzarella. Mix gently. Prepare the dressing. Add all dressing ingredients into a blender and mix for 1 minute on high speed. Season to taste. Pour dressing into the salad and mix gently. Place spinach leaves onto a serving tray and add salad. Garnish with orange rings around the tray. Sprinkle with croutons and chopped parsley over salad.

Smoked Tongue with Shredded Vegetable Vinaigrette Oil Dressing

Ingredients

16 oz. smoked tongue, small cubes
6 oz. fresh green beans, cooked
½ cup sundried tomatoes
¼ cup chopped walnuts
1 small carrot, finely grated
1 small red pepper, chopped
½ cup fresh pineapple, small cubes
1 small seedless cucumber, cubed
2 radishes, sliced into thin rings

Dressing

⅓ cup wine vinaigrette
⅓ cup oil
⅓ cup water
⅛ tsp. hot crushed red pepper
1 tsp. garlic, chopped
1 tsp. horseradish
Salt, pepper, and sugar to taste

Garnish

3 cups spring lettuce
2 beets, cooked and julienned
2 Tbsp. Italian parsley, chopped

Instructions

Place smoked tongue into a mixing bowl. Cook the green beans in a pot of water for 4 to 5 minutes. Drain, cool, and place into the mixing bowl with the tongue. Add sundried tomatoes, walnuts, carrot, red pepper, pineapple, seedless cucumber, and radishes. Mix gently. Prepare the dressing. Add all dressing ingredients into a blender and mix for 1 ¼ minutes on high speed. Season to taste. Place spring lettuce onto a serving tray and add salad on top. Before serving, pour dressing over the salad. Garnish with beets around the edge of the tray and sprinkle with Italian parsley.

Tenderloin Tips with Tropical Fruit and Curry Picante

Ingredients

16 oz. tenderloin tips, broiled or sautéed
½ cup fresh pineapple, cut into small cubes
1 persimmon, cubed
1 medium mango, cubed
½ cup papaya, cubed
1 Tbsp. fresh tarragon, chopped
3 Tbsp. roasted coconut, shredded

Dressing

¼ cup lemon juice
¼ cup olive oil
¼ cup orange juice
¼ cup mango juice
2 garlic cloves, chopped
1 tsp. curry powder
Salt, pepper, and sugar to taste

Garnish

6 iceberg lettuce leaves
½ cup pomegranate seeds
½ cup smoked cheese, julienned
2 Tbsp. parsley, chopped

Instructions

Place beef tenderloin tips into a mixing bowl. Add pineapple, persimmon, mango, papaya, tarragon, and roasted coconut. Mix gently. Prepare the dressing. Add all dressing ingredients into a blender and mix for 1 ¼ minutes on high speed. Season to taste. Place iceberg lettuce onto a serving tray and add salad on top. Before serving, pour dressing over the salad. Garnish with pomegranate seeds on top of the salad. Sprinkle with smoked cheese and parsley.

PORK

Pork Loin Cubes with Vegetable and Herb Dressing

Ingredients

20 oz. roasted pork loin, cubed (may used leftover, if available)
4 oz. provolone cheese, julienned
½ cup fresh cranberries, chopped
2 scallion onions, chopped
1 medium carrot, cooked and cut into rings
1 celery stalk, chopped
4 oz. crunchy bacon

Dressing

¾ cup mayonnaise
¼ cup white vinegar
¼ cup half & half cream
Salt, pepper, and sugar to taste
1 tsp. garlic, chopped

Garnish

2 cups fresh spinach
1 medium red pepper, cut into strips
2 Tbsp. fresh parsley

Instructions

Place pork loin into a mixing bowl. Add provolone cheese, cranberries, scallion onions, carrot, celery, and bacon. Mix gently. Prepare the dressing. Add all dressing ingredients into a blender and mix for 1 minute on high speed. Season to taste. Place spinach leaves onto a serving tray and add salad. Before serving, pour dressing over the salad. Garnish by placing red pepper strips on top of the salad and sprinkle with parsley.

Pork Loin Salad with Fruit Cranberry and Honey Dressing

Ingredients

16 oz. pork loin thin strips, cooked
½ cup pineapple, cut into small cubes
½ cup fresh cranberries
1 tsp. mint leaves, chopped
¼ cup chopped walnuts
1 celery stalk, chopped
½ cup papaya, cubed

Dressing

⅓ cup honey
⅓ cup olive oil
⅛ cup mustard
1 small lemon for juice
1 oz. fresh cranberries
Dash of fresh nutmeg
Salt, pepper, and sugar to taste

Garnish

3 cups spinach leaves
¼ cup fresh crunchy raspberries
1 Tbsp. dill, chopped

Instructions

Place pork loin strips into a mixing bowl. (Leftover pork can be substitute). Add pineapple, cranberries, mint leaves, walnuts, celery, and papaya. Mix gently. Prepare the dressing. Add all dressing ingredients into a blender and mix for 1 minute on high speed. Season to taste. Place spinach leaves onto a serving tray and add salad on top. Before serving, pour dressing over the salad. Garnish with raspberries on top and sprinkle with dill.

Pork Loin Strips with Vegetable and Cream of Herb Dressing

Ingredients

20 oz. roasted pork loin, thinly sliced
1 small carrot, grated
1 pickle, chopped
1 red pepper, chopped
1 cup fresh spinach, chopped
2 scallion onions, chopped
1 small cucumber, finely cubed

Dressing

½ cup mayonnaise
1 cup sour cream
1 small onion, chopped
1 Tbsp. garlic, chopped
⅛ cup vinegar
1 Tbsp. Worcester sauce
1 tsp. fresh garlic, chopped
Salt, pepper, and sugar to taste

Garnish

2 cups red cabbage, shredded
3 Tbsp. grated parmesan
1 Tbsp. parsley, grated

Instructions

Place pork loin into a mixing bowl. Add carrot, pickle, red pepper, spinach, scallion onions, and cucumber. Mix gently. Prepare the dressing. Add all dressing ingredients into a blender and mix for 1 minute on high speed. Season to taste. Place red cabbage onto a serving tray and add salad. Before serving, pour dressing over the salad. Garnish by sprinkling with parmesan and parsley.

Smoked Ham Pineapple Fresh Cherry Honey Lemon Dressing

Ingredients

1 ½ lbs. smoked ham, julienned
1 cup fresh pineapple, cubed
1 cup fresh seedless cherries
1 cup spinach leaves, whole

Dressing

½ cup honey
1 Tbsp. mustard
½ cup olive oil
1 large lemon for juice
1 tsp. lemon skin, grated
1 tsp. fresh rosemary, chopped
Salt, pepper, and sugar to taste

Garnish

5 iceberg lettuce leaves
2 persimmon, cut into rings
1 Tbsp. parsley, chopped

Instructions

Place smoked ham into a mixing bowl. Add pineapple, seedless cherries, and spinach leaves. Mix gently. Prepare the dressing. Add all dressing ingredients into a blender and mix for 1 ½ minutes on high speed. Season to taste. Place lettuce leaves onto a serving tray and add salad. Before serving, pour dressing over the salad. Garnish by placing persimmon rings around the edges of the tray and sprinkle with parsley.

LAMB

Chopped Leg of Lamb Leftover with Spinach and Raisin Balsamic Dressing

Ingredients

20 oz. leftover boneless leg of lamb, small cubes
2 cups fresh spinach
¼ cup raisins
2 small scallion onions, chopped
1 medium red pepper, chopped
1 medium mango, cubed
4 Roma tomatoes, cut in half lengthwise

Dressing

¼ cup balsamic vinegar
¼ cup olive oil
¼ cup water
2 Tbsp. raisins
1 tsp. garlic, chopped
1 tsp. curry powder
Salt, pepper, and sugar to taste

Garnish

5 leaves lettuce
½ cup rosemary, crunchy and sour
1 lime, wedged

Instructions

Place lamb into a mixing bowl. Add spinach, raisins, scallion onions, red pepper, and mango. Mix gently. Clean tomato halves by carefully scooping out the insides with a spoon. Fill tomato halves evenly with the salad. Prepare the dressing. Add all dressing ingredients into a blender and mix for 1 minute on high speed. Prepare a serving tray with lettuce leaves and add stuffed tomatoes on top. Before serving, pour dressing evenly over the tomato halves. Garnish by sprinkling crunchy rosemary over tomatoes and place lime wedges around the tray.

Roasted Leg of Lamb with Kalamata and Curry Dressing Picante

Ingredients

24 oz. leftover boneless leg of lamb, cut into small cubes
½ cup seedless Kalamata olives, chopped
1 medium Granny Smith apple, julienned
1 celery stalk, chopped
1 cup papaya, cubed
1 tsp. fresh tarragon, chopped

Dressing

½ cup olive oil
½ cup white vinaigrette
½ cup water
1 Tbsp. garlic, chopped
1 tsp. curry powder
Salt, pepper, and sugar to taste

Garnish

6 leaves lettuce
6 pineapple rings with skin, cut in half
1 cup fresh spinach leaves, julienned

Instructions

Place lamb cubes into a mixing bowl. Add Kalamata olives, Granny Smith apple, celery, papaya, and tarragon. Mix gently. Prepare the dressing. Add all dressing ingredients into a blender and mix for 1 ½ minutes on high speed. Season to taste. Prepare a serving tray with lettuce leaves and add salad on top. Pour dressing over the salad. Garnish with pineapple slices around the edges of the tray and sprinkle spinach leaves down the center of the salad.

POTATOES

Baby Potatoes with Coconut Fresh Cucumber Dill Lemon Dressing

Ingredients

20 oz. baby potatoes, cooked or roasted and sliced in half
¼ cup roasted coconut, shredded
1 medium seedless cucumber, cubed
3 Tbsp. dill, chopped
½ cup red cabbage, chopped
1 cup spinach leaves, chopped
1 small carrot, coarsely grated
2 scallion onions, chopped

Dressing

¼ cup lemon juice
¼ cup olive oil
¼ cup water
1 tsp. garlic, chopped
1 Tbsp. lemon skin, finely grated
Salt, pepper, and sugar to taste

Garnish

6 Romaine or Iceberg lettuce leaves
1 tomato, cut into rings
3 Tbsp. poppy seeds

Instructions

Place potatoes into a mixing bow. Add roasted coconut, cucumber, dill, red cabbage, spinach leaves, carrot, and scallion onions. Mix gently. Prepare the dressing. Add all dressing ingredients into a blender and mix for 1 minute on high speed. Season to taste. Place lettuce leaves onto a serving tray and add salad. Before serving, pour dressing over the salad. Garnish with tomato slices around the edges of the tray and sprinkle with poppy seeds.

Baby Potatoes with Smoked Turkey Bacon and Lemon

Ingredients

1 ½ lbs. baby potatoes, cooked or roasted
½ lb. smoked turkey
½ cup crispy bacon, chopped
1 red pepper, cut into strips
2 celery stalks, chopped
3 scallion onions, coarsely chopped

Dressing

⅓ cup lemon juice
⅓ cup oil
⅓ cup water
1 tsp. sugar
Salt and pepper to taste
½ tsp. nutmeg

Garnish

1 ½ cups red cabbage
1 Tbsp. dill
1 lemon, cut into 8 wedges

Instructions

Wash the potatoes and boil them or roast them. Let cool. Put the potatoes into a mixing bowl and add the rest of the ingredients; turkey, red pepper, bacon, celery and scallions. Prepare a serving tray with red cabbage then add potato salad on top. Blend all dressing ingredients in the blender for approximately 1 minute. Adjust flavor if needed. Before serving pour dressing on salad. Garnish with chopped dill and place the lemon wedges around the tray.

Marinated Red-Skinned Potatoes with Smoked Dry Herring

Ingredients

6 medium red-skinned potatoes, cooked and thinly sliced
1 cup smoked dry herring, chopped
½ onion, finely chopped
2 Tbsp. dill, chopped
1 tsp. capers
1 small Granny Smith apple, grated
1 ¼ cup mayonnaise
1 tsp. mustard
1 tsp. garlic, chopped
1 lemon for juice
1 Tbsp. lemon skin, finely grated

Garnish

2 cups lettuce, julienned
2 beets, cooked and julienned
¼ cup walnuts, chopped

Instructions

Place potatoes into a mixing bowl. Add smoked herring, onion, dill, kipper, apple, mayonnaise, mustard, garlic, lemon juice, and lemon skin. Season to taste. Mix gently until thoroughly combined. Place the lettuce onto a serving tray and add salad. Garnish with beets around the edges of the tray and sprinkle with walnuts.

Potato Salad and Parmesan with Bacon and Olive Oil Vinaigrette Dressing

Ingredients

6 medium potatoes, cooked, peeled and cubed
¾ cup fresh parmesan, grated
½ cup crunchy bacon, chopped
1 celery stalk, chopped
½ small onion, chopped
½ cup carrots, shredded

Dressing

½ cup tarragon vinaigrette
½ cup olive oil
½ cup water
1 tsp. garlic, chopped
Salt, pepper, and sugar to taste

Garnish

4 iceberg lettuce leaves
1 medium pickle, chopped
1 lemon, cut into rings

Instructions

Wash potatoes in cold water. Place potatoes in a pot and add enough water to cover the potatoes. Cook for 35 to 40 minutes. Remove from heat. Rinse in cold water, drain. Cut potatoes into cubes. Place potatoes into a mixing bowl. Add parmesan cheese, crunchy bacon, onion, and carrots. Mix gently. Prepare the dressing. Add all dressing ingredients into a blender and mix for 1 minute on high speed. Season to taste. Place lettuce leaves onto a serving tray and add salad. Before serving, pour dressing over the salad. Garnish by sprinkling pickles and placing lemon rings around the tray.

Potato Salad with Anchovy and Mayonnaise

Ingredients

6 medium potatoes, cooked
½ cup anchovies, chopped
1 tsp. capers
2 Tbsp. Italian parsley
2 scallion onions, chopped
1 medium pickle, finely chopped

Dressing

2 Tbsp. horseradish
1 cup mayonnaise
¼ cup white vinegar
½ cup sour cream
3 Tbsp. half & half cream
Salt and pepper to taste

Garnish

2 beets, julienned
2 Tbsp. dill, chopped
1 lime, cut into wedges and twisted

Instructions

Wash potatoes and place into a pot. Fill the pot with water to cover the potatoes and cook for 30 to 40 minutes. Remove from heat, rinse with cold water, and drain. Peel and cut into cubes. Place potatoes into a mixing bowl. Add anchovies, pepper, parsley, scallion onions, and pickle. Mix gently. Prepare the dressing. Add all dressing ingredients into a blender and mix for 1 ½ minutes on high speed. Season to taste. Place salad onto a serving tray. Before serving pour dressing over the salad. Garnish with beets around the edges of the tray. Place lime wedges down the center of the salad and sprinkle with dill.

Potato Salad with Fruit and Veggies Marinated

Ingredients

16 oz. baby potatoes, cooked, peeled and cubed
1 fresh peach, cut into thin wedges
1 small carrot, coarsely grated
1 large plum, cut into thin wedges
1 cup spinach, julienned
1 small cucumber, chopped
½ cup seedless black grapes
1 Tbsp. mint leaves, chopped

Dressing

¼ cup lemon juice
¼ cup olive oil
1 tsp. fresh rosemary, chopped
1 orange for juice
Salt, pepper, and sugar to taste

Garnish

1 lime, thinly sliced
¼ cup black olives, chopped
2 Tbsp. parsley, chopped

Instructions

Place potatoes into a mixing bowl. Add peach, carrot, plum, spinach, cucumber, seedless black grapes, and mint leaves. Mix gently. Prepare the dressing. Add all dressing ingredients into a blender and mix for 2 to 2 ½ minutes on high speed. Season to taste. Pour dressing over the salad and mix gently. Place salad onto a serving tray and arrange lime rings around the edges of the tray. Garnish by sprinkling with black olives and parsley on top.

Potato Salad with Pastrami and Sundried Tomatoes

Ingredients

4 large potatoes, cooked
1 cup pastrami, julienned thin
½ cup sundried tomatoes, chopped
3 Tbsp. parsley, chopped
1 celery stalk, chopped
1 small carrot, cooked and grated
1 small pickle, cubed

Dressing

¼ cup olive oil
½ cup sundried tomatoes
¼ cup vinegar
¼ cup water
Salt, pepper, and to taste
Dash of grated nutmeg
3 strips crispy bacon, chopped

Garnish

4 lettuce leaves, whole
1 tomato, cut into thin rings
Dash of sweet paprika

Instructions

Wash the potatoes and boil for 35 minutes. Pour out the water and cook potatoes under cold water. Peel and cut into cubed. Put into a mixing bowl and add the pastrami, sundried tomatoes, parsley, celery carrots and pickles. Toss gently. Prepare a serving tray with iceberg lettuce, and add salad on top. Put all dressing ingredients in a blender on high speed. Adjust flavor if needed. Pour dressing over salad before serving. Place tomato slices and paprika on top.

Potato Salad with Roasted Tomatoes Garlic

Ingredients

6 medium red-skinned potatoes, cooked and cut into medium-sized rings
½ cup sundried tomatoes
1 cup roasted tomatoes
2 scallion onions, chopped
3 Tbsp. Italian parsley
3 Tbsp. parmesan, grated

Dressing

¼ cup olive oil
¼ cup wine vinaigrette
¼ cup water
Salt, black pepper, and sugar to taste
1 Tbsp. lemon skin
1 tsp. garlic, chopped

Garnish

1 cup fresh spinach, julienned
1 beet, cooked and cut into thin rings
1 carrot, coarsely grated

Instructions

Wash potatoes and place in a pot. Fill the pot with water to cover the potatoes. Cook for 35 minutes. Remove from heat and rinse with cold water. Drain and slice into medium-sized rings. Place spinach onto a serving tray. Evenly add the potato slices on top of the spinach. In a sauté pan, add sundried tomatoes and roasted tomatoes. Cook on high heat for 3 to 4 minutes. Remove from heat and cool. Add tomatoes on top of the potatoes. Add scallion onions, parsley, and parmesan on top of the tomatoes. Prepare the dressing. Add all dressing ingredients into a blender and mix for 45 seconds on high speed. Season to taste. Before serving, pour dressing over the salad. Garnish with beet slices around the tray and sprinkling with carrots.

Potato Salad with Smoked Meat Wine Vinaigrette Dressing

Ingredients

4 large potatoes, cooked, peeled, and cubed
4 oz. smoked turkey, julienned
4 oz. hard salami, julienned
1 small green pepper, cut into strips
½ cup onion, thinly sliced
1 small pickle, chopped

Dressing

¼ cup red wine vinegar
¼ cup olive oil
¼ cup water
1 tsp. garlic, chopped
1 tsp. oregano, chopped
Salt, pepper, and sugar to taste

Garnish

5 lettuce leave, whole
½ cup parmesan, shredded
1 orange, thinly sliced
Dash of paprika

Instructions

Place potatoes into a mixing bowl. Add the smoked turkey, hard salami, green pepper, onion, and pickle. Mix gently. Prepare the dressing. Add all the dressing ingredients into a blender and mix for 45 seconds on high speed. Season to taste. Pour dressing over the salad and mix gently. Place lettuce leaves onto a serving tray and add salad on top. Garnish with orange slices on the edges of the tray. Sprinkle with parmesan and paprika.

Potatoes and Bacon with a Cream Dressing Picante

Ingredients

4 large potatoes, cooked
¾ cup crispy bacon
2 medium celery stalks, chopped
1 small onion, chopped
2 Tbsp. tarragon, chopped

Dressing

½ cup mayonnaise
1 cup sour cream
¼ cup vinegar
1 Tbsp. garlic, chopped
Salt and pepper to taste
Dash of hot red pepper

Garnish

1 red apple, sliced into rings
2 Tbsp. dill, chopped
1 Tbsp. parmesan

Instructions

Boil the potatoes cool them and then peel. Cut into small cubes and put into a mixing bowl, add bacon, celery, onion, tarragon and mix gently. Prepare your dressing. Blend all ingredients in the blender for about 1 minute. Adjust the flavor as needed. Prepare a serving tray with julienned lettuce. Pour salad on top of the lettuce. Pour the dressing on top . Garnish with red apple, sprinkle chopped dill and parmesan.

Potatoes and Corned Beef with Red Wine Vinegar Dressing

Ingredients

4 large potatoes, cooked and cubed
8 oz. smoked corned beef, julienned
4 strips crunch bacon, chopped
¼ cup onion, chopped
2 Tbsp. chives, chopped
1 pickle, chopped
3 hard-boiled eggs, sliced

Dressing

¼ cup wine vinegar
¼ cup avocado oil
¼ cup water
1 tsp. garlic, chopped
1 tsp. mustard
Salt, pepper, and sugar to taste
Dash of nutmeg

Garnish

3 cups spinach, julienned
1 cucumber, sliced
2 tsp. parsley

Instructions

Wash potatoes and cook for 40 to 50 minutes. Remove from stove and cool under cold water. Slice into cubes and place into a mixing bowl. Add corned beef, bacon, onion, chives, and hard-boiled egg. Prepare dressing in a blender and mix well. Prepare a serving tray with the spinach leaves and add salad on top. Pour dressing over the salad. Garnish with cucumber slices and parsley.

Potatoes and Grilled Chicken Breast with Picante Veggie Dressing

Ingredients

5 large potatoes, cooked
8 oz. grilled chicken breast
1 green pepper, cut into strips
1 small red onion, chopped

Dressing

½ cup mayonnaise
½ cup sour cream
½ cup red wine vinegar
1 red pepper, roasted
2 tsp. garlic, chopped
½ tsp. crushed red pepper
Salt to taste
1 Tbsp. oregano

Garnish

1 lemon, sliced
3 sprigs of Italian parsley
½ cup croutons
Dash of paprika

Instructions

Boil potatoes for approximately 35 to 40 minutes. Let cool under cold water and then peel. Cut into round slices or cubes. Grill the breast of chicken and then cut into strips when done. Put into a mixing bowl with the potatoes. Add the green peppers and onion. Mix gently and transfer to serving tray. Put all dressing ingredients into a blender and blend for 1 minute. Adjust flavor as needed. Before serving pour dressing on top of salad and add garnish. Put the lemon rings around the edge of the tray and sprinkle croutons, parsley and paprika.

Potatoes in Spinach Sour Cream Picante

Ingredients

24 oz. baby potatoes , cooked
4 oz. fresh spinach
1 scallion onion, chopped
1 small red pepper, chopped
1 small carrot, coarsely grated
½ tsp. hot crushed red pepper

Dressing

1 ½ cups sour cream
1 tsp garlic, chopped
2 Tbsp. white vinaigrette
1 Tbsp. fresh rosemary, chopped
1 tsp. nutmeg, grated
Salt and pepper to taste

Garnish

5 iceberg lettuce leaves
1 medium pickle, cut into rings
2 Tbsp. parsley chopped
3 hard-boiled eggs, wedged

Instructions

Wash potatoes and place into a pot. Fill with enough water to cover the potatoes. Cook 17 to 20 minutes. Remove from heat, rinse with cold water, drain, and cut potatoes in half. Place potatoes into a mixing bowl. Add spinach, scallion onion, red pepper, carrot, and hot crushed red pepper. Mix gently. Prepare the dressing. Place all dressing ingredients into a blender and mix for 1 ¼ minutes on high speed. Season to taste. Place lettuce leaves onto a serving tray and add salad. Before serving, pour dressing over the salad. Garnish by placing the pickles on top of the salad. Arrange egg slices around the edge of the tray and sprinkle with parsley.

Red-Skinned Potatoes with Vegetable and Mayonnaise

Ingredients

5-6 medium potatoes with skin, cooked and thin-medium sliced
1 medium carrot, grated
½ onion, finely chopped
1 small pickle, chopped
2 hard-boiled eggs, cut into rings
1 tsp. garlic, chopped
1 tsp. mustard
1 ¼ cups mayonnaise
Salt and pepper to taste
2 Tbsp. white vinegar
1 Tbsp. tabasco sauce

Garnish

2 tomatoes, cut into rings
2 hard-boiled eggs, cut into wedges
2 Tbsp. fresh parsley, chopped

Instructions

Place potatoes into a mixing bowl. Add carrot, onion, pickle, hard-boiled eggs, garlic, mustard, mayonnaise, white vinegar, and tabasco sauce. Season to taste. Mix gently until thoroughly combined. Place salad onto a serving tray. Garnish with tomato rings around the edges of the tray. Place egg wedges down the center of the salad and sprinkle with parsley.

White Potato Salad with Spicy Mustard and Red Pepper

Ingredients

6 medium white potatoes, cooked and cubed
1 medium red pepper, chopped
½ small onion, chopped
½ tsp. garlic, chopped
¼ cup walnuts, chopped
1 small pickle, chopped
½ tsp. crushed hot red pepper

Dressing

¼ cup spicy mustard
3 Tbsp. honey
¼ cup olive oil
2 Tbsp. water
Salt and sugar to taste

Garnish

8 corn husks
2 Tbsp. dill, chopped
1 small pickle, chopped
2 hard-boiled eggs, cut into wedges

Instructions

Place potatoes into a mixing bowl. Add red pepper, onion, garlic, walnuts, pickle, and crushed hot red pepper. Mix gently. Prepare the dressing. Add all dressing ingredients into a blender and mix for 45 seconds on high speed. Season to taste. Place corn husks onto a serving tray from the center to the edges and add salad. Before serving, pour dressing over the salad. Garnish by arranging the eggs around the tray. Sprinkle with dill and pickle.

Potatoes Sour Cream and Sundried Tomatoes Picante

Ingredients

6-7 medium potatoes, cooked and cubed
2 cups sour cream
2 scallion onions, chopped
1 Tbsp. fresh oregano, chopped
1 small red pepper, chopped
½ cup relish
2 Tbsp. dill, chopped
½ cup sundried tomatoes, chopped
Salt and pepper to taste

Garnish

4 lettuce leaves
3 hard-boiled eggs, wedged
2 Tbsp. Italian parsley
3 Tbsp. peanuts, chopped

Instructions

Place potatoes into a pot and fill with water to cover potatoes. Cook 30 to 35 minutes. Remove from heat. Rinse under cold and drain. Cut into cubes and place into a mixing bowl. Add sour cream, scallion onions, oregano, red pepper, relish, dill, and sundried tomatoes. Mix gently. Season to taste. Place lettuce leaves onto a serving tray and add salad. Before serving, pour dressing over the salad. Garnish with hard-boiled eggs face-up around the tray. Sprinkle with parsley and peanuts.

BEANS

Black Bean Salad with Roasted Jalapenos and Red Pepper Dressing

Ingredients

16 oz. black beans, cooked
2 medium jalapeños, roasted and chopped
1 medium firm avocado, cubed
1 medium orange, cubed
½ cup feta cheese, crumbled
2 scallion onions, chopped

Dressing

1 large red pepper, fried or broiled and chopped
¼ cup olive oil
¼ cup lemon juice
¼ cup tomato juice
1 Tbsp. garlic, chopped
Salt, pepper, and sugar to taste

Garnish

1 cup green cabbage, shredded
2 Tbsp. fresh parsley, chopped
1 tomato rings, cut into half moon slices

Instructions

Place beans into a pot, fill with water and add 1 tsp. baking soda. Let soak overnight. Drain beans, rinse, and refill pot with water above the beans. Cook for 1 hour. Remove from heat, rinse with cold water and then drain. If using canned beans, drain and rinse well, and drain again. Place beans into a mixing bowl. Add jalapeños, avocado, orange, feta cheese, and scallion onions. Mix gently. Prepare the dressing. Add all dressing ingredients into a blender and mix for 2 minutes on high speed. Season to taste. Add dressing to the salad and mix gently. Place green cabbage onto a serving tray and add salad. Garnish with tomato rings around the tray and sprinkle with parsley.

Black Bean Salad with Red Wine Sauce and Olive Oil Picante

Ingredients

16 oz. black beans
1 cup fresh spinach, julienned
1 cucumber, cubed
1 medium carrot, grated
1 red pepper, chopped
1 celery stalk, chopped
½ cup yellow onion, chopped

Dressing

½ cup wine vinaigrette
½ cup olive oil
¼ cup water
1 Tbsp. garlic, chopped
1 Tbsp. fresh oregano, chopped
Dash of nutmeg, grated
Salt, pepper, and sugar to taste

Garnish

1 ½ cups red cabbage, shredded
1 lemon, cut into rings and twisted
2 Tbsp. parmesan, grated

Instructions

Place beans into a pot, fill with water and add 1 tsp. baking soda. Let soak overnight. Drain beans, rinse, and refill pot with water above the beans. Cook for 1 hour. Remove from heat, rinse with cold water and then drain. If using canned beans, drain and rinse well, and drain again. Remove from heat, let cool and then drain. Place pinto beans into a mixing bowl. Add spinach, cucumber, carrot, red pepper, celery, and onion. Mix gently. Prepare the dressing. Add all dressing ingredients into a blender and mix for 1 ½ minutes on high speed. Season to taste. Add dressing to the salad and mix gently. Place red cabbage onto a serving tray and add salad. Garnish with lemon twists around the tray and sprinkling with grated parmesan.

Garbanzo Beans with Tropical Fruit Marinated

Ingredients

16 oz. garbanzo beans, cooked
1 cup papaya, chopped
1 cup mango, cubed
1 cup persimmon, cubed
2 Tbsp. Italian parsley
1 scallion onion, chopped
¾ cup spinach leaves, julienned
5 strawberries, soured and halved

Dressing

¼ cup olive oil
¼ cup lemon juice
¼ cup lime juice
¼ cup orange juice
1 tsp. tarragon, chopped
Salt, pepper, and sugar to taste

Garnish

5 lettuce leaves, whole
¼ cup pecans, chopped
1 Roma tomato, cut into rings

Instructions

If using dry garbanzo beans, let soak in water overnight. Place in a pot and cook for approximately 1 hour. Remove from heat, let cool and then drain. Canned beans may also be used by strain all the juice, rinse under cold water and drain beans. Place pinto beans into a mixing bowl. Add papaya, mango, persimmon, Italian parsley, scallion onion, spinach leaves, and soured strawberries. Mix gently. Prepare the dressing. Add all dressing ingredients into a blender and mix for 1 ½ minutes on high speed. Season to taste. Add dressing to the salad and mix gently. Place lettuce leaves onto a serving tray and add salad. Garnish with tomato rings around the tray and sprinkle with chopped pecans.

Garbanzo Beans Veggie Olive Oil Lemon Lime Dressing

Ingredients

16 oz. beans, cooked
1 medium carrot, grated
1 red pepper, chopped
1 apple, coarsely grated
3 Tbsp. parsley, chopped
3 scallion onions, chopped
1 large plum, cut into thin wedges

Dressing

½ cup olive oil
¼ cup lime juice
¼ cup lemon juice
¼ cup water
1 tsp. cumin
⅛ tsp. crushed hot red pepper
1 Tbsp. garlic, chopped
Salt, pepper, and sugar to taste

Garnish

1 ½ cups red pepper, julienned
1 medium lemon, wedged
2 Tbsp. parmesan cheese, grated
Dash of paprika

Instructions

If using dry Garbanzo beans, let soak in water overnight. Place in a pot and cook for approximately 1 ¼ to 1 ½ hours. Remove from heat, let cool and then drain. Canned beans may also be used by strain all the juice, rinse under cold water and drain beans. Place Garbanzo beans into a mixing bowl. Add carrot, red pepper, apple, parsley, scallion onions, and plum. Mix gently. Prepare the dressing. Add all dressing ingredients into a blender and mix for 1 minute on high speed. Season to taste. Add dressing to the salad and mix gently. Place red peppers onto a serving tray and add salad. Garnish with lemon wedges on top of the salad. Sprinkle with grated parmesan and paprika.

Humus Salad with Veggie Picante

Ingredients

16 oz. garbanzo beans, cooked
1 medium pickle, chopped
½ cup sundried tomatoes, chopped
2 Tbsp. parsley, chopped
2 scallion onions, chopped
1 small tomato, cubed
½ tsp. crushed hot red pepper
½ cup Kalamata olives, chopped

Dressing

¼ cup olive oil
¼ cup lemon juice
1 Tbsp. cumin
1 ½ Tbsp. garlic, chopped
Salt and pepper to taste

Garnish

4 lettuce leaves
1 lemon, wedged
2 Tbsp. parsley, chopped
Dash of paprika

Instructions

If using dry garbanzo beans, let soak in water overnight. Place in a pot and cook for approximately 1 hour. Remove from heat, let cool and then drain. Canned beans may also be used by strain all the juice, rinse under cold water and drain beans. Place pinto beans into a blender. Mix high speed 3 to 4 minutes. Remove from blender and place into a mixing bowl. Add pickle, sundried tomatoes, parsley, scallion onions, tomato, crushed hot red pepper, and Kalamata olives. Mix gently. Prepare the dressing. Add all dressing ingredients into a blender and mix for 1 ½ to 2 minutes on high speed. Season to taste. Add dressing to the salad and mix gently until well combined well. Place lettuce leaves onto a serving tray and add salad. Garnish with lemon rings around the tray. Sprinkle with parsley and paprika.

Kidney Beans with Julienned Pastrami Marinated Balsamic Dressing

Ingredients

16 oz. kidney beans, cooked
8 oz. pastrami smoked, julienned
½ cup medium onion, thin sliced
2 Tbsp. fresh Italian parsley, chopped
1 tsp. oregano, chopped
5 strips crunchy bacon, chopped
1 celery stalk, chopped
1 medium carrot, coarsely grated

Dressing

½ cup balsamic vinegar
½ cup olive oil
½ cup avocado
¼ cup water
1 Tbsp. garlic, chopped
1 tsp. fresh oregano, chopped
2 Tbsp. fresh jalapeños, chopped
Salt, pepper, and sugar and to taste

Garnish

2 cups lettuce, julienned
1 small seedless cucumber, skinned and cut into rings
½ cup Kalamata olives, chopped

Instructions

If using dry pinto beans, let soak in water overnight. Place in a pot and cook for approximately 1-1 ¼ hours. Remove from heat, let cool, and then drain. If using canned beans, strain all the juice, rinse under cold water and drain beans. Place kidney beans into a mixing bowl. Add smoked pastrami, onion, Italian parsley, oregano, crunchy bacon, celery, and carrot. Mix gently. Prepare the dressing. Add all dressing ingredients into a blender and mix for 1 minute on high speed. Season to taste. Place lettuce leaves onto a serving tray. Pour dressing over top of the salad. Garnish with cucumber rings around the tray and sprinkle with olives.

Pinto Bean with Spinach Sour Cream and Cheese

Ingredients

16 oz. pinto beans, cooked
1 ½ cups spinach, julienned
1 small lime, peeled and cubed
1 tsp. lime skin, finely grated
¾ cup shredded white cheddar cheese
1 tsp. fresh rosemary, chopped
1 scallion onion, chopped
1 small carrot, coarsely grated

Dressing

1 cup sour cream
¼ cup lemon juice
¼ cup half & half cream
½ cup white cheddar cheese, grated
1 tsp. garlic, chopped
Salt and pepper to taste

Garnish

5 lettuce leaves
2 Tbsp. ground peanuts
1 tomato, cut into rings

Instructions

If using dry pinto beans, let soak in water overnight. Place in a pot and cook for approximately 1 hour. Remove from heat, let cool and then drain. Canned beans may also be used by strain all the juice, rinse under cold water and drain beans. Place pinto beans into a mixing bowl. Add spinach, lime cubes, lime skin, white cheddar cheese, rosemary, scallion onion, and carrot. Mix gently. Prepare the dressing. Add all dressing ingredients into a blender and mix for 1 minute on high speed. Season to taste. Add dressing to the salad and mix gently. Place lettuce leaves onto a serving tray and add salad. Garnish with tomato rings around the tray and sprinkling with ground peanuts.

Red Bean Salad with Tomato and Lemon Dressing

Ingredients

16 oz. red beans, cooked
10 oz. tomatoes, cubed
2 Tbsp. Italian parsley, chopped
1 medium lemon, peeled and cubed
1 tsp. lemon skin, finely grated
1 seedless cucumber, thinly sliced
½ tsp. crushed hot red pepper

Dressing

¼ cup olive oil
½ cup lemon juice
¼ cup water
1 Tbsp. garlic, chopped
Salt, pepper, and sugar to taste

Garnish

2 cups red cabbage, julienned
2 Tbsp. parsley, chopped
1 lemon, cut into rings

Instructions

If using dry beans, soak them overnight in water. The next day, cook for 1 hour. If using beans from the can, drain and rinse with cold water. Place red beans into a mixing bowl. Add tomatoes, Italian parsley, lemon cubes, lemon skin, cucumber, and crushed hot red pepper. Mix gently. Prepare the dressing. Add all dressing ingredients into a blender and mix for 1 minute on high speed. Season to taste. Place red cabbage onto a serving tray and add salad. Before serving, pour dressing over the salad. Garnish with lemon rings on the edges of the tray and sprinkle with parsley.

FRUIT

Apple and Smoked Trout with Sundried Tomatoes

Ingredients

4 medium Granny Smith apples, julienned
8 oz. smoked dried trout
8 oz. sundried tomatoes, chopped
1 Tbsp. dill, chopped
1 small cucumber, finely cubed

Dressing

¼ cup fresh lemon juice
¼ cup olive oil
1 small red pepper, roasted and chopped
Dash of crushed hot red pepper
1 tsp. garlic, chopped
2 Tbsp. orange skin, chopped
Salt, pepper, and sugar to taste

Garnish

2 cups fresh spinach
1 lemon, cut into medium wedges
1 small cucumber, chopped

Instructions

Wash apples, peel and slice julienned. Place into a mixing bowl. Add smoked trout, sundried tomatoes, dill, and cucumber. Mix gently. Prepare the dressing. Add all dressing ingredients into a blender and mix for 2 minutes on high speed. Season to taste. Place spinach leaves onto a serving tray and add salad. Before serving, pour dressing over the salad. Garnish with lemon wedges around the tray and sprinkle with chopped cucumber.

Apple Crabmeat and Sundried Tomatoes with Mayonnaise

Ingredients

3 medium Granny Smith apples, peeled and julienned
12 oz. backfin crabmeat or lump
½ cup sundried tomatoes, chopped
1 small red pepper, chopped
2 Tbsp. dill, chopped
2 Tbsp. lemon juice
Dash of Old Bay Seasoning
Salt and pepper taste
¾ cup mayonnaise
2 garlic cloves, chopped

Garnish

3 cups spring lettuce
¼ cup chopped walnuts
1 small seedless cucumber, cut into rings

Instructions

Peel Granny Smith apple, cut in half, remove seeds, slice into half rings and julienned. Place into a mixing bowl. Add backfin crabmeat, sundried tomatoes, red pepper, dill, lemon juice, Old Bay Seasoning, salt and pepper to taste, mayonnaise, and garlic. Mix gently, careful not to mush ingredients together. Place spring onto a serving tray and add salad to the center. Garnish with cucumber rings around the tray and sprinkle with walnuts.

Apple Pecan in Celery Mayonnaise Base

Ingredients

4 medium to large granny Smith apples, julienned
¼ cup pecans, chopped
2 celery stalks, chopped
¼ cup raisins
2 hard-boiled eggs, coarsely grated
¾ cup mayonnaise
1 lemon for juice
Salt, pepper, and sugar to taste

Garnish

2 ½ cups spring lettuce
1 lemon, cut into rings
1 tsp. dill, chopped
1 small red apple, cut into rings

Instructions

Wash apples, cut in half, remove seeds, and slice julienned. Place into a mixing bowl. Add pecans, celery, raisins, hard-boiled eggs, mayonnaise, lemon juice, salt, pepper, and dash of sugar. Mix gently. If you would like a thicker base, add small amount of additional mayonnaise. Place spring lettuce onto a serving tray and add salad. Garnish with apple rings around the edges of the tray. Place lemon rings on top of the salad and sprinkle with dill.

Apricot with Grilled Chicken Breast with Mayonnaise and Herb Dressing

Ingredients

8 large apricots, wedged
12 oz. grilled or broiled chicken breast, cut into thin strips
1 scallion onion, chopped
1 celery stalk, chopped
1 tsp. dill, chopped
¼ cup sundried tomatoes, chopped

Dressing

¾ cup mayonnaise
1 large lemon for juice
1 tsp. garlic, chopped
1 tsp. fresh rosemary, chopped
2 soft apricots
Salt and pepper to taste

Garnish

2 cups spinach, julienned
1 small seedless cucumber, cut into rings
1 Tbsp. parsley, chopped

Instructions

Wash apricots in cold water, peel, cut in half lengthwise, remove seeds, and slice into thin wedges. Place into a mixing bowl. Add chicken, scallion onion, celery, dill, and sundried tomatoes. Mix gently. Prepare the dressing. Add all dressing ingredients into a blender and mix for 1 ½ minutes on high speed. Season to taste. Place spinach onto a serving tray and add salad on top. Before serving, pour dressing over the salad. Garnish with cucumber rings on top and sprinkle with parsley.

Avocado Fruit and Veggie Picante

Ingredients

3 medium avocado, cubed
1 medium Granny Smith apple, peeled and julienned
2 small red plums, cubed
1 small carrot, coarsely grated
1 scallion onion, chopped
1 tsp. lime skin, grated
2 Tbsp. Italian parsley, chopped
1 persimmon, cut into small cubes

Dressing

¼ cup balsamic vinegar
⅓ cup olive oil
1 small dill pickle, chopped
1 tsp. garlic, chopped
Salt, pepper, and sugar to taste

Garnish

5 lettuce leaves, whole
1 medium tomato, cut into rings
2 Tbsp. pomegranate seeds
½ cup seasoned croutons

Instructions

Wash avocado, cut in half lengthwise, remove seeds, and scoop the fruit out with a spoon. Place the fruit onto a cutting board and slice into medium-sized cubes. Place lettuce leaves onto a serving tray and add the avocado evenly over top. Add apples, plums, carrots, scallion onions, lime skin, Italian parsley, and persimmon over avocado. Prepare the dressing. Add all dressing ingredients into a blender and mix for 35 seconds minutes on high speed or in a mixing bowl. Season to taste. Before serving, pour dressing over the salad. Garnish with tomato rings around the salad. Sprinkle with pomegranate seeds and croutons.

Blackberries with Cheddar Cheese Dressing

Ingredients

20 oz. blackberries, crunchy and sour
¾ cup yellow sharp cheddar cheese
1 cup spinach, chopped
1 small carrot, coarsely grated
1 tsp. lemon skin, finely grated

Dressing

¼ cup lemon juice
¼ cup olive oil
1 Tbsp. lemon skin, grated
1 tsp. tarragon
¼ cup sweet red wine
Salt, pepper, and sugar to taste

Garnish

6 leaves lettuce, whole
2 Persimmon, cut into thin rings
1 small red pepper, thinly sliced

Instructions

Wash blackberries in cold water, drain, and place into a mixing bowl. Add sharp cheddar cheese, spinach, carrot, and lemon skin. Mix gently. Prepare the dressing. Add all dressing ingredients into a blender and mix for 1 minute on high speed. Season to taste. Place lettuce leaves onto a serving tray and add salad. Before serving, pour dressing over the salad. Garnish with Persimmon rings around the edges and place red peppers on top.

Blackberries with Feta Cheese and Avocado Picante

Ingredients

16 oz. blackberries, hard and sour
10 oz. feta cheese, small cubes
1 large avocado or 2 medium, firm and cubed
1 scallion onion, chopped
1 Tbsp. dill, chopped
1 small seedless cucumber with skin, cubed

Dressing

⅓ cup avocado oil
⅓ cup white wine vinegar
⅓ cup water
1 tsp. jalapeños, chopped
2 garlic cloves, chopped
Salt, pepper, and sugar to taste

Garnish

2 ½ cups spinach leaves, julienned
1 Tbsp. parsley, chopped
2 Tbsp. chopped walnuts

Instructions

Wash blackberries in cold water, strain, and place into a mixing bowl. Add feta cheese, avocado, scallion onion, dill, and seedless cucumber. Mix gently. Prepare the dressing. Add all dressing ingredients into a blender and mix for 1 minute on high speed. Season to taste. Place spinach leaves onto a serving tray and add salad. Before serving, pour dressing over the salad. Garnish by sprinkling parsley and walnuts on top.

Blueberries with Sour Cream Picante Lemon Dressing

Ingredients

20 oz. crunchy blueberries, soured if possible
1 small red pepper, chopped
1 tsp. dill, chopped
1 small granny Smith apple, cubed

Dressing

¾ cup sour cream
1 large lemon for juice
¼ cup half & half cream
1 Tbsp. olive oil
2 oz. cream cheese
Salt and pepper to taste

Garnish

8 cornhusks
¼ cup walnuts, chopped
1 lime, cut into rings and twisted

Instructions

Wash blueberries, drain and place into a mixing bowl. Add red pepper, dill, and Granny Smith apple. Mix gently. Prepare the dressing. Add all dressing ingredients into a blender and mix for 1 ½ minutes on high speed. Season to taste. Place cornhusks onto a serving tray and add salad. Before serving, pour dressing over the salad. Garnish with lime twists around the tray and sprinkle with walnuts.

Cantaloupe and Cranberry with Lemon Dressing

Ingredients

1 small cantaloupe, peeled and cubed
1 cup fresh cranberries
2 Tbsp. Italian parsley
1 lime, peeled and finely cubed

Dressing

¼ cup olive oil
¼ cup lemon juice
1 Tbsp. fresh basil, chopped
¼ cup fresh orange juice
Salt, pepper, and sugar to taste

Garnish

2 cups spinach leaves
1 lemon, cut into thin rings
¼ cup chopped walnuts

Instructions

Wash cantaloupe, peel, slice lengthwise and remove all seeds. Cut into small-medium-size cubes and place into a mixing bowl. Add cranberries into a pot of boiling water and cook for 1 minute. Remove from heat, drain, rinse with cold water, drain, and add to the cantaloupe. Add Italian parsley and lime. Mix gently. Prepare the dressing. Add all dressing ingredients into a blender and mix for 1 minute on high speed. Season to taste. Place spinach leaves onto a serving tray and add salad. Before serving, pour dressing over the salad. Garnish with lemon rings around the edges and sprinkle chopped walnuts.

Cantaloupe and Smoked Turkey with Cherry Cranberry Dressing

Ingredients

4 cups cantaloupe, cubed
8 oz. smoked turkey breast, julienned
3 oz. smoked cheese, julienned
¾ cup seedless fresh cherries, whole
2 oz. fresh cranberries, chopped
2 Tbsp. Italian parsley, chopped

Dressing

¼ cup cranberries
¼ cup fresh seedless cherries
¼ cup olive oil
¼ cup fresh lemon juice
¼ cup water
3 Tbsp. cherry brandy
Salt, pepper, and sugar to taste

Garnish

6 Romaine lettuce leaves
¼ cup chopped pecans
2 medium plums, wedged

Instructions

Place cantaloupe into a mixing bowl. Add smoked turkey, smoked cheese, fresh cherries, fresh cranberries, and Italian parsley. Mix gently. Prepare the dressing. Add all dressing ingredients into a blender and mix for 2 minutes on high speed. Season to taste. Place lettuce onto a serving tray and add salad on top. Before serving, pour dressing over the salad. Garnish with plums around the edges of the tray and sprinkle with pecans.

Cherry Spinach and Plum with Sour Feta Cheese Dressing

Ingredients

12 oz. fresh seedless cherries
2 cups spinach, julienned
4 sour green plums, thinly wedged
1 tsp. fresh tarragon, chopped
1 small carrot, coarsely grated

Dressing

6 oz. feta cheese
1 oz. cream cheese
⅓ cup olive oil
⅓ cup lemon juice
⅓ cup half & half cream
2 garlic cloves, chopped
Salt and pepper to taste

Garnish

4 lettuce leaves
1 tomato, thinly sliced
2 Tbsp. parsley, chopped

Instructions

Wash cherries, remove stems, and place into a mixing bowl. Wash spinach leaves, slice julienned, and add to cherries. Add plums, tarragon, and carrot. Mix gently. Prepare the dressing. Add all dressing ingredients into a blender and mix for 2 ½ minutes on high speed. Season to taste. Place lettuce onto serving tray and add salad on top. Before serving, pour dressing over the salad. Garnish with tomato wedges around the salad and sprinkle with parsley.

Cranberry Avocado and Smoked Turkey Picante

Ingredients

10 oz. fresh cranberries
2 medium avocado, peeled and cubed
8 oz. smoked turkey, julienned
⅛ tsp. crushed hot red pepper
1 small green pepper, small cubes
1 scallion onion, chopped
1 tsp. lemon skin, finely grated

Dressing

¼ cup lemon juice
1/3 cup olive oil
¼ cup fresh cranberries
¼ cup fresh orange juice
1 Tbsp. dill, chopped
2 garlic cloves, chopped
Salt, pepper, and sugar to taste

Garnish

2 cups spinach julienned
2 Tbsp. chopped walnuts
2 Tbsp. parsley, chopped
1 medium lemon, thinly sliced

Instructions

Wash cranberries and place into a pot filled with 2 quarts of water. Bring to a boil and cook for 1 ½ to 2 minutes. Remove from heat, strain, and let cool to room temperature. Place the cranberries into a mixing bowl. Wash avocado, cut lengthwise and remove seeds. Scoop fruit from the inside using a spoon. Place fruit onto a cutting board, cut into cubes, and add to the cranberries. Add avocado, smoked turkey, crushed hot red pepper, green pepper, scallion onion, and lemon skin. Mix gently. Prepare the dressing. Add all dressing ingredients into a blender and mix for 1 minute on high speed. Season to taste. Place spinach onto a serving tray and add salad on top. Before serving, pour dressing over the salad. Garnish with lemon rings around the tray. Sprinkle with walnuts and parsley.

Cranberry Spinach and Feta with Sour Cream Dressing Picante

Ingredients

16 oz. fresh cranberries
2 cups fresh spinach, whole
8 oz. feta cheese, crumbled
1 scallion onions, chopped
5 strips crunchy bacon, chopped

Dressing

1 ½ cups sour cream
1 large lemon for juice
1 large green pepper, roasted
1 tsp. garlic, chopped
2 Tbsp. jalapeños, chopped
2 Tbsp. shredded roasted coconut
Salt and pepper to taste

Garnish

5 lettuce leaves, julienned
3 hard-boiled eggs, cut into wedges
1 small carrot, coarsely grated

Instructions

Wash cranberries and place into a pot with 2 ½ quarts of water. Bring to a boil. Add dash of lemon juice and dash of sugar. Cook 2 to 3 minutes. Remove from heat, strain, and let cool to room temperature. Place the cranberries into a mixing bowl. Add spinach, feta, scallion onions, and bacon. Mix gently. Prepare the dressing. Add all dressing ingredients into a blender and mix for 1 ¼ minutes on high speed. Season to taste. Place lettuce onto a serving tray and add salad. Before serving, pour dressing over the salad. Garnish with carrots over salad and place egg wedges (yellow side up) evenly around the tray.

Persimmon Pasta and Spinach Picante

Ingredients

3 medium Persimmon, cubed
10 oz. small rotini pasta, cooked
1 cup spinach, chopped
1 medium tomato, cubed
4 shallots, cut into rings
1 seedless cucumber, thin rings
1 small red pepper, chopped
1 small carrot, coarsely grated

Dressing

⅓ cup olive oil
⅓ cup balsamic vinegar
1 large lime for juice
1 tsp. lime skin, grated
Dash of crushed hot red pepper
1 tsp. garlic, chopped
¼ cup water
Salt, pepper, and sugar to taste

Garnish

5 lettuce leaves
2 hard-boiled eggs, wedged
1 Tbsp. parsley chopped
2 Tbsp. parmesan, grated

Instructions

Place Persimmon into a mixing bowl. Place 2 quarts of water in a pot and bring to a boil. Add pasta and cook 10 to 12 minutes. Remove from heat. Rinse with cold water, strain, and add to Persimmon. Add spinach, tomato, shallots, seedless cucumber, red pepper, and carrot. Mix gently. Prepare the dressing. Add all dressing ingredients into a blender and mix for 1 ¼ minutes on high speed. Season to taste. Place lettuce onto a serving tray and add salad on top. Before serving, pour dressing over the salad. Garnish with hard-boiled eggs wedges on the center of the salad. Sprinkle with parsley and parmesan.

Persimmon Swiss Cheese and Pastrami with Tomato Dressing Picante

Ingredients

5 Persimmon, cut in medium cubes
6 oz. swiss cheese, julienned
6 oz. pastrami, julienned
¼ cup sundried tomatoes, chopped
1 tsp. fresh rosemary, chopped

Dressing

¼ cup olive oil
¼ cup white wine vinegar
½ cup tomato juice
1 small tomato
1 tsp. fresh oregano, chopped
Salt, pepper, and sugar to taste

Garnish

4 red cabbage leaves, whole
1 persimmon, cut into rings
1 tomato, wedged
1 Tbsp. parsley, chopped

Instructions

Wash Persimmon in cold water, cut into rings and place in a mixing bowl. Add swiss cheese, pastrami, sundried tomatoes, and rosemary. Mix gently. Prepare the dressing. Add all dressing ingredients into a blender and mix for 1 minute on high speed. Season to taste. Place red cabbage leaves onto a serving tray and gently add salad on top. Before serving, pour dressing over the salad. Garnish with persimmon rings around the edges. Place tomato wedges across the middle of the salad and sprinkle with parsley.

Persimmon with Smoked Corned Beef Cream of Herb Dressing

Ingredients

5 medium Persimmon, cubed
10 oz. smoked corned beef, julienned
¼ cup red onion, chopped
2 Tbsp. dill, chopped
1 small red pepper, julienned
1 tsp. lemon skin, finely grated

Dressing

¾ cup mayonnaise
⅓ cup sour cream
1 large lemon for juice
1 tsp. garlic, chopped
3 Tbsp. half & half cream
Salt, pepper, and sugar to taste

Garnish

2 cups spring lettuce
2 hard-boiled eggs, wedged
2 Tbsp. parsley, chopped

Instructions

Wash Persimmon, cut into cubes and place into a mixing bowl. Add smoked corned beef, red onion, dill, red pepper, and lemon skin. Mix gently. Prepare the dressing. Add all dressing ingredients into a blender and mix for 1 minute on high speed. Season to taste. Place spring lettuce onto a serving tray and add salad on top. Before serving, pour dressing over the salad. Garnish with hard-boiled around the tray with yellow side up. Sprinkle with parsley on top.

Figs and Feta Cheese with Veggie Dressing

Ingredients

8 large figs, wedged
12 oz. feta cheese, crumbled
1 scallion onion, chopped
1 Tbsp. dill, chopped
1 Tbsp. mint leaves, chopped

Dressing

¼ cup olive oil
2 medium lemon for juice
¼ cup orange juice
1 tsp lemon skin, finely grated
2 garlic cloves, chopped
1 small carrot
1 small seedless cucumber
2 Tbsp. raisins
Salt, pepper, and sugar to taste

Garnish

3 cups spring lettuce
2 Tbsp. black olives, chopped
2 Tbsp. Italian parsley, chopped
1 medium red apple, wedged

Instructions

Wash figs, cut top off, and cut into wedges. Place spring lettuce onto a serving tray and add figs on top. Add feta cheese, scallion onion, dill, and mint leaves. Prepare the dressing. Add all dressing ingredients into a blender and mix for 1 minute on high speed. Season to taste. Before serving, pour dressing over the salad. Garnish with black olives and parsley. Dip apple wedges into lemon juice and place on top.

Fresh Marinated Apricots with Lobster Picante

Ingredients

10 medium apricots, wedged
2 medium-large lobster tails, broiled or grilled
1 small green pepper, roasted
1 scallion onion, chopped
2 Tbsp. Italian parsley, chopped

Dressing

¼ cup sesame oil
¼ cup lemon juice
¼ cup water
1 small orange for juice
¼ cup sundried tomatoes
1 tsp. garlic, chopped
1 tsp. lemon skin, grated
Salt, pepper, and sugar to taste

Garnish

3 cups lettuce, julienned
1 tomato, cut into thin rings
2 Tbsp. chopped peanuts

Instructions

Wash apricots, cut in half, remove seeds, slice into wedges, and place into a mixing bowl. To prepare lobster tail: use a sharp knife to make a cut on top of shell to crack. Broil. As it cooks, the shell will crack. Once cooked, remove from shell, cut into cubes, and add to apricots. Add roasted green pepper, scallion onion, and Italian parsley. Mix gently. Prepare the dressing. Add all dressing ingredients into a blender and mix for 1 ¼ minutes on high speed. Season to taste. Place lettuce leaves onto a serving tray and add salad on top. Before serving, pour dressing over the salad. Garnish with tomato rings around the tray and sprinkle with peanuts.

Fresh Peaches with Smoked Corned Beef Olive Oil Kalamata Dressing

Ingredients

4 medium peaches, thin sliced wedges
12 oz. smoked corned beef, julienned thin
½ cup Kalamata olives
1 scallion onion, chopped
1 small red pepper, thinly sliced
1 Tbsp. parsley, chopped

Dressing

⅔ cup olive oil
⅔ cup wine vinegar
2 garlic cloves, chopped
1 tsp. oregano, chopped
Salt, pepper, and sugar to taste

Garnish

5-6 fresh grape leaves
1 large lime, cut into wedges
1 Tbsp. parmesan, shredded
1 small tomato, cut into cubes

Instructions

Wash peaches, cut lengthwise, remove seeds, and cut into thin slices. Place into a mixing bowl. Add corned beef, Kalamata olives, scallion onions, red pepper, and parsley. Mix gently. Prepare the dressing. Add all dressing ingredients into a blender and mix for 1 minute on high speed. Season to taste. Place grape leaves onto a serving tray and add salad. Before serving, pour dressing over the salad. Garnish with lime wedges around the tray. Add tomato cubes down the center of the salad and sprinkle with parmesan.

Fried Papaya with Prosciutto and Honey Dressing

Ingredients

1 medium papaya, cut into strips
1 cup prosciutto, julienned
1 cup spinach, julienned
½ cup white flour
3 egg beaten
1 cup plain bread crumbs
1 ¼ cups oil

Dressing

½ cup honey
1 large lemon for juice
3 Tbsp. dry red wine
1 tsp. rosemary, chopped
¼ cup vegetable oil
1 tsp. yellow mustard
2 Tbsp. water
Salt, pepper, and sugar to taste

Garnish

2 cups spring lettuce
1 lime, thinly wedged
1 Tbsp. dill, chopped
3 Tbsp. pecans, chopped

Instructions

Peel papaya, cut in half lengthwise, remove seeds, slice into 4 inch strips. Prepare three plates: 1 with flour, 1 with beaten eggs, and 1 with bread crumbs. Dip each papaya piece into flour, eggs, then bread crumbs. In a sauté pan, heat vegetable oil, and add papaya slices. Cook until golden brown. Remove from oil, place on paper towel to drain excess oil from fruit. Place spring lettuce onto a serving tray and add papaya evenly on top. Add prosciutto and spinach over papaya. Prepare the dressing. Add all dressing ingredients into a blender and mix for 1 minute on high speed. Season to taste. Before serving, pour dressing over the salad. Garnish with lime wedges around the tray. Sprinkle with dill and pecans on top.

Fried Pineapple with Parmesan and Spinach Kalamata Dressing

Ingredients

6-8 pineapples rings, cut medium thin
½ cup white flour
3 large eggs, beaten
¾ cup bread crumbs
1 cup vegetable oil

Dressing

¼ cup canola oil
1 large lemon for juice
2 Tbsp. parmesan cheese
¼ cup orange juice
¼ cup seedless Kalamata olive
½ cup spinach
2 garlic cloves, finely chopped
Salt, pepper, and sugar to taste

Garnish

5 lettuce leaves, julienned
1 lemon cut into rings and twisted
1 Tbsp. parsley, chopped

Instructions

Peel pineapple and make sure there are no black dots on it. Cut into ⅛ to ½ inch slices. Prepare three plates: 1 with flour, 1 with beaten eggs, and 1 with bread crumbs. Dip each pineapple piece into flour, eggs, then bread crumbs. In a sauté pan, heat vegetable oil, and add pineapple slices. Cook until golden brown. Remove from oil, place on paper towel, and let cool. Place lettuce onto a serving tray and add fried pineapple rings evenly over the lettuce. Prepare the dressing. Add all dressing ingredients into a blender and mix for 1 ½ to 2 minutes on high speed. Season to taste. Before serving, pour dressing over the salad. Garnish with lemon twist on each pineapple ring and sprinkle with parsley.

Fruit and Cheese with Chambord Liquor

Ingredients

1 Granny Smith apple, julienned
1 medium pear, julienned
12 oz. ¼ inch cheese wine balls
3 Tbsp. chopped walnuts
2 plums, cut into thin strips
1 Tbsp. mint leaves, chopped
8 strawberries, halved
½ cup fresh cherries with stems and seeds
¼ cup Chambord liquor

Garnish

5 lettuce leaves, whole
1 large lemon, thinly sliced
1 Tbsp. dill, chopped
4 Tbsp. whipped cream

Instructions

Wash all fruit. Peel and julienned slice the Granny Smith apple and place into a mixing bowl. Prepare cheese balls by rolling into chopped walnuts and add to apples. Add pear, plum, mint leaves, strawberries, cherries, and Chambord liquor. Dash of sugar may be added, if desired for taste. Mix gently. Place lettuce leaves onto a serving tray and add salad. Garnish with lemon slices around the edges of the salad and sprinkle with parsley. Add whipped cream by spoonful onto the center of the salad. Lightly flatten each dab of whipped cream by pressing down lightly on each with the backside of the spoon.

Note: Prepare your own cheese balls by mixing 16 oz. cheddar cheese, 2 to 3 Tbsp. chopped walnuts, sweet red wine, dash of a salt, if needed. Mix in a blender for 3 to 4 minutes, until stiff and mushy. Roll into ¼" balls and roll in walnuts, pecans, or poppy seeds.

Fruit and Lobster with Honey and Lemon

Ingredients

½ cup pomegranate seeds
14 oz. lobster meat, broiled and cubed
1 plum, thinly wedged
½ cup blueberries, whole
½ cup raspberries, whole
3 apricots, thinly edged
1 tsp. rosemary, chopped

Dressing

¼ cup lemon juice
1/3 cup honey
¼ cup olive oil
¼ cup fresh orange juice
Salt, pepper, and sugar to taste

Garnish

5 lettuce leave, julienned
1 lemon, wedged
2 Tbsp. parsley, chopped

Instructions

Place pomegranate seeds, lobster meat, plum, blueberries, raspberries, apricots, and rosemary into a mixing bowl. Mix gently. Prepare the dressing. Add all dressing ingredients into a blender and mix for 1 minute on high speed. Season to taste to sweet and sour. Place lettuce leaves onto a serving tray and add salad on top. Before serving, pour dressing over the salad. Garnish with lemon wedges face-up around the tray and sprinkle with parsley.

Fruit and Smoked Meat Marinated

Ingredients

1 medium Granny Smith apple, julienned
½ cup crunchy blueberries
1 persimmon, cut into small cubes
1 celery stalk, chopped
6 oz. smoked turkey, julienned
6 oz. smoked pastrami, julienned
6 oz. smoked ham, julienned

Dressing

¼ cup olive oil
¼ cup white vinegar
¼ cup water
1 tsp. garlic, chopped
1 tsp. tarragon, chopped
1 tsp. lime skin, grated
Salt, pepper, and sugar to taste

Garnish

5 lettuce leaves
1 tomato, cut into thin rings
2 Tbsp. parsley, chopped

Instructions

Wash apple, peel, cut in half, remove seeds, and cut julienned. Place apples into a mixing bowl. Wash and drain blueberries. Add blueberries, persimmon, celery, smoked turkey, smoked pastrami, and smoked ham to the apples. Mix gently. Prepare the dressing. Add all dressing ingredients into a blender and mix for 1 minute on high speed. Season to taste. Pour dressing over the salad and mix gently. Place lettuce leaves onto a serving tray and add salad. Garnish with tomato rings around the tray and sprinkle parsley over top.

Fruit and Spinach with Sweet and Sour Dressing

Ingredients

2 large plums, thinly wedged
½ cups pineapple, cubed
1 medium nectarine, cubed
1 Granny Smith apple, peeled and julienned
1 medium pear, julienned
2 cups spinach leaf lettuce

Dressing

¼ cup olive oil
¼ cup fresh lemon juice
¼ cup pomegranate seeds
1 Tbsp. honey
⅛ cup pomegranate juice
Salt, pepper, and sugar to taste

Garnish

5 lettuce leaves, whole
¼ cup pomegranate seeds
1 lemon, wedged
1 Tbsp. fresh rosemary, chopped

Instructions

Wash all fruit and spinach leaves. Slice plums into wedges, pineapple and nectarine into cubes. Cut the Granny Smith apple and pear julienned in half, remove seeds, slice into cubes, and place all into a mixing bowl. Add spinach leaves and mix gently. Prepare the dressing. Add all dressing ingredients into a blender and mix for 1 minute on high speed. Season to taste. Place lettuce leaves onto a serving tray and add salad on top. Before serving, pour dressing over the salad. Garnish with lemon wedges around the edges of the salad. Add pomegranate seeds on top and sprinkle with rosemary.

Fruit and Veggie Patty Salad Avocado Lemon Dressing

Ingredients

1 small apple, grated
1 small pear, grated
1 small nectarine, grated
1 cup spinach leaves, julienned
1 medium carrot, finely grated
1 cup green cabbage, chopped
2 scallion onions, chopped
1 cup bread crumbs
¼ cup flour
2 eggs beaten
Dash salt and pepper
1 1/2 cup oil

Dressing

1 small moist avocado
¼ cup lemon juice
¼ cup olive oil
1 ¼ cup water
1 Tbsp. oregano, chopped
1 tsp. honey
Salt, pepper, and sugar to taste

Garnish

4 iceberg lettuce leaves
3 Tbsp. grated parmesan cheese
3 Tbsp. sesame seeds
2 hard-boiled eggs, wedges

Instructions

Wash and prepare all fruit as directed. Place into a mixing bowl. Add spinach leaves, carrot, green cabbage, scallion onion, bread crumbs, and flour. Mix gently to combine all ingredients. Shape mixture into patties. Heat oil in a sauté pan and add patties. Cook until golden brown. Remove from the pan, place onto paper towel to remove excess oil. Place iceberg lettuce onto a serving tray and add the patties evenly on top. Prepare the dressing. Add all dressing ingredients into a blender and mix for 1 ½ minutes on high speed. Season to taste. Before serving, pour dressing over the patties. Garnish with hard-boiled egg wedges around the salad. Sprinkle with parmesan and sesame seeds.

Fruit and Veggie with Tahini Dressing

Ingredients

1 medium Granny Smith Apple, peeled and julienned
1 peach, cubed
½ cup seedless red grapes
1 small seedless cucumber, cubed
1 small red pepper, thinly sliced
2 Tbsp. parsley, chopped
1 scallion onion, chopped

Dressing

⅓ cup tahini paste
¼ cup lemon juice
⅓ cup water
1 tsp. garlic, chopped
1 tsp. grated lemon skin
Salt and pepper to taste

Garnish

2 cups spring lettuce
2 Tbsp. sesame seeds
1 medium tomato, cut into rings
1 Tbsp. dill, chopped

Instructions

Place apples into a mixing bowl. Add peach, seedless red grapes, seedless cucumber, red pepper, parsley, and scallion onion. Mix gently. Prepare the dressing. Add all dressing ingredients into a blender and mix for 1 ½ to 2 minutes on high speed. Season to taste. Place spring lettuce onto a serving tray and add salad. Before serving, pour dressing over salad. Garnish with tomato rings around the edge of the salad. Sprinkle with sesa

Fruit, Rice and Crabmeat Picante

Ingredients

2 large plums, cubed
1 Granny Smith apple, julienned
4 large strawberries, quartered
1 cup cooked wild rice
16 oz. backfin crabmeat without shell
2 Tbsp. Italian parsley, chopped

Dressing

¾ cup sour cream
¼ cup mayonnaise
1 large lemon for juice
2 Tbsp. half & half cream
Dash of Old Bay Seasoning
1 tsp. fresh tarragon, chopped
1 tsp. lemon skin, finely grated
Salt and pepper to taste

Garnish

2 ½ cups fresh spinach leaves
1 scallion onion, chopped
1 lemon, wedged

Instructions

Wash all fruit. Cut and peel the Granny Smith apple. Cut remaining fruit, as specified. Place all fruit into a mixing bowl. Add cooked wild rice, backfin crabmeat, and parsley. Mix gently to blend all ingredients well. Prepare the dressing. Add all dressing ingredients into a blender and mix for 1 ½ minutes on high speed. Season to taste. Place spinach leaves onto a serving tray and add salad on top. Before serving, pour dressing over the salad. Garnish with lemon wedges around the tray and sprinkle scallion onions on top.

Grape Salad with Blue Cheese Sour Picante

Ingredients

20 oz. small seedless red and yellow grapes
12 oz. blue cheese, crumbled
1 medium red pepper, cubed
2 Tbsp. dill chopped
1 Tbsp. mint leaves, chopped

Dressing

¼ cup olive oil
¼ cup fresh lemon juice
¼ cup water
1 Tbsp. honey
⅛ tsp. crushed hot red pepper
1 tsp. fresh oregano, chopped
1 tsp. fresh, garlic, chopped
1 small orange for juice
Salt, pepper, and sugar to taste

Garnish

6 grape leaves
½ cup blueberries, crunchy
2 Tbsp. chopped walnuts

Instructions

Wash grapes in cold water, strain and place into a mixing bowl. Add blue cheese, red pepper, dill, and mint leaves. Mix gently. Prepare the dressing. Add all dressing ingredients into a blender and mix for 2 minutes on high speed. Season to taste. Place grape leaves onto a serving tray and add salad on top. Before serving, pour dressing over the salad. Garnish with crunchy blueberries around the tray and sprinkle walnuts on top.

Green Plums with Shrimp Domino Dressing

Ingredients

7 medium-large plums, cut into thin wedges
6 oz. medium shrimp, cooked, peeled and deveined
2 scallion onions, chopped
1 small red pepper, chopped
2 Tbsp. carrots, coarsely grated
1 medium Roma tomato, cubed
2 Tbsp. Italian parsley

Dressing

¼ cup olive oil
1 large lemon for juice
1 lime for juice
1 tsp. lemon skin, finely grated
1 clove fresh garlic, coarsely grated
Dash of Old Bay Seasoning
Salt, pepper, and sugar to taste

Garnish

5 lettuce leaves
1 tomato, cut into wedges
3 Tbsp. white sharp cheddar cheese, shredded

Instructions

Wash plums in cold water, cut in half, remove seed, slice in thin wedges. Place plums into a mixing bowl. Add shrimp, scallion onions, red pepper, carrot, tomatoes, and Italian parsley. Mix gently. Prepare the dressing. Add all dressing ingredients into a blender and mix for 1 minute on high speed. Season to taste. Pour dressing on top of the salad and mix gently. Place lettuce leaves onto a serving tray and add salad. Garnish with tomato wedges around the tray and sprinkle with sharp cheddar cheese.

Guava Salad with Lemon Dressing

Ingredients

6-8 medium guava, cut into thin slices
1 red pepper, roasted
3 Tbsp. onion, chopped
1 Tbsp. dill, chopped

Dressing

¼ cup olive oil
¼ cup lemon juice
¼ cup water
1 tsp. oregano, chopped
1 tsp. garlic, chopped
Salt, pepper, and sugar to taste

Garnish

1 ½ cups spinach leaves
1 lime, wedged
3 Tbsp. peanuts, chopped

Instructions

Wash guava and cutting the head and tail off. Make sure there are not any black dots on the skin. Cut into slices. Place spinach leaves onto a serving tray and evenly add guava onto the spinach. Add red pepper, onion, and dill on top of the guava. Prepare the dressing. Add all dressing ingredients into a blender and mix for 1 ½ minutes on high speed. Season to taste sweet and sour. Before serving, pour dressing over the salad. Garnish with lime wedges around the tray and sprinkle with chopped peanuts.

Guava with Roasted Carrot Dressing

Ingredients

6 medium guava, cut into thin rings
4 medium carrots, roasted
1 scallion onion, chopped
½ cup olives, chopped
1 small green pepper, chopped
2 Tbsp. parsley, chopped

Dressing

2 medium carrots, fried
1 small onion, chopped
1 tsp. garlic, chopped
¼ cup olive oil
¼ cup balsamic vinaigrette
¼ cup carrot juice
Salt, pepper, and sugar to taste

Garnish

5 lettuce leaves
¼ cup chopped walnuts
1 lemon, cut into thin rings

Instructions

Wash guavas, cut off tops and bottoms, peel making sure there are no black spots and slice into cubes. Place lettuce leaves onto a serving tray and add guava on top. Add carrots, scallion onion, olives, green pepper, and parsley. Prepare the dressing. Add all dressing ingredients into a blender and mix for 1 ½ minutes on high speed. Season to taste. Before serving, pour dressing over the salad. Garnish with lemon rings down the center of the salad and sprinkle with walnuts.

Honeydew and Strawberry Dressing Olive Oil Lemon

Ingredients

1 small honeydew, cubed
10 strawberries, hard (sour if possible) cut into halves
1 tsp. dill chopped
¼ cup red onion, finely chopped

Dressing

¼ cup light olive oil
⅛ cup fresh lemon juice
⅛ cup water
⅛ cup fresh orange juice
3 large strawberries
1 tsp. fresh rosemary, chopped
Salt, pepper, and sugar to taste

Garnish

6 lettuce leaves
1 lime, cut into rings and twisted
1 Tbsp. parsley, chopped

Instructions

Wash honeydew with cold water, peel, and cut in half lengthwise. Remove the seeds and rinse again with cold water. Cut into cubes and place into a mixing bowl. Rinse strawberries in cold water and remove any leaves. Slice in half and add to the honeydew. Add dill and red onion. Mix gently. Prepare the dressing. Add all dressing ingredients into a blender and mix for 45 seconds on high speed. Season to taste. Place lettuce leaves onto a serving tray and add salad. Before serving, pour dressing over the salad. Garnish with lime twists around the tray and sprinkle with parsley.

Honeydew Spinach Red Pepper Avocado Lemon Dressing

Ingredients

1 small honeydew, peeled and cubed small
1 cup spinach leaves, julienned
1 small red pepper, cubed
1 Tbsp. dill, chopped
1 tsp. lemon skin, finely grated

Dressing

¾ cup sour cream
¼ cup lemon juice
1 small avocado, chopped
1 clove garlic, chopped
2 Tbsp. orange juice
Salt, pepper, and sugar to taste

Garnish

2 cups spinach, julienned
¼ cup pomegranate seeds
1 Tbsp. dill, chopped
¼ cup golden brown bread crumbs

Instructions

Wash honeydew, peel, cut in half lengthwise, remove seeds, slice into small cubes, and place into a mixing bowl. Add spinach leaves, red pepper, dill, and lemon skin. Mix gently. Prepare the dressing. Add all dressing ingredients into a blender and mix for 1 minute on high speed. Season to taste. Place spinach onto a serving tray and add salad on top. Before serving, pour dressing over the salad. Garnish by sprinkling pomegranate seeds, dill, and bread crumbs on top.

Julienned Nectarine with Avocado Dressing

Ingredients

6 large sour nectarines, julienned
1 celery stalk, chopped
2 Tbsp. dill, chopped

Dressing

1 small avocado, chopped
1 small Granny Smith apple, chopped
¼ cup olive oil
¼ cup lemon juice
¼ cup sweet white wine
⅛ cup half & half cream
2 cloves garlic, chopped
Salt, pepper, and sugar to taste

Garnish

1 cup spinach, julienned
3 Tbsp. ground peanuts
2 Tbsp. parsley, chopped

Instructions

Wash nectarines, cut in half, remove seeds, slice julienned, and place into a mixing bowl. Add celery and dill. Mix gently. Prepare the dressing. Add all dressing ingredients into a blender and mix for 2 minutes on high speed. Season to taste. Place spinach onto a serving tray and add salad. Before serving, pour dressing over the salad. Garnish by sprinkling with ground peanuts and parsley.

Kiwi Salad with Roasted Red Pepper Cream Cheese Feta Cream Dressing

Ingredients

8 kiwi, peeled and cut into rings
1 large red pepper, fried or grilled and cut into strips
1 Tbsp. dill, chopped
1 scallion onion, chopped

Dressing

¼ cup lime juice
½ cup mayonnaise
½ cup feta cheese
1 small orange for juice
1 tsp. lime skin, finely grated
1 lemon for juice
1 tsp. fresh parsley, chopped
Salt, pepper, and sugar to taste

Garnish

2 cups large fresh spinach leaves
1 orange, cut into thin rings
1 Tbsp. parsley, chopped
¼ cup, chopped pecans

Instructions

Wash kiwi in cold water, peel and cut into rings. Place the spinach leaves onto a serving tray and place the kiwi evenly on top. Add the red pepper, dill, and scallion onion over the kiwi. Prepare the dressing. Add all dressing ingredients into a blender and mix for 1 to 1 ½ minutes on high speed. Season to tastes. Before serving, pour dressing over the salad. Garnish with orange rings around the edges. Sprinkle with pecans and parsley.

Kiwi Avocado and Feta Picante

Ingredients

5 kiwi, peeled and cut into rings
1 medium avocado, cubed
6 oz. feta cheese, crumbled
1 small carrot, grated coarsely
¼ cup red onion, chopped

Dressing

¼ cup olive oil
¼ cup lemon juice
¼ cup water
1 tsp. lemon skin, grated
Dash of crushed hot red pepper
Salt, pepper, and sugar to taste

Garnish

6 lettuce leave, whole
1 lime, cut into rings and twisted
1 Tbsp. dill, chopped

Instructions

Wash kiwi, peel, and cut into medium rings. Place lettuce leaves onto a serving tray and add kiwi evenly over top. Cut avocado in half, remove seeds, and slice into cubes. Place on top of kiwi. Add feta, carrots, and red onion on top of avocado. Prepare the dressing. Add all dressing ingredients into a blender and mix for 1 minute on high speed. Season to taste. Before serving, pour dressing over the salad. Garnish with lime twists around the edges of the salad. Sprinkle with dill.

Mango and Brown Rice Picante

Ingredients

1 large mango, cubed
2 ½ cup, brown rice, cooked
2 scallion onions, chopped
½ cup sundried tomatoes, chopped
1 small Granny Smith apple, julienned
1 Tbsp. fresh rosemary, chopped
1 tsp. lemon skin, finely grated

Dressing

¾ cup avocado oil
¼ cup lemon juice fresh
1 small mango, chopped
1 tsp. garlic, chopped
1 tsp. jalapeños, chopped
1 tsp. curry powder
Salt, pepper, and sugar to taste

Garnish

2 cups spinach leaves
2 Tbsp. parsley, chopped
1 lime, cut into rings and twisted

Instructions

Peel mango, remove skin, and remove skin from the seed. Cut into cubes and place into a mixing bowl. Prepare rice by adding 5 cups of water into a pot, and bring to a boil. Add rice, stir and bring to a boil again. Reduce heat to medium simmer, cover and cook for approximately 30 minutes. (Brown rice cooking time is longer than regular rice). Remove from heat, mix with long fork and cool to room temp. Add rice to the mango and stir. Add scallions onions, sundried tomatoes, Granny Smith apple, rosemary, and lemon skin. Mix gently. Prepare the dressing. Add all dressing ingredients into a blender and mix for 1 ½ minutes on high speed. Season to taste. Place spinach leaves onto a serving tray and add salad on top. Before serving, pour dressing over the salad. Garnish with lime twists around the edges of the tray and sprinkle with parsley.

Mango and Fried Eggplant Curry Picante Dressing

Ingredients

2 medium mango, cubed
16 oz. eggplant, fried and cubed
1 small red pepper, chopped
1 scallion onion, chopped
1 medium tomato, cubed
1 cup oil
1 cup white flour

Dressing

¼ cup olive oil
¼ cup lemon juice
¼ cup water
1 tsp. curry powder
1 tsp. garlic, chopped
2 Tbsp. parmesan
Salt, pepper, and sugar to taste

Garnish

2 cups spinach, julienned
2 hard-boiled eggs, sliced
2 Tbsp. dill, chopped
1 Tbsp. poppy seeds

Instructions

Wash mango, peel, remove the fruit from the seeds, slice into cubes, and place into a mixing bowl. Add red pepper, scallion onion, and tomato. Mix gently. Peel eggplant and cut into cubes. Heat 1 cup of oil in a sauté pan. Dip cubes into flour and place in hot oil. Cook until golden brown. Remove using a spoon and place onto paper towel to drain excess oil. Place spinach onto a serving tray and add eggplant on top. Add mango mixture on top of eggplant. Prepare the dressing. Add all dressing ingredients into a blender and mix for 1 minute on high speed. Season to taste. Before serving, pour dressing over the salad. Garnish with hard-boiled eggs across the center of the salad. Sprinkle with dill and poppy seeds.

Mango and Spinach with Orange Olive Oil Dressing

Ingredients

3 large mango, peeled and cubed
2 cups spinach, julienned
1 large orange, peeled and cubed
1 red pepper, cut into thin strips
2 scallion onions, chopped

Dressing

½ cup fresh orange juice
½ cup olive oil
¼ cup fresh lemon juice
1 tsp. lemon skin, finely grated
Salt, pepper, and sugar to taste

Garnish

4 iceberg lettuce leaves
2 Tbsp. dill chopped
1 lemon, cut into thin rings

Instructions

Wash, peel and remove seeds from the enter of mango. Cut into cubes. Place mango into a mixing bowl. Add spinach, orange, red pepper, and scallion onions. Mix gently. Prepare the dressing. Add all dressing ingredients into a blender and mix for 1 ½ to 2 minutes on high speed. Season to taste. Place lettuce leaves onto a serving tray and add salad. Pour dressing over top of the salad. Garnish with lemon rings around the salad edges and sprinkle with dill.

Mango Tomatoes and Feta Picante

Ingredients

3 large mangos, peeled and strips
3 medium Roma tomatoes, cut into half moon
1 cup feta cheese, cut into small cubes
1 tsp. fresh oregano, chopped
2 Tbsp. fresh Italian parsley, coarsely chopped

Dressing

¼ cup olive oil
1 large lemon for juice
1 tsp. garlic, chopped
Dash of curry powder
Salt and pepper to taste

Garnish

2 cups spinach leaves
½ cup seedless Kalamata olives, whole
1 large lemon, cut into thin rings

Instructions

Wash mango and tomatoes in cold water. Peel mangos, remove seeds and cut into strips. Slice tomatoes in half and cut into half moon. Place mango and tomatoes into a mixing bowl. Add feta cheese, oregano, parsley, and dressing ingredients into the salad. Mix gently and season to taste. Place spinach leaves onto a serving tray and add salad on top. Garnish with Kalamata olives down the center of the salad and arranging lemon twists around the edges of the tray.

Marinated Persimmon with Smoked Pastrami Lime Dressing

Ingredients

7 Persimmon, cubed
1 small lime, peeled and cubed
1 cup pomegranate seeds
6 oz. smoked pastrami, julienned
2 Tbsp. fresh parsley, chopped

Dressing

¼ cup fresh lime juice
¼ cup olive oil
⅛ cup lemon juice
1 tsp. fresh rosemary, chopped
Salt, pepper, and sugar to taste

Garnish

5 lettuce leaves
2 kiwi, peeled and cut into rings
¼ cup chopped walnuts

Instructions

Wash the Persimmon and cut into cubes. Place into a mixing bowl. Add lime, pomegranate seeds, smoked pastrami, and parsley. Mix gently. Prepare the dressing. Add all dressing ingredients into a blender and mix for 1 ½ minutes on high speed. Season the taste to sweet and sour. Place lettuce leaves onto a serving tray and add salad. Pour dressing over the salad. Garnish with kiwi rings around the edges of the salad and sprinkle with chopped walnuts.

Marinated Lime Spinach and Carrots with Kalamata Olive Oil Dressing

Ingredients

5 medium limes with skin, cut int thin rings
1 cup spinach, julienned
1 medium carrot, coarsely grated
½ cup Kalamata olives
2 scallion onions, chopped
½ cup olive oil
2 Tbsp. salt

Dressing

½ cup lemon juice
½ cup water
½ cup olive oil
1 Tbsp. fresh rosemary
1 tsp. fresh garlic, chopped
¼ cup Kalamata olives, chopped Salt and pepper to taste

Garnish

4 lettuce leaves, whole
2 tomatoes, wedged
2 kiwi, cubed

Instructions

This salad must be prepared three (3) days prior to serving. Place a layer of limes into a mixing bowl and sprinkle with salt. Add another layer of limes and add more salt. Repeat one more time. Pour olive oil over top and let sit for approximately three (3) days either on the counter in the refrigerator. On the third day, remove the limes from the mixing bowl. Place lettuce leaves to a serving tray. Add limes evenly over the lettuce. Add spinach, carrot, Kalamata olives, and onions on top of the limes. Prepare the dressing. Add all dressing ingredients into a blender and mix for 1 ½ to 2 minutes on high speed. Season to taste. Before serving, pour dressing over the salad. Garnish with tomato wedges around the tray and sprinkle with kiwi.

Marinated Plums with Feta Cheese

Ingredients

4 large sour plums, cubed small
12 oz. feta cheese, cubed small
1 small carrot, grated
1 Tbsp. dill, chopped
4 stalks fresh green asparagus, cut into 1 inch pieces
1 small red pepper, chopped
1 scallion onion, chopped
4 strips crunchy bacon, crumbled

Dressing

¼ cup olive oil
2 medium lemon for juice
2 small sour plums, no seeds
1 tsp. garlic, chopped
¼ cup fresh orange juice
Salt, pepper, and sugar to taste

Garnish

4 iceberg lettuce leaves
6 large strawberries with stems, halved
2 Tbsp. Italian parsley, chopped

Instructions

Wash plums, cut in half, remove seeds, slice into small cubes, and place into a mixing bowl. Add feta, carrot, dill, asparagus, red pepper, scallion onion, and bacon. Mix gently. Prepare the dressing. Add all dressing ingredients into a blender and mix for 1 ¼ minutes on high speed. Season to taste. Place lettuce leaves onto a serving tray and add salad. Before serving, pour dressing over the salad. Garnish with strawberries on top of the salad and sprinkle with parsley.

Marinated Red Plums and Feta Cheese

Ingredients

8 large sour plums, thinly wedged
8 oz. feta cheese, crumbled
½ cup Kalamata olives, chopped
¼ cup onion, chopped
2 Tbsp. parsley, chopped
1 Tbsp. lime skin, grated

Dressing

½ cup olive oil
2 lemons for juice
1 medium orange for juice
Salt, pepper, and sugar to taste

Garnish

5 lettuce leaves
6-8 watermelon, thinly sliced
1 Tbsp. orange skin, coarsely grated

Instructions

Wash plums, cut in half and remove seeds. Slice the plum into thin wedges and place into a mixing bowl. Add feta cheese, Kalamata olives, onions, parsley, and lime skin. Mix gently. Place all dressing ingredients into a mixing bowl and stir well, seasoning to taste. Place lettuce leaves onto a serving tray and add salad. Before serving, pour dressing over the salad. Garnish with watermelon slices around the tray and sprinkle with orange skin.

Mediterranean Grapefruit Salad

Ingredients

3 medium grapefruit, filet
½ cup Kalamata olives, chopped
¾ cup feta cheese, crumbled
1 cup spinach, julienned
½ cup seedless red grapes
1 scallion onion, chopped
1 tsp. fresh oregano
1 tsp. lemon skin, finely grated

Dressing

¼ cup sesame oil
¼ cup lemon juice
¼ cup water
2 figs
2 garlic cloves, chopped
Salt, pepper, and sugar to taste

Garnish

4 iceberg lettuce leaves, whole
6 red figs, halved
1 tsp. parsley, chopped
1 small lime, cut into rings and twisted

Instructions

Peel grapefruit, separate the fruit from the skin, and place into a mixing bowl. Add Kalamata olives, feta cheese, spinach, seedless red grapes, scallion onion, oregano, and lemon skin. Mix gently. Prepare the dressing. Add all dressing ingredients into a blender and mix for 2 minutes on high speed. Season to taste. Place iceberg lettuce onto a serving tray and add salad on top. Before serving, pour dressing over the salad. Garnish with fig halves around the salad. Sprinkle with parsley and place lime twists down the center of the salad.

Nectarine and Blue Cheese Olive Oil Dressing

Ingredients

6 medium nectarines, cut into cubes
6 oz. blue cheese, crumbled
½ cup Kalamata olives, chopped
1 celery stalk, chopped
1 scallion onion, chopped
1 cup spinach, julienned
2 oz. pepperoni, sliced thin

Dressing

¼ cup olive oil
¼ cup white wine vinegar
¼ cup Kalamata olives
1 small nectarine, chopped with no seeds
1 tsp. fresh oregano, chopped
1 tsp. brown mustard
Salt, pepper, and sugar to taste

Garnish

2 medium beets, cooked and julienned
1 lime, cut into rings and twisted
2 Tbsp. Italian parsley, chopped

Instructions

Wash nectarines, cut in half, remove seeds, slice into cubes, and place into a mixing bowl. Add blue cheese, Kalamata olives, celery, scallion onion, spinach, and pepperoni. Mix gently. Prepare the dressing. Add all dressing ingredients into a blender and mix for 1 ½ minutes on high speed. Season to taste. Place salad onto a serving tray and add beets on top. Before serving, pour dressing over the salad. Garnish with lemon twists down the center of the salad and sprinkle with parsley.

Nectarine with Grilled Chicken Picante Dressing

Ingredients

4 medium nectarines, julienned
12 oz. chicken breast, grilled or broiled
1 scallion onion, chopped
1 celery stalk, julienned
1 medium red pepper, julienned

Dressing

¼ cup olive oil
¼ cup lemon juice
¼ cup water
1 tsp. rosemary, chopped
1 Tbsp. dill, chopped
Dash of crushed hot red pepper
1 tsp. garlic, chopped
Salt, pepper, and sugar to taste

Garnish

2 ½ cups lettuce leaves, julienned
1 lemon, cut into rings and twisted
2 Tbsp. chopped pecans
1 small carrot, coarsely grated

Instructions

Wash nectarines in cold water, cut lengthwise and remove seeds. Cut julienned into thin strips and place into a mixing bowl. Add chicken, scallion onion, celery stalk, and red pepper. Mix gently. Prepare the dressing. Add all dressing ingredients into a blender and mix for 45 seconds on high speed. Season to taste. Place lettuce onto a serving tray and add salad. Before serving, pour dressing over the salad. Garnish with lemon twists around the tray. Sprinkle with pecan and carrots over top of the salad.

Orange Spinach and Rosemary Orange Dressing

Ingredients

4 large seedless oranges, peeled and cut into medium-sized cubes
2 cups spinach leaves, julienned
2 cups raspberries, hard and sour
1 celery stalk, julienned

Dressing

⅛ cup olive oil
¾ cup orange juice
1 large lemon for juice
1 tsp. lemon skin, finely grated
1 tsp. rosemary, chopped
Salt, pepper, and sugar to taste

Garnish

5 iceberg lettuce leaves
1 large lime, cut into wedges
1 Tbsp. parsley, chopped
3 Tbsp. chopped walnuts

Instructions

Wash oranges, spinach, and rosemary. Peel the orange, cut and slice into cubes. Place into a mixing bowl. Add spinach leaves, raspberries, and celery. Mix gently. Prepare the dressing. Add all dressing ingredients into a blender and mix for 1 ½ minutes on high speed. Season to taste. Place lettuce leaves onto a serving tray and add salad. Before serving, pour dressing over the salad. Garnish with lime wedges around the tray. Sprinkle with parsley and walnuts.

Orange and Lettuce Rosemary Olive Oil Dressing

Ingredients

3 medium oranges, peeled and cubed into medium-sized pieces
8 large Romaine lettuce, julienned
5 pieces of red figs, quartered

Dressing

¼ cup olive oil
¼ cup lemon juice
¼ cup fresh orange juice
1 tsp. garlic, chopped
2 Tbsp. rosemary, chopped
Salt, black pepper, and sugar to taste

Garnish

1 medium orange, cut into thin rings
2 Tbsp. oregano, chopped
¼ cup red onion, chopped
3 Tbsp. shredded parmesan
½ cup small croutons

Instructions

Place lettuce onto a serving tray. Add oranges on top of the lettuce. Place figs on top of the oranges. Prepare the dressing. Add all dressing ingredients into a blender and mix for 1 ½ minutes on high speed. Season to taste. Before serving, pour dressing over the salad. Garnish with oranges slices around the edges. Sprinkle with red onion, shredded parmesan, and croutons.

Papaya with Figs Sour Cream Dill Dressing

Ingredients

1 medium papaya, cubed
2 Tbsp. dill, chopped
5 medium figs, halved
1 small scallion onion, finely chopped

Dressing

1 cup sour cream
¼ cup lemon juice
⅛ cup half & half cream
1 Tbsp. dill, chopped
Salt and pepper and to taste

Garnish

1 cup carrots, coarsely grated
1 nectarine, wedged
¾ cup spinach, chopped

Instructions

Wash papaya, cut in half lengthwise to remove the seeds and cube. Place into a mixing bowl. Add dill, figs, and scallion onion. Mix gently. Prepare the dressing. Add all dressing ingredients into a blender and mix for 45 seconds to 1 minute on high speed. Season to taste. Place carrots onto a serving tray and add salad. Before serving, pour dressing over the salad. Garnish with nectarine wedges face up around edges of the tray. Add spinach down the center of the salad.

Papaya with Lime and Olive Dressing

Ingredients

1 medium papaya, cut into ½-inch cubes
1 scallion onion, chopped
2 tsp. fresh mint leaves, chopped
¼ cup provolone cheese, grated

Dressing

¼ cup olive oil
¼ cup fresh lime juice
1 medium orange for juice
1 tsp. grated orange skin
3 Tbsp. water
2 garlic cloves, chopped
Dash of crushed hot red pepper
Salt and sugar to taste

Garnish

5 medium lettuce leaves, whole
1 medium beet, cooked and cut into small cubes
1 tsp. dill, chopped

Instructions

Wash papaya in cold water, peel, cut in half lengthwise, and remove seeds. Slice the papaya into ½" cubes and place into a mixing bowl. Add scallion onion, mint leaves, and provolone cheese. Mix gently. Prepare the dressing. Add all dressing ingredients into a blender and mix for 1 ½ minutes on high speed. Season to taste. Place lettuce leaves onto a serving tray and add salad. Before serving, pour dressing over the salad. Garnish with beets around the tray and sprinkle dill on top.

Papaya with Pastrami and Cheese Roasted Red Pepper Dressing

Ingredients

1 medium papaya, peeled and cubed
12 oz. pastrami, cubed
4 oz. white sharp cheddar cheese, grated
2 Tbsp. parsley, chopped
1 scallion onion, chopped
1 small carrot, finely grated

Dressing

¼ cup avocado oil
¼ cup white wine vinegar
3 Tbsp. honey
1 medium red pepper, fried
1 tsp. garlic, chopped
⅛ cup orange juice
Salt, pepper, and sugar to taste

Garnish

2 cups lettuce, julienned
1 tomato, cut into rings
1 Tbsp. rosemary, chopped

Instructions

Peel papaya cut lengthwise, remove seeds, slice into medium cubes, and place into a mixing bowl. Add pastrami, white sharp cheddar cheese, parsley, scallion onion, and carrot. Mix gently. Prepare the dressing. Add all dressing ingredients into a blender and mix for 1 ½ minutes on high speed. Season to taste. Place lettuce onto a serving tray and add salad on top. Before serving, pour dressing over the salad. Garnish with tomato rings around the tray and sprinkle rosemary on top.

Pineapple and Prosciutto with Lemon Dressing

Ingredients

4 cups pineapple, cubed
1 cup prosciutto, julienned
½ lb. smoked ham
¼ cup raisins

Dressing

¼ cup olive oil
¼ cup honey
¼ cup lemon juice
¼ cup water
1 Tbsp. garlic, chopped
Salt and pepper to taste
1 Tbsp. brown mustard

Garnish

5 lettuce leaves
3 Tbsp. roasted shredded coconut

Instructions

Wash the pineapple and peel. Cut into cubes. Do not use the center of pineapple. Put into a mixing bowl add prosciutto, ham and raisins. Toss gently. Prepare a platter for serving. Lay lettuce leaves on it and pour salad on top. Put dressing ingredients into a blender for 1 minutes. Adjust flavor if needed. Pour dressing on salad before serving. Garnish with coconut.

Pineapple Ham and Blackberry Sweet and Sour

Ingredients

¾ qt. pineapple, small cubes
1 cup smoked ham, cubed
1 cup sour blackberries
1 celery stalk, chopped
½ cup swiss cheese, shredded

Dressing

¼ cup canola oil
¼ cup fresh lemon juice
¼ cup honey
2 Tbsp. dill, chopped
1 tsp. lemon skin, finely grated
Salt, pepper, and sugar to taste

Garnish

5 lettuce leaves
2 Tbsp. mint leaves
1 small cucumber, cut into rings

Instructions

Peel pineapple and cut into cubes. Place into a mixing bowl. Add smoked ham, sour blackberries, celery, and swiss cheese. Mix gently. Prepare the dressing. Add all dressing ingredients into a blender and mix for 1 ½ minutes on high speed. Season to taste. Place lettuce onto a serving tray and add salad on top. Before serving, pour dressing over the salad. Garnish with cucumber rings around the edges of the salad and sprinkle with mint leaves.

Plum and Shrimp in Sour Lemon Dressing

Ingredients

6 large plums, thin wedges
1 tsp. lemon skin, finely grated
1 cup cheddar cheese, cubed
1 tsp. dill, chopped
2 cups baby shrimp, cooked, peeled, and deveined
½ cup sundried tomatoes, chopped

Dressing

¼ cup lemon juice
¼ cup olive oil
¼ cup orange juice
3 Tbsp. water
Dash of Old Bay Seasoning
2 cloves garlic, chopped
Salt, pepper, and sugar to taste

Garnish

5 iceberg lettuce leaves, whole
2 fresh beets, cooked and julienned
2 Tbsp. parsley, chopped

Instructions

Wash plums in cold water, cut in half, remove seeds, and slice into thin wedges. Place into a mixing bowl. Add lemon skin, cheddar cheese, dill, shrimp, and sundried tomatoes. Mix gently. Prepare the dressing. Add all dressing ingredients into a blender and mix for 1 ½ minutes on high speed. Season to taste. Place lettuce onto a serving tray and add salad. Before serving, pour dressing over the salad. Garnish with beets around the edges of the tray and sprinkle with parsley.

Pomegranate and Fresh Mozzarella Picante

Ingredients

3 cups pomegranate seeds
1 ½ cups fresh mozzarella, shredded coarsely
1 small seedless cucumber, cubed
1 scallion onion, chopped
2 small beets, cooked and cubed
2 Tbsp. Italian parsley, chopped
1 small green pepper, cubed
1 tsp. fresh oregano, chopped

Dressing

¼ cup olive oil
¼ cup balsamic vinegar
1 medium-large lime for juice
1 tsp. lime skin, finely grated
1 tsp. mustard
1 tsp. garlic, chopped
Salt, pepper, and sugar to taste

Garnish

2 ½ cups spinach, julienned
1 medium tomato, wedged
1 small lemon, cut into rings and twisted

Instructions

Crack pomegranate in the center to split in half. Use your fingers to remove skin and seeds. Make sure there is no skin, as it is very bitter. Place seeds into a mixing bowl, wash with cold water, drain, and place into another mixing bowl. Add mozzarella, seedless cucumber, scallion onion, beets, Italian parsley, green pepper, and oregano. Mix gently. Prepare the dressing. Add all dressing ingredients into a blender and mix for 45 seconds on high speed. Season to taste. Place spinach onto a serving tray and add salad on top. Before serving, pour dressing over the salad. Garnish with tomatoes around the tray. Place lemon twists down the center of the salad.

Pomegranate Beets and Smoked Turkey Honey Mustard Dressing

Ingredients

12 oz. pomegranate seeds
3 medium beets, cooked and julienned
12 oz. smoked turkey julienned
1 scallion onion chopped
1 Tbsp. fresh dill, chopped

Dressing

¼ cup yellow mustard
¼ cup honey
½ cup canola oil
1 medium lemon for juice
Salt, pepper, and sugar to taste

Garnish

2 cups spinach leaves
1 large lemon, cut into rings
2 Tbsp. sliced roasted almond

Instructions

Place pomegranate seeds into a mixing bowl. Add beets, smoked turkey, scallion onion, and dill. Mix gently. Prepare the dressing. Add all dressing ingredients into a blender and mix for 45 seconds on high speed. Season to taste with additional honey, if needed. Place spinach leaves onto a serving tray and add salad. Before serving, pour dressing over salad. Garnish with lemon rings around the tray and sprinkle almonds.

Pomegranate with Feta Cheese Sour Picante

Ingredients

4 cups pomegranate seeds
1 ½ cups feta cheese, crumbled
1 green pepper, chopped
¼ cup red onion, chopped
2 Tbsp. Italian parsley, chopped
1 medium carrot, finely grated
1 small seedless cucumber, cut into small cubes

Dressing

¼ cup lemon juice
¼ cup orange juice
⅛ cup olive oil
⅛ tsp. garlic
1 tsp. parmesan cheese
Salt, pepper, and sugar to taste

Garnish

3 cups spring lettuce
1 orange, cut int rings and twisted
1 hard-boiled egg, cut into 8 wedges

Instructions

Wash pomegranate, remove the skin and remove seeds being careful to not get any skin, as the skin is very bitter. Place seeds into a mixing bowl. Add feta cheese, green pepper, red onion, Italian parsley, carrot, and cucumber. Mix gently. Prepare the dressing. Add all dressing ingredients into a blender and mix for 1 minute on high speed. Season to taste. Place spring lettuce onto a serving tray and add salad. Before serving, pour dressing over the salad. Garnish with orange twists around the tray and place egg wedges in the center of the salad.

Pumpkin Apricot and Red Pepper Picante

Ingredients

16 oz. pumpkin, cubed and cooked
2 medium apricot, thinly wedged
1 medium red pepper, roasted and chopped
¼ cup red onion, chopped
2 Tbsp. Italian parsley, chopped
1 Tbsp. jalapeños, chopped

Dressing

¾ cup sour cream
¼ cup fresh lemon juice
1 tsp. garlic, chopped
1 tsp. rosemary, chopped
Salt and pepper and to taste

Garnish

1 ½ cups red cabbage, shredded
1 lemon, wedged
2 Tbsp. Italian parsley, chopped

Instructions

Place a pot of water on the stove and bring to a boil. Add pumpkin cubes to the boiling water and cook for 5 to 6 minutes. Remove from heat, strain, and let cool. Place pumpkin onto a cutting board and chop coarsely. Place into a mixing bowl. Add apricots, red pepper, red onion, Italian parsley, and jalapeños. Mix gently. Prepare the dressing. Add all dressing ingredients into a blender and mix for 2 minutes on high speed. Season to taste. Place red cabbage onto a serving tray and add salad on top. Leave enough room on the side to let some of the red cabbage show. Before serving, pour dressing over the salad. Use a spoon to gently combine the salad and the dressing. Garnish with lemon wedges around the tray and sprinkle with parsley.

Raspberry with Boil Egg and Cream Herb Dressing

Ingredients

16 oz. raspberries, soured and hard
5 hard-boiled eggs, wedged
4 oz. swiss cheese, grated

Dressing

¼ cup cream cheese
¼ cup lemon juice
¼ cup sour cream
¼ cup half & half cream
1 tsp. fresh rosemary, chopped
Salt and pepper and to taste

Garnish

4 lettuce leaves, whole
2 Tbsp. parmesan, grated
1 lemon, cut into rings and twisted

Instructions

Wash raspberries, strain, and pat dry. Place lettuce onto a serving tray and add raspberries on top. Add hard-boiled eggs evenly over the raspberries and sprinkle with swiss cheese. Prepare the dressing. Add all dressing ingredients into a blender and mix for 1 minute on high speed. Season to taste. Before serving, pour dressing over the salad. Garnish with lemon twists around the edges and sprinkle with parmesan.

Raspberry and Shrimp with Sundried Tomatoes

Ingredients

16 oz. raspberries, hard and sour
12 oz. baby shrimp, cooked, peeled and deveined
½ cup sundried tomatoes, coarsely chopped
½ cup fresh spinach, julienned
1 tsp. fresh rosemary, chopped
1 celery stalk, chopped
2 Tbsp. Italian parsley, chopped

Dressing

¾ cup mayonnaise
1 large lemon for juice
Dash of Old Bay Seasoning
Salt and pepper to taste

Garnish

6 lettuce leaves
1 medium cucumber, cut into rings
2 Tbsp. sesame seeds
2 hard-boiled eggs, wedged

Instructions

Wash raspberries in cold water, strain, and place into a mixing bowl. Add shrimp, sundried tomatoes, spinach, rosemary, celery, and Italian parsley. Mix gently. Prepare the dressing. Add all dressing ingredients into a blender and mix for 2 minutes on high speed. Season to taste. If dressing is too thick, add approximately 2 Tbsp. of half & half cream. Mix gently. Place lettuce leaves onto a serving tray and gently add salad on top. Before serving, pour dressing over the salad. Garnish with cucumber rings around the edges of the salad. Sprinkle sesame seeds and place hard-boiled eggs (yellow side facing up) across the center.

Red Fig with Roasted Red Pepper Lime Lemon Dressing

Ingredients

10 large red figs, cut into wedges
1 large fresh red pepper, roasted and julienned
1 scallion onion, chopped
1 celery stalk, julienned thin

Dressing

2 lemons for juice
⅛ cup olive oil
¼ cup water
1 lime for juice
1 tsp. grated lime skin
2 cloves garlic, chopped
Salt, pepper, and sugar to taste

Garnish

5 lettuce leaves, whole
1 medium tomato, cut into rings
2 Tbsp. Italian parsley, chopped

Instructions

Wash figs in cold water and cut the tops off. Slice into quarters and place into a mixing bowl. Place red peppers into a sauté pan and cook. Remove from heat and cool. Place on top of figs in mixing bowl. Add scallion onion and celery stalk. Mix gently. Prepare the dressing. Add all dressing ingredients into a blender and mix for 1 ½ minutes on high speed. Season to taste. Pour into the salad and mix gently. Place lettuce leaves onto a serving tray and add salad. Before serving, pour dressing over the salad. Garnish with tomato rings around the edges of the salad. Sprinkle with Italian parsley.

Sabres Salad with Feta and Oil Dressing

Ingredients

6-7 large sabres, peeled, cut into cubes or rings
½ cup feta cheese, crumbled
½ cup pomegranate seeds

Dressing

¼ cup olive oil
¼ cup balsamic vinegar
¼ cup water
2 cloves garlic, chopped
Salt, pepper, and sugar to taste

Garnish

3 cups spring lettuce
2 large figs, cut into rings
1 tsp. fresh Italian parsley

Instructions

Sabres fruit is desirable in the Mediterranean and Middle East. Wear gloves due to needles on the skin. Place fruit into ice water, then take out and make a cut lengthwise. Cut head, tail and peel off the skin. Wash again with cold water. Cut into cubes or rings. Place lettuce onto a serving tray and add sabres on top. Add feta cheese and pomegranate seeds over the sabres. Prepare the dressing. Add all dressing ingredients into a blender and mix for 45 seconds on high speed. Season to taste. Before serving, pour dressing over the salad. Garnish with fig slices around the edges of the tray and sprinkle with Italian parsley.

Sour Apple Pecan Celery and Grilled Chicken

Ingredients

4 med Granny Smith apples, peeled and julienned
¼ cup pecans, chopped
¼ cup raisins
2 medium celery stalks, chopped
10 oz. chicken breast grilled or broiled and cut into strips

Dressing

⅓ cup mayonnaise
½ cup lemon juice
1 Tbsp. fresh mint leaves, chopped
½ Tbsp. half & half cream
Salt, black pepper, and sugar to taste

Garnish

1 ½ cups red cabbage, shredded
6 mint leaves, whole
1 lemon, cut into thin rings

Instructions

Wash apples, peel, cut in half, and remove seeds. Cut apples, slice julienned, and place into a mixing bowl. Add pecans, raisins, celery, and chicken breast strips. Mix gently. Prepare the dressing. Add all dressing ingredients into a blender and mix for 1 minute on high speed. Season to taste. Place red cabbage onto a serving tray and add salad. Before serving, pour dressing over the salad. Garnish with lemon rings around the tray and add mint leaves down the center of the salad.

Strawberries with Sour Cream and Feta Lime Dressing

Ingredients

16 oz. strawberries, crunchy and soured
¾ cup feta cheese, crumbled
1 small seedless cucumber, finely cubed
2 Tbsp. dill, chopped

Dressing

1 ¼ cups sour cream
¼ cup fresh lime juice
1 tsp. lime skin, finely grated
1 Tbsp. dill, chopped
¼ cup feta cheese
Salt, pepper, and sugar to taste

Garnish

5 lettuce leaves, whole
1 orange, cut into rings
2 Tbsp. poppy seeds

Instructions

Wash strawberries, remove tops and leaves, and cut in half. Place lettuce leaves onto a serving tray and add strawberries on top. Add feta, seedless cucumber, and dill over the strawberries. Prepare the dressing. Add all dressing ingredients into a blender and mix for 1 minute on high speed. Season to taste. Before serving, pour dressing over the salad. Garnish with orange rings around the edges and sprinkle with poppy seeds.

Strawberry and Crab Meat with Cream Wine Sauce

Ingredients

12 oz strawberries, hard, cut into thin slices
6 oz. backfin crab meat, no shells
2 Tbsp. Italian parsley
1 tsp. grated lime skin

Dressing

¼ cup mayonnaise
½ cup sour cream
2 Tbsp. lemon juice
1 Tbsp. red wine vinaigrette
1 Tbsp. dry red wine
Dash of Old Bay Seasoning
Salt and pepper to taste

Garnish

1 ½ cups fresh spinach leaves
1 lemon, cut into thin rings
Dash of paprika
2 Tbsp. parmesan, grated

Instructions

Wash strawberries with cold water, remove any leaves, slice thin and place into a mixing bowl. Add crabmeat, Italian parsley, and lime skin. Mix gently. Prepare the dressing. Add all dressing ingredients into a blender and mix for 1 minute. Season to taste. Place spinach leaves onto a serving tray and add salad. Before serving, pour dressing over the salad. Garnish with lemon rings arounds the tray. Sprinkle with parmesan and paprika.

Stuffed Grape Leaves with Pecan and Lemon Olive Dressing

Ingredients

16 grape leaves, cooked
2 ½ cups white rice, cooked
½ cup raisins
2 Tbsp. fresh parsley
2 Tbsp. pecans, chopped
Dash of salt

Dressing

¼ cup fresh lemon juice
½ cup olive oil
¼ cup water
½ cup sour cream
Salt and pepper to taste
1 tsp. garlic, chopped

Garnish

5 lettuce leaves, whole
3 Tbsp. pecans pieces
1 lemon, cut into rings and twisted
Dash of paprika

Instructions

Boil 2 to 3 quarts of water with dash of lemon. Dip grape leaves for 5-6 minutes. Remove, place in strainer to drain. Place separately onto a cutting board. Place into a mixing bowl the cooked rice, raisins, parsley, and pecans. Mix gently. Place mixture evenly into the center of each grape leaf. Fold each leaf to center, then fold the two sides into the center, and gently roll up. Prepare the dressing. Add all dressing ingredients into a blender and mix for 1 minute on high speed. Season to taste. Place lettuce leaves onto a serving tray and add the rolled grapes leaves on top. Before serving, pour dressing over the salad. Garnish by adding the pecan pieces over salad, placing lemon twists on top, and sprinkling with paprika.

Tropicana Cocktail with a Citrus Dressing

Ingredients

1 mango, peeled, cubed
1 cup pineapple, cubed
1 cup papaya, cubed
2 persimmon, cubed
2 kiwi, cubed

Dressing

½ cup grapefruit juice
½ cup orange juice
1 lemon for juice
1 lime for juice
Sugar to taste
1 Tbsp. mint leaves
3 Tbsp. cherry brandy

Garnish

2 cups strawberries, sliced
1 lemon, wedged
¼ cup walnuts, chopped
¼ cup pomegranate
6-8 champagne glasses
8 mint leaves, whole

Instructions

Wash fruit, peel, cut into cubes and place into a mixing bowl. Prepare the dressing in a blender for 2 minutes, Adjust sugar and lemon flavor if needed. Before serving, fill 6 to 8 champagne glasses with the fruit. Add strawberries for garnish around the glass and stick one lemon wedge on the side of each glass. Sprinkle with pomegranate seeds and walnuts. Pour dressing over each salad. Place a mint leaf on top each serving.

Tropical Fruit with Grilled Fresh Tuna Lemon Dressing

Ingredients

1 medium mango, cubed
2 medium Persimmon, cubed
½ cup fresh pineapple, small cubes
1 cup papaya, cubed
12 oz. grilled tuna filets, cooked and cubed
1 tsp. lime skin, grated

Dressing

¼ cup olive oil
¼ cup lemon juice
1 cup orange juice
3 Tbsp. water
1 Tbsp. dill, chopped
1 Tbsp. coconut, roasted and shredded
Salt, pepper, and sugar to taste

Garnish

3 cups spinach leaves
4 medium oranges, halved and cleaned
3 Tbsp. chopped pecans
2 Tbsp. parsley, chopped
1 lemon, wedged

Instructions

Wash all the fruit. Peel mango, remove fruit from the seeds, and cut into cubes. Place into a mixing bowl. Add Persimmon, pineapple, papaya, grilled tuna, and lime skin. Mix gently. Prepare the dressing. Add all dressing ingredients into a blender and mix for 1 minute on high speed. Season to taste. Evenly fill orange halves with the salad mixture. Pour dressing over the salad. Place spinach leaves onto a serving tray. Add orange halves on top of the spinach leaves. Garnish by sprinkling with pecans and parsley. Place lemon wedge on top of each orange half.

Watermelon Blue Cheese Mediterranean

Ingredients

30 oz. watermelon, cut into medium cubes
10 oz. blue cheese, crumbled
1 scallion onion, chopped
½ cup Kalamata olives, chopped

Dressing

¼ cup olive oil
¼ cup lemon juice
⅛ cup fresh orange juice
1 garlic clove, chopped
Salt, pepper, and sugar to taste

Garnish

4 iceberg lettuce leaves
1 tsp. dill, chopped
3 Tbsp. poppy seeds
½ cup crunchy blackberries

Instructions

Peel watermelon, cut into cubes, and place into a mixing bowl. Add blue cheese, scallion onion, and Kalamata olives. Mix gently. Prepare the dressing. Add all dressing ingredients into a blender and mix for 45 seconds on high speed. Season to taste. Pour dressing over the salad. Place iceberg lettuce onto a serving tray and add salad on top. Garnish by sprinkling with dill, poppy seeds, and crunchy blackberries.

Watermelon with Feta and Spinach Lemon Dressing

Ingredients

24 oz. seedless watermelon, small cubes
1 cup feta cheese, small cubes
1 cup fresh spinach, julienned

Dressing

¼ cup lemon juice
¼ cup olive oil
¼ cup water
1 tsp. garlic, chopped
1 tsp. fresh oregano, chopped
Salt, pepper, and sugar to taste

Garnish

4 lettuce leaves, whole
1 small lemon, peeled and cubed
1 Tbsp. parsley, chopped

Instructions

Place watermelon into a mixing bowl. Add feta, and spinach. Mix gently. Prepare the dressing. Add all dressing ingredients into a blender and mix for 1 minute on high speed. Season to taste. Place lettuce leaves onto a serving tray and add salad. Before serving, pour dressing over the salad. Garnish by sprinkling lemon cubes and parsley over top.

Watermelon with Kalamata Feta and Dill Dressing

Ingredients

1 ½ qt. watermelon, cut into small to medium cubes
½ cup Kalamata olives, chopped
½ cup feta cheese, crumbled
1 scallion onion, finely chopped
5 strips crunchy bacon, chopped

Dressing

¼ cup olive oil
¼ cup fresh lemon juice
¼ cup pomegranate juice
2 Tbsp. dill, chopped
2 garlic cloves, chopped
Dash of hot crushed red pepper
Salt, pepper, and sugar to taste

Garnish

4 red cabbage leaves, whole
1 Tbsp. Italian parsley, chopped
¼ cup Kalamata olives, whole

Instructions

Peel watermelon and cut into small to medium cubes. Place into a mixing bowl. Add Kalamata olives, feta cheese, scallion onion, and crunchy bacon. Mix gently. Prepare the dressing. Add all dressing ingredients into a blender and mix for 1 ¼ minutes on high speed. Season to taste. Place red cabbage onto a serving tray and add salad on top. Before serving, pour dressing over the salad. Garnish with Kalamata olives on top of the salad and sprinkle with parsley.

Yellow Figs with Cream of Herb Avocado Dressing

Ingredients

10 large yellow figs, quartered
2 Tbsp. parsley, chopped
2 Tbsp. red onion, chopped

Dressing

½ cup mayonnaise
½ medium avocado
¼ cup half & half cream
1 small kiwi, peeled and chopped
1 Tbsp. parmesan
1 medium lemon for juice
1 tsp. fresh rosemary, chopped
½ tsp. grated lemon skin
Salt, pepper, and sugar to taste

Garnish

8 cornhusks leaves
1 medium orange, cut into rings
2 Tbsp. Italian parsley, chopped

Instructions

Wash figs in cold water, cut the tops off and slice into quarters. Place into a mixing bowl. Add parsley and red onion. Mix gently. Prepare the dressing. Add all dressing ingredients into a blender and mix for 1 ½ minutes on high speed. Season to taste. Place cornhusk onto a serving tray and add salad. Before serving, pour dressing over the salad. Garnish with orange rings around the edges and sprinkle Italian parsley on top.

RECIPE INDEX

Vegetables

Alfalfa Sprouts with Veggie Cream Dressing	2
Artichoke Bottom with Feta, Cream Cheese and Avocado Dressing	3
Artichoke Heart with Roquefort Kalamata	5
Artichoke Heart with Sundried Tomatoes and Mozzarella	6
Artichoke Hearts with Crab Meat and Sour Cream Dressing Picante	7
Artichoke Hearts with Raisins and Fresh Grapes	8
Avocado and Baby Spinach	9
Avocado and Feta with Lemon Lime Dressing	10
Avocado and Granny Smith Apples with Parmesan Dressing	11
Avocado and Melon Sweet and Sour	13
Avocado and Tropical Fruit Sweet and Sour	14
Avocado and Veggie Lemon Lime Dressing	15
Avocado and Wild Rice Dates Spicy	17
Avocado and Wild Rice Picante	18
Avocado on Toast with Lemon and Persimmon Dressing	19
Avocado with Cranberry and Ham Red Pepper Dressing	20
Avocado with Smoked White Fish and Roasted Red Pepper Dressing	21
Avocado with Tahini Sesame Dressing	22
Baby Spinach with Raspberry Cream Dressing	23
Baby Corn with Granny Smith Apples and Lemon Dressing	25
Baby Tomatoes Cooked Kale and Cheddar Cheese	26
Breaded Zucchini with Roasted Red Pepper Dressing	27
Beet Salad with Anchovies and Sour Cream	29
Broccoli and Egg with Avocado Cream Dressing	31
Broccoli and Persimmon with Herb Parmesan Dressing	32
Broccoli and Smoked Ham with Parmesan Cream Dressing	33
Broccoli with Shrimp, Walnuts and Picante Cream Dressing	34
Broccoli with Smoked Turkey and Mango Dressing	35
Broccoli with Tomato, Basil and Blue Cheese Dressing	36
Brussel Sprouts and Fruit with Lemon Olive Dressing	37
Brussel Sprouts with Fruit and Kalamata Lemon Dressing	39
Carrot and Fruit with Honey Sour Dressing	41
Carrot and Hard Boiled Eggs with Mayonnaise Base	42
Carrot and Pineapple with Honey Mustard Raisin Dressing	43
Cauliflower with Feta Cheese and Cream of Tomato Rosemary Dressing	45
Cauliflower with Parmesan and Herb Dressing	47
Cauliflower with Olive Oil and Feta Dressing	48
Cherry Tomatoes, Blue Cheese and Feta with Poppy Seeds	49
Cherry Tomatoes, Kalamata and Cream Cheese Dressing Picante	51
Collard Greens with Sour Cream and Bacon	53

Chick Peas, Poppy Seed and Cheddar Cheese with Olive Oil Dressing 54
Cooked Spinach with Parmesan and Sundried Tomatoes 55
Cooked Zucchini and Pear with Balsamic Dressing 56
Cucumber and Anchovy with Sour Cream Dressing 57
Cucumber and Parmesan with Dill Dressing 59
Cucumber and Carrot Salad with Cream Cheese Dill Dressing 60
Cucumber Salad with Feta and Olive Oil Lemon Dressing 61
Cucumber Salad with Smoked Salmon and Sour Cream Dressing 62
Cucumber with Blue Cheese and Tarragon Dressing 63
Cucumber with Cream Cheese and Lemon Dressing 65
Eggplant and Veggie Eggs Carrots Tomato Dressing 66
Eggplant with Feta Cheese with Oil and Vinegar Dressing 67
Eggplant with Domino Picante Dressing 69
Eggplant with Spicy Sour Cream 70
Eggplant with Sundried Tomatoes and Sesame Dressing 71
Espanol Tomato Rice Picante 72
Fresh Asparagus with Sundried Tomatoes Picante Lemon 73
Fried Artichokes with Sundried Tomato Dressing 74
Fried Avocado with Cucumber and Brie Cheese Dressing 75
Fried Green Pepper and Feta Cheese with Red Onion Lemon Dressing 76
Fried Pumpkin with Lime Blackberry Dressing 77
Fried Red Pepper Salad with Wine Vinegar and Hot Crushed Pepper 78
Fried Squash with Sour Cream and Dill Dressing 79
Fried Zucchini Salad with Lemon and Jalapenos Dressing 80
Garbanzo Spinach and Tomato Picante Flavor 81
Grated Beets with Eggs and Carrots and Horseradish Mayonnaise Dressing 83
Grated Radishes with Feta and Olives with Lime Dressing 84
Grated Radishes with Spinach and Fresh Mozzarella with Sour Cream and Lemon Dressing 85
Green Asparagus and Hard Salami Kalamata Pepper Dressing 87
Green Asparagus with Veggie Mediterranean Lemon Dressing 89
Grated Zucchini with Fruit Cream Cheese Olive Oil Dressing 90
Green Bean Salad with Marinated Red Pepper 91
Green Beans with Cranberry and Honey Mustard Dressing 93
Green Beans with Red Pepper Olive and Lemon Dressing 94
Green Cabbage with Apples and Carrots with Marinated Rosemary 95
Green Cabbage with Grapes and Plum Mayonnaise Base 97
Green Cabbage with Smoked Pastrami, Egg and Mayonnaise 98
Grilled Tomatoes with Parmesan, Kalamata and Olive Oil Dressing Picante 99
Heart of Palm with Corned Beef and Lemon Red Pepper Dressing 101
Heart of Palm and Persimmon with Kalamata Olive Dressing 102
Julienned Carrots with Shredded Vegetable Dressing 103
Kale Salad with Sour Cream Dressing 104
Kohlrabi Balsamic Dressing 105

Kohlrabi Cabbage with Egg and Mayonnaise 106
Leftover Stuffed Cabbage with Spicy Tomato Oregano Dressing 107
Leftover Stuffed Pepper Salad with Olive Oil Picante Dressing 108
Marinated Beet Salad with Mustard and Honey Dressing 109
Marinated Cucumber Picante Cream Dressing 110
Marinated Fruit, Vegetables and Feta 111
Marinated Okra Salad with Lime Picante Dressing 112
Mediterranean Carrot Salad with Parmesan and Picante Mayonnaise 113
Mediterranean Chopped Veggie and Fruit Salad with Feta, Olive Oil and Vinegar Dressing 115
Mountain Mushroom with Spinach Sour Cream Dressing Picante 117
Mushroom Feta and Cucumber with Dill Lemon Dressing 118
Mushroom Salad with Cream of Herbs 119
Napa Cabbage with Grilled Tuna Marinated with Vinaigrette Oil Dressing 120
Okra and Apples with Curry Picante Dressing 121
Okra Salad with Marinated Tomato Dressing 123
Orzo Artichoke and Spinach with Spicy Tomato Dressing 124
Pea Salad with Shredded Vegetables and Kalamata Dressing 125
Pea Salad with Tomato, Mozzarella and Tarragon Dressing 126
Pearl Onion with Blue Cheese Dressing and Rosemary 127
Portobella Mushrooms with Egg Picante and Cumin 129
Pearl Onion with Red Pepper and Fresh Mozzarella Picante 130
Pumpkin and Apple Salad with Lemon and Olive Oil 131
Pumpkin Salad with Sour Cream and Parmesan Dressing 133
Pumpkin Patty Salad with Cream of Herb Dressing 134
Pumpkin with Veggie, Lemon and Cheddar Cheese Dressing 135
Radishes and Cheddar Cheese with Kalamata Dressing 137
Radishes and Grated Swiss Cheese with Smoked Dry Herring 138
Red Beans with Sundried Tomatoes Picante 139
Red Cabbage Salad with Beets Cheese and Mayonnaise 141
Red Onion with Feta Cheese and Olive Lime Dressing 143
Red Cabbage with Mango Papaya Apple and Mayonnaise Dressing 144
Roasted Portobella Mushrooms with Red Wine Dressing Picante 145
Roasted Portobella Mushrooms with Red Pepper Picante Dressing 147
Root Salad with Shrimp and Tomato, Mayonnaise Dressing 148
Scallion Onion with Julienned Corned Beef Red Wine Vinegar Dressing 149
Scallion and Feta with Basmati Rice Picante 151
Spicy Carrots with Beet Olive Oil Tarragon Dressing 152
Spicy Carrots with Curry and Olive Oil Dressing 153
Spicy Eggplant with Sour Cream Avocado Dressing 154
Spinach and Anchovy with Red Pepper Raspberry Dressing 155
Squash Salad with Tarragon Dressing 157
Squash Sour Cream Feta Cheese Cheddar Dressing 158
Squash with Walnuts, Celery Onion and Cheese Dressing 159

Stuffed Roma Tomatoes with Crab Meat and Sour Cream Lemon Dressing 160
Tomato and Rosemary with Hot Pepper Dressing 161
Tomato and Feta with Garden Cream Dressing 163
Tomato Mozzarella with Balsamic Dressing 164
Tomato Picante with Sour Cream and Lemon Dressing 165
Tomato Salad with Tahini Dressing Picante 166
Tomato, Spinach and Turkey with Lemon Dressing 167
Tomatoes and Cucumber with Humus Tahini Dressing Spicy 169
Vegetable Root Salad with Balsamic Dressing 170
Wax Beans with Tomato Picante 171
Wax Beans, Granny Smith and Sour Cream Dressing 172
White Asparagus Granny Smith and Cheddar Cheese Dressing 173
White Asparagus with Grilled Chicken Tarragon Dressing 174
White Asparagus with Spinach and Sundried Tomato Dressing 175
Zucchini with Balsamic Dressing Picante 176

Fish & Seafood

Anchovy, Egg and Kalamata with Cream Dressing 179
Breaded Flounder with Avocado Picante Dressing 180
Breaded Mahi Mahi Fish with Mango Lemon Dressing.. 181
Crab and Plum Salad Cocktail Mayonnaise Dressing 182
Crab Meat and Persimmon Herb Dressing 183
Crab Meat Cocktail with Fried Ham and Cream Veggie Dressing 184
Crab Meat, Potato and Mayonnaise Picante 185
Crab Meat with Shredded Vegetable Mayonnaise and Sundried Tomatoes 186
Escargot and Tomato with Spicy Dressing 187
Flounder Filet and Orzo Picante 188
Flounder Filet Picante with Herb Dressing 189
Flounder Filet with Papaya and Cream Dressing 190
Fresh Escargot with Wild Rice, Vegetables and Olive Oil Dressing 191
Fresh Tuna Salad with Roasted Red Pepper and Wine Vinegar Dressing 192
Fresh Tuna Salad with Spinach and Roasted Red Pepper 193
Fried Spicy Calamari with Lemon Dressing 195
Fried Oyster Salad with Lemon Picante Dressing 196
Herring Filet Stuffed Tomatoes with Red Wine Dressing 197
Herring Filet with Sour Cream Picante Dressing 198
Herring Filet with Vegetable and Olive Oil Dressing 199
Lobster Salad with Fig Picante 200
Lobster Salad with Sundried Tomatoes and Sour Cream Dressing 201
Lobster Stuffed Tomatoes with Mayonnaise 202
Lobster with Veggie and Fruit Cream Picante Dressing 203

Mahi Mahi Filet with Spaghetti Picante 204
Mahi Mahi with Veggie Curry and Lemon Dressing with Tahini 205
Marinated Herring Fillet with Beet Olive Oil Dressing 206
Marinated Spicy Shrimp Picante 207
Mediterranean Fried Sardines with Red Wine Dressing 208
Red Snapper Cocktail with Fruit 209
Red Snapper Filet with Avocado Persimmon Sour Picante 210
Salmon Filet with Spicy Mango Tahini Dressing 211
Salmon Fish Filet with Marinated Mango 212
Salmon Salad with Fruit, Veggies and Cream of Lemon Dill Dressing 213
Salmon Salad with Honey Chambord Dressing 214
Salmon with Vegetable and Cream Dressing 215
Salmon with Potatoes Fruit and Vegetables 217
Seafood Cocktail with Cocktail Dressing 218
Shark Meat Salad with Curry and Sundried Tomato Dressing 219
Shark Meat Salad with Red Wine Dressing Picante 220
Shrimp and Sundried Tomatoes Picante 221
Shrimp with Roasted Green Pepper and Parmesan 222
Smoked Spicy Oysters with Orzo 223
Smoked White Fish with Scallion, Avocado and Olive Oil Dressing 224
Snow Crab Legs with a Cream Vegetable Dressing 225
Snow Crab Legs with Fruit and Lemon 226
Spicy Claw Crabmeat with Sundried Tomatoes and Cream Dressing 227
Spicy Shrimp 228
Traditional Jewish Carp Salad with Celery Horseradish Dressing 229
Tuna Cocktail with Veggie and Parmesan Cream Dressing 230
Tuna, Fruit and Vegetables with Lemon Dressing 231

Pasta

Bow Pasta with Sundried Tomatoes and Pomegranate 234
Cheese Tortellini with Ham and Parmesan with Red Wine Dressing 235
Couscous and Spicy Tomato 237
Couscous Salad with Chopped Smoked Ham and Lemon Mayonnaise Dressing 238
Couscous Salad with Domino Dressing 239
Couscous with Artichoke and Garbanzo Picante 240
Dumplings with Spinach and Cream of Herb Dressing 241
Gluten Free Pasta with Marinated Scallops and Vegetables 242
Gluten Free Pasta with Sour Cream Dressing 243
Gnocchi Veggie and Fruit with Raspberry Dressing 245
High Gluten Pasta, Broccoli and Kalamata with Lemon Dressing 246
Leftover Dumplings with Roasted Green Pepper Picante 247

Linguine with Avocado and Pomegranate Dressing 248
Macaroni Pasta with Avocado, Papaya Picante 249
Macaroni Salad with Shrimp and Lemon Sour Cream Dressing Picante 251
Macaroni with Vegetables, Cheddar Cheese and Pepperoni with Mayonnaise Dressing 252
Multi Colored Pasta with Spicy Clams and Mushrooms 253
Multi Color Spiral Pasta with Vegetable and Avocado Olive Oil Dressing 255
Orzo and Grilled Chicken with Curry Lemon Dressing 256
Orzo and Vegetables Marinated 257
Orzo Salad with Avocado, Sundried Tomatoes and Oil and Vinegar Dressing 258
Orzo Salad with Fruit and Vegetables with Mayonnaise 259
Orzo with Figs and Red Pepper Mayonnaise 260
Orzo, Tomato and Kalamata Olives with Lemon Lime Dressing 261
Pasta Spaghetti Pasta with Spicy Tomatoes 263
Pasta Spinach with Sour Picante Roquefort Cheese 264
Penne Pasta with Grilled Salmon and Pomegranate Picante Dressing 265
Ravioli and Grilled Chicken with Tomatoes Picante Dressing 266
Ravioli and Sundried Tomatoes with Lemon and Cilantro Dressing 267
Ravioli Salad with Tomatoes Picante 268
Roasted Orzo with Snow Crab Legs with Vegetable and Curry Picante Dressing 269
Shell Pasta with Veggies and Fruit Marinated 271
Spaghetti Cheese Nuts and Gavrilovic Salami Picante Dressing 273
Spaghetti and Crab Meat Salad with Cream of Herb Dressing 274
Spinach Pasta with Avocado Sour Cream and Cheese 275
Spinach Pasta with Herb and Avocado Dressing 276
Spinach Pasta with Ricotta and Lemon Dressing 277
Spiral Whole Wheat Pasta with Broccoli and Shrimp with Olive Oil and Vinegar Dressing .. 278
Sweet Linguini Pasta with Brown Sugar and Cocoa 279
Tortellini, Egg and Spinach with Cream of Herb Dressing 280
Tortellini and Smoked Beets with Sundried Tomato Dressing 281
Tortellini Salad with Corned Beef, Sundried Tomatoes and Sour Cream 282
Tortellini with Cheese and Veggie Kalamata Picante 283
Vermicelli Pasta with Clams, Bacon and Sour Cream Parmesan Dressing 284
Vermicelli Pasta with Hard Salami and Cheddar Cheese with Cucumber Dill Dressing 285
Whole Wheat Pasta Spaghetti with Tomato, Parmesan and Basil Dressing 286

Rice

Basmati Rice with Fruit Oriental Picante 289
Basmati Rice with Grilled Salmon Lemon-Lime Dressing 290
Basmati with Rice Avocado Spinach and Mayonnaise Based 291
Brown Rice with Shrimp and Sundried Tomatoes Picante Lemon Dressing 293
Chopped Rice Salad with Apple and Raisin Curry Dressing 295

Brown Rice with Roasted Vegetable and Dill Dressing 296
Rice Mediterranean Style Spicy 297
Rice with Avocado and Turkey with Cream of Herb Dressing 298
Rice with Shredded Vegetables and Lemon Dressing 299
Tomato and Basmati Rice Fruit and Veggie with Smoked Salmon 300
White Rice with Chick Peas and Tomatoes Cumin 301
White Rice with Curry and Mango Picante 302
Wild Rice with Beets Sour Cream Lime Dressing 303
Wild Rice with Black Beans and Broiled Salmon Picante Dressing 304
Wild Rice with Orzo Veggie and Fruit Olive Oil and Lemon Dressing 305
Wild Rice with Prosciutto and Smoked Cheese Picante 306
Wild Rice with Vegetable and Spicy Dressing 307
Wild Rice with Tahini and Vegetable Dressing 308
Wild Rice with Seafood and Vegetables Spicy 309

Eggs

Boiled Eggs with Grilled Tuna Mayonnaise Picante Dressing 312
Egg and Sundried Tomatoes on Toast Picante 313
Egg and White Fish Mayonnaise Picante 314
Egg Salad Avocado and Cheese Sour Cream Dill Dressing 315
Egg Salad Ham and Bacon with Sun-Dried Tomatoes 316
Egg Salad Hard-Boiled Egg with Roasted Red Pepper Mayo and Tomatoes 317
Egg Salad with Beets and Horseradish 318
Egg Salad with Dill and Sour Cream 319
Fried Egg Salad with Feta and Spinach Mayonnaise Dressing 320
Hard-Boiled Egg with Fried Eggplant Tahini Dressing 321
Hard-Boiled Egg with Spinach Chopped Salad Cream of Herbs 322
Hard-Boiled Eggs with Granny Smith Apple Feta and Tomato Mayonnaise Dressing 323
Leftover Omelet with Veggies, Cheese, and Bacon Herb Dressing 324
Simple Egg Salad with Relish and Mayo 325
Spicy Egg Salad 326

Poultry

Boneless Breast of Chicken with Dominos Picante Dressing 328
Breast of Chicken Salad Mayonnaise and Celery–Simple Chicken Salad 329
Breast of Cornish Hen with Light Orange Dressing 330
Cornish Hen Salad with Sundried Tomatoes Picante 331
Dark Pieces of Chicken with Spicy Tomato Dressing 332
Dark Pieces of Cornish Hen Boneless with Spicy Lime Dressing 333

Grilled Breast of Chicken with Vegetable Lemon Dressing 334
Roasted Turkey with Potato Mayonnaise Picante 335
Turkey Breast with Mango and Mayonnaise 336
Turkey Breast with Portabella Mushroom Grated Vegetable Vinaigrette Oil Dressing 337
Turkey Breast with Veggie and Fruit Tarragon Dressing 338
Turkey Legs with Spicy Curry Dressing 339

Beef & Venison

Beef Strip with Veggie and Fruit Fig Lemon Dressing 342
Chopped Beef on Garlic Toast with Tahini Dressing Picante 343
Leftover American Goulash with Cheese and Herb Dressing 344
Leftover Beef Schnitzel with Tarragon Wine Dressing 345
Leftover Hungarian Beef Spicy with Tomatoes and Basil 347
Leftover Meatballs with Tomatoes Red Pepper Spicy Dressing 349
Nonfat Roast Beef with Spicy Vegetable Dressing 350
Roasted Eye Round Beef with Sour Fruit Oil Vinegar Dressing 351
Roasted Venison with Shredded Vegetables and Balsamic Picante Dressing 352
Smoked Tongue with Shredded Vegetable Vinaigrette Oil Dressing 353
Tenderloin Tips with Tropical Fruit and Curry Picante 354

Pork

Pork Loin Cubes with Vegetable and Herb Dressing 356
Pork Loin Salad with Fruit Cranberry and Honey Dressing 357
Pork Loin Strips with Vegetable and Cream of Herb Dressing 359
Smoked Ham Pineapple Fresh Cherry Honey Lemon Dressing 360

Lamb

Chopped Leg of Lamb Leftover with Spinach and Raisin Balsamic Dressing 362
Roasted Leg of Lamb with Kalamata and Curry Dressing Picante 363

Potatoes

Baby Potatoes with Coconut Fresh Cucumber Dill Lemon Dressing 367
Baby Potatoes with Smoked Turkey Bacon and Lemon 368
Marinated Red-Skinned Potatoes with Smoked Dry Herring 369
Potato Salad and Parmesan with Bacon and Olive Oil Vinaigrette Dressing 370
Potato Salad with Anchovy and Mayonnaise 371

Potato Salad with Fruit and Veggies Marinated	372
Potato Salad with Pastrami and Sundried Tomatoes	373
Potato Salad with Roasted Tomatoes Garlic	374
Potato Salad with Smoked Meat Wine Vinaigrette Dressing	375
Potatoes and Bacon with a Cream Dressing Picante	376
Potatoes and Corned Beef with Red Wine Vinegar Dressing	377
Potatoes and Grilled Chicken Breast with Picante Veggie Dressing	378
Potatoes in Spinach Sour Cream Picante	379
Red-Skinned Potatoes with Vegetable and Mayonnaise	381
White Potato Salad with Spicy Mustard and Red Pepper	383
Potatoes Sour Cream and Sundried Tomatoes Picante	384

Beans

Black Bean Salad with Roasted Jalapenos and Red Pepper Dressing	387
Black Bean Salad with Red Wine Sauce and Olive Oil Picante	388
Garbanzo Beans with Tropical Fruit Marinated	389
Garbanzo Beans Veggie Olive Oil Lemon Lime Dressing	391
Humus Salad with Veggie Picante	392
Kidney Beans with Julienned Pastrami Marinated Balsamic Dressing	393
Pinto Bean with Spinach Sour Cream and Cheese	395
Red Bean Salad with Tomato and Lemon Dressing	397

Fruit

Apple and Smoked Trout with Sundried Tomatoes	400
Apple Crabmeat and Sundried Tomatoes with Mayonnaise	401
Apple Pecan in Celery Mayonnaise Base	402
Apricot with Grilled Chicken Breast with Mayonnaise and Herb Dressing	403
Avocado Fruit and Veggie Picante	404
Blackberries with Cheddar Cheese Dressing	405
Blackberries with Feta Cheese and Avocado Picante	406
Blueberries with Sour Cream Picante Lemon Dressing	407
Cantaloupe and Cranberry with Lemon Dressing	409
Cantaloupe and Smoked Turkey with Cherry Cranberry Dressing	411
Cherry Spinach and Plum with Sour Feta Cheese Dressing	412
Cranberry Avocado and Smoked Turkey Picante	413
Cranberry Spinach and Feta with Sour Cream Dressing Picante	415
Persimmon Pasta and Spinach Picante	416
Persimmon Swiss Cheese and Pastrami with Tomato Dressing Picante	417
Persimmon with Smoked Corned Beef Cream of Herb Dressing	418

Figs and Feta Cheese with Veggie Dressing 419
Fresh Marinated Apricots with Lobster Picante 420
Fresh Peaches with Smoked Corned Beef Olive Oil Kalamata Dressing 421
Fried Papaya with Prosciutto and Honey Dressing 422
Fried Pineapple with Parmesan and Spinach Kalamata Dressing 423
Fruit and Cheese with Chambord Liquor 424
Fruit and Lobster with Honey and Lemon 425
Fruit and Smoked Meat Marinated 426
Fruit and Spinach with Sweet and Sour Dressing 427
Fruit and Veggie Patty Salad Avocado Lemon Dressing 428
Fruit and Veggie with Tahini Dressing 429
Fruit, Rice and Crabmeat Picante 430
Grape Salad with Blue Cheese Sour Picante 431
Green Plums with Shrimp Domino Dressing 432
Guava Salad with Lemon Dressing 433
Guava with Roasted Carrot Dressing 434
Honeydew and Strawberry Dressing Olive Oil Lemon 435
Honeydew Spinach Red Pepper Avocado Lemon Dressing 436
Julienned Nectarine with Avocado Dressing 437
Kiwi Salad with Roasted Red Pepper Cream Cheese Feta Cream Dressing 439
Kiwi Avocado and Feta Picante 440
Mango and Brown Rice Picante 441
Mango and Fried Eggplant Curry Picante Dressing 442
Mango and Spinach with Orange Olive Oil Dressing 443
Mango Tomatoes and Feta Picante 444
Marinated Persimmon with Smoked Pastrami Lime Dressing 445
Marinated Lime Spinach and Carrots with Kalamata Olive Oil Dressing 446
Marinated Plums with Feta Cheese 447
Marinated Red Plums and Feta Cheese 448
Mediterranean Grapefruit Salad 449
Nectarine and Blue Cheese Olive Oil Dressing 450
Nectarine with Grilled Chicken Picante Dressing 451
Orange Spinach and Rosemary Orange Dressing 453
Orange and Lettuce Rosemary Olive Oil Dressing 454
Papaya with Figs Sour Cream Dill Dressing 455
Papaya with Lime and Olive Dressing 456
Papaya with Pastrami and Cheese Roasted Red Pepper Dressing 457
Pineapple and Prosciutto with Lemon Dressing 458
Pineapple Ham and Blackberry Sweet and Sour 459
Plum and Shrimp in Sour Lemon Dressing 461
Pomegranate and Fresh Mozzarella Picante 462
Pomegranate Beets and Smoked Turkey Honey Mustard Dressing 463
Pomegranate with Feta Cheese Sour Picante 464

Pumpkin Apricot and Red Pepper Picante 465
Raspberry with Boil Egg and Cream Herb Dressing 467
Raspberry and Shrimp with Sundried Tomatoes 468
Red Fig with Roasted Red Pepper Lime Lemon Dressing 469
Sabres Salad with Feta and Oil Dressing 470
Sour Apple Pecan Celery and Grilled Chicken 471
Strawberries with Sour Cream and Feta Lime Dressing 473
Strawberry and Crab Meat with Cream Wine Sauce 474
Stuffed Grape Leaves with Pecan and Lemon Olive Dressing 475
Tropicana Cocktail with a Citrus Dressing 477
Tropical Fruit with Grilled Fresh Tuna Lemon Dressing 478
Watermelon Blue Cheese Mediterranean 479
Watermelon with Feta and Spinach Lemon Dressing 481
Watermelon with Kalamata Feta and Dill Dressing 483
Yellow Figs with Cream of Herb Avocado Dressing 484

www.ingramcontent.com/pod-product-compliance
Lightning Source LLC
Chambersburg PA
CBHW041323110526
44592CB00021B/2797